TALES
of the
BROTHERS
GRIMM

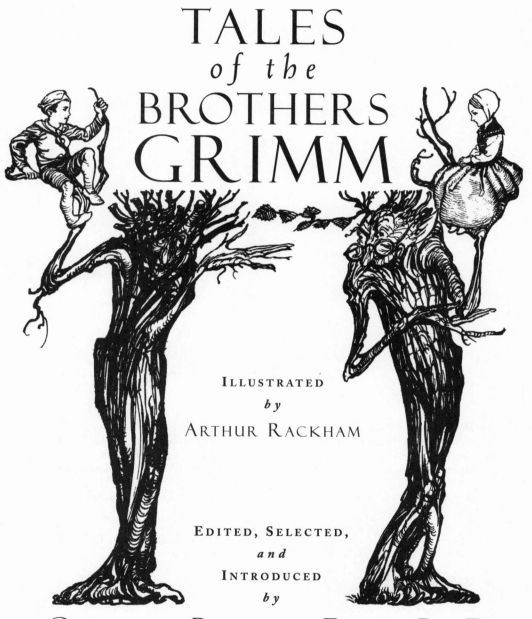

ILLUSTRATED
by
ARTHUR RACKHAM

EDITED, SELECTED,
and
INTRODUCED
by

CLARISSA PINKOLA ESTÉS, PH.D.

QUALITY PAPERBACK BOOK CLUB
NEW YORK

Book design by Felicia Telsey

Quality Paperback Book Club
1271 Avenue of the Americas
New York, NY 10020

Printed in the United States of America

DEDICATION

Para Angela Carter, *la cuentera grande,*
y mi comadre,
con cariño y amor.

CONTENTS

THE MEDICINE OF THE TALES
BY CLARISSA PINKOLA ESTÉS, PH.D.

"Though fairy tales end after ten pages, our lives do not. We are multi-volume sets. In our lives, even though one episode might culminate in a crash and burn, there is always another episode awaiting us, and then another. There are always more opportunities to get it right, to fashion our lives in the ways we soulfully deserve. Do not waste your time hating a failure. Failure is a greater teacher than success. Listen. Learn. Go on. That is every tale's essence. As we listen to these ancient messages, we learn about deteriorative patterns, and we learn to go on with the strength of one who senses the traps, cages, and baits before we are upon them, or caught in them."[1]

THE IMPERISHABLE FAIRY TALE

In fairy tales are embedded the most infinitely wise ideas that, over the centuries, have refused to be shorn, worn down, or killed off. The most imperishable and wise ideas are gathered together in the silvery nets we call stories. Since the first fire, human beings have been drawn to mystical tales. Why? Because they all point to a single great fact—that is, although the soul on its journey may stumble or become lost, it will ultimately find its heart, its divinity, its strength, its Godly pathway through the dark woods again—no matter that it may take several episodes of "two steps forward, and one step back" in order to discover and retrieve such.

Whether we understand a fairy tale culturally, cognitively, or spiritually—or in many ways, as I am so inclined—there remains one certainty: Fairy tales have survived political aggression and oppressions, the fall and rise of civilizations, massacres of generations, and immense overland and oceanic migrations. They have survived argument, augmentation, and fragmentation. How very diamond-hard these multifaceted jewels truly are. Perhaps this is their greatest mystery and *milagro*, miracle: The great soulful facts imbedded in the tales act exactly like the rhizome of the green plant whose hidden food source remains alive underground—even during the winter, when the plant appears to live no discernible life above ground. The ever-alive hidden essence remains, no matter the weather: *that* is the power of story.

MODERN WISDOM FROM ANCIENT TALES

Though one might think that reading and listening to fairy tales simply transfers their content to both young and ageless hearts and souls alike, it is a much more complex process. The hearing and remembering of tales has an effect more like that of throwing an internal electrical switch to "On." Once activated, the tales evoke from the psyche a deeper subtext, a sagacity that, via the collective unconscious, arrived *inborn*, whether before, during, or just after the first little breeze flowed over the babe's moist little body just fresh from the womb. Though we do not know the exact moment of infusion, we *do* know that deep understandings of the essences contained in stories can be palpably felt by the heart and mind and soul of the listener.

When people listen to tales, they become *encantado*, meaning to become enchanted. Although the word *enchanted* is often misused today, its original sense remains pure—from the Latin, *incantare*, upon, + *cantare*, to sing; to sing upon or about ... in order to create. It is related to the word for *chant*. It speaks of entering onto mysterious ground with one's wits intact. This is quite opposite from having one's mind frozen by an obsession, for instance, and thereby losing dominion over one's wits entirely.

When people hear tales, they are not so much "hearing," as they are remembering; remembering innate ideals. When a body hears stories, something interior knells. A powerful *viento dulce*, the sweet wind of the breath that carries the story, reveals the true soulfulness that lies under the surface of the story. Amongst some of the circumpolar region people, this quality is called *anerca*, the power of the essence of the poem amplified as it is carried outward on the breath of the teller.

Why do we tell and listen to stories over and over? Stories are like little generators that remind us of the essential knowings about soul life—those we may often temporarily forget, lose touch with, and many times so, over an entire lifetime.

A tale invites the psyche to dream upon something that seems familiar, yet often finds its origins rooted far away in time. In entering the tales, listeners are re-visioning the meanings of them, "reading with the heart" these important metaphoric guidances about the life of the soul.

TALES AND THE CREATIVE IMAGINATION

Think about fairy tales too as magic-lantern glass plates that record the zeitgeist, the spirit of the times. Some folklorists examine fairy tales, mythology, and legends in an effort to perceive their cultural underpinnings. For instance, one dear friend folklorist I know writes about "Rumpelstiltskin" as a fairy tale that she feels originated during a time when the jobs of women weavers were being overrun by machines. Men began to take over what was formerly considered "women's work." In this way, the fairy tale may be a cultural snapshot, as well as carrying timeless psychological ideas.

To add to the latter interpretation, from my viewpoint as a

psychoanalyst, and as a *Mexicana-Magyar* from deeply ethnic oral-traditioned cultures, I understand the Rumpelstiltskin story too, as one about putting one's life on the line, about giving one's daunting life's work over to a small but powerful demonic creature who shows up promising, "I'll do this for you, but you have to give me your firstborn child." As the story moves along, we see the demon's desire is not to assist, but to steal the life's blood of the creative soul.

An entirely different way to relate to tales that is distinct from the ones noted above, is to tell for pure entertainment's sake alone. This, by far, is the raison d'être of most modern tellers of stories. Some tales are told because they are simply fun to tell. They are told to enable people to laugh together as the dummling falls off the mountain for the third time because he or she is constantly walking backwards and not paying attention. In this way, certain fairy tales are the prototypes for the slapstick dummlings in media and in politics—The Three Stooges, Abbott and Costello, Cheech and Chong, "The Emperor's New Clothes," and any other number of intentionally and unintentionally comedic single acts, duos, and trios.

We find the roots of true comedy in the oldest stories known to humankind, wherein the fool—often a very good-hearted but unconscious soul—stumbles about, and yet often accidentally finds his or her way to win the crown, the gold, or the prize. No matter how foolish the means, they are somehow just right, for they come straight from the heart, or from faithfulness to God, or from a great intuition, or through a magnificent imagination. The use of tales to entertain finds its depth in the word *entertain*, from the Latin *intertenere*, meaning *inter*, among, + *tenere*, to hold. To *entertain* means to beautifully hold something mutually, to bring together in an intertwined way. The word carries the idea of reciprocity, meaning that each one keeps the other in a certain desired state or condition; that such a condition maintains the heart; that the openness of laughter renews faith in goodness. It is in this way that "to be entertaining" can be understood as a fine necessity, a great revivifying, healing pleasure and presence.

SOME AGE-OLD QUESTIONS
ABOUT TALES

In my travels throughout the world, I have come to appreciate that there are several aspects of fairy tales that audiences want to know more about.

THE APPLICATION OF MORALITY TO TALES

Since time out of mind, certain tales have been used to proselytize a certain way of being, behaving, and thinking. We call these morality tales. Aesop's fables are often understood as such. Think of Aesop's fable of the big black crow who spies a shiny glass jar filled with enormous juicy grapes. He inserts his beak into the mouth of the vessel in order to seize as many as he can. But, because his beak is overfilled with grapes, and is thereby gaping wide open, he cannot remove his bill from the jar. He must either take less of the grapes, or else never taste the luscious grapes and remain forever with his bill lodged in the container.

The tale indicates that, if one tries to take all that one sees, or imagines, the result may be that one will not be able to enjoy any of it. The age-old idea that passion and appetite can entrap the soul in the most deleterious ways emphasizes that greed is the absence of a fair assessment of need.

As in all art, the interpretation of any tale can be made either base or articulate—depending on the artfulness or lack of art in the teller/interpreter. A base way of interpreting Aesop's crow tale might be: "It is bad if one tries to take more than one can really hold. People who do this are bad. You should never do this because you would not want to be bad, would you?"

Truly, children are able to understand more articulate renderings of morality than this. They are able to understand tales as instructive, and as examples for success and/or failure to follow one's heart, to preserve one's soul, to love others, and to not faint in the midst of it all.

In fact, we see in many tales—for example in C. S. Lewis's "Chronicles of Narnia" series featuring the little boy Eustace—children who are shamed or humiliated into goodness, and who have thereby never really learned goodness. They have only learned fear. They have never developed nor amplified the goodness that is already in themselves. They live in fear of being found "not good," or being "found out" as a self who is somehow thoroughly defective. This is not the same as striving towards goodness. Developing mercy, compassion, justice, prudence, temperance, boundaries—all of these qualities develop the greater goodness. These traits are demonstrated in one way or another in the old tales.

Moral interpretation of fairy tales and fables is good. But base and humiliating interpretations that feature threats to the listener, rather than inviting the soul to see at greater depths, shaming rather than teaching, would not be a wise use of these ancient stories that have survived so very many contretemps throughout the eons.

BIAS AND BIGOTRY IN FAIRY TALES

Broad historical distortions can be found in many tales throughout the world. Folk "collectors" of long ago, like the old-fashioned anthropologists, archeologists, and psychologists, often carried and inserted into their works their own biases, especially racial and class ones, that were egregious in some cases and stone-cold ignorant at best. Even without comparing the zeitgeist of "then" with the consciousness of "now," it is sometimes difficult to understand why careful and accurate observations and assessments were not made— ones that one would expect from a true heart and a fair mind.

The inclusion and repetition of strong biases and bigotries in the Grimm collections seemed to be a sine qua non in earlier times, but cannot be tolerated today for any reason, especially since other tales carry the same core teachings, but without the lethal scorn. A particular tale in the original Grimm collection, "The Jew Among the Thorns," is so filled with such deeply murderous racial and religious slurs that one can only say it ought to exist in archives only, for study by serious students of the history of stories of malevolence and the sad failure of humans to reach for the eternal heart. Such tales profane human life, invite the excitement of harming others, and definitely dehumanize us. Absenting such a tale from modern collections is not a matter of censorship—the tales exist in old collections for all to see if they so desire. It is far more so a matter of consciousness and *misereicordia*, mercy for others.

THE ORAL TRADITION, AND THE EVOLUTION OF FINDING MEANING IN TALES

As a soul born into an oral-traditioned, nonliterate family, my way of seeing story is first order, face to face. The Brothers Grimm were second- and third-order observers. Sometimes those who observe the tellers of tales, and the culture of the tellers of tales, stand somewhat or quite outside the very phenomenon they are trying to see. They stand outside because they are—whether beloved or only merely tolerated—visitors, rather than ongoing kin, sharing completely in the day-to-day tragedies and triumphs of the community from generation through generations.

Because the telling of tales is a subjective phenomenon at its true heart, in order to truly understand, one would have to try to live *inside* the culture of the storytellers, as much as possible *inside* the minds of the storytellers, and within the circle of warmth of the teller in "forever relationship."

Once inside the phenomenon, in the best of all worlds, it would be best if one were oneself an organic teller of tales, neither solely a reader of books of tales, nor only a recorder—for there is much to be conveyed in learning the works firsthand at the knees and near the hips of the elders, sitting with, yes, but more so, striving through the everyday household, yard, and field works with the ones who are the master tellers. Growing up naturally in a family life of tales and oral communications, such as stories, songs, and poetry, allows one to see, feel, and benefit from the many nuances one finds in a single fairy tale over a long period of time. As one develops and matures, and continually finds more and more layers of meaning in the tales, one begins to attain a true mastery. Count decades of practice, to achieve such, not single years alone.

Here is an example. So far in my lifetime, I have viewed Ingmar Bergman's film *The Seventh Seal* four times. I first saw it when I was twenty-five years old. I saw it again when I was thirty, then again when I was forty, and again when I was in my early fifties. Each time I discerned additional meaning in the film. I saw more, thought more, much more than ever before.

Fairy tales carry the same capacity. The fairy tale "Red Riding Hood" means a certain something to an eight year old. It can mean something more to a fifteen year old; be found even more complex by a twenty-five year old; so much more seen and understood and "switched on" in a fifty year old, an eighty year old.

This is not to say we categorize the understanding of story by the number of years lived—for often the young are very wise, and sometimes an old person can remain very dense. Rather, the tale can contribute to life-learning and to the development of insight into matters large and small. Learning and insight are what cause a life to develop a sense of *meaningfulness*. That stories can evoke all of these in the mind of the listeners is reason enough to understand them as renewing forces.

In little children we know there exists a developmental stage during which they think very concretely. If you say to children, "It's raining and snowing elephants outside," the little ones run to the window to see the elephants. But, by the time the same children are eight and nine years old, they know that when people use such metaphors, they are not necessarily reflecting a concrete reality. The child has learnt that images are often used to describe the essence of an idea, a kind of imaginative symbol. So the little ones may not run to the windows anymore expecting to see elephants, but rather rain or snow. However they have not lost the image of elephants falling out of the sky; only now has it been translated into a wonderful symbolic language.

Even though we eventually move away from a solely concretistic way of thinking as we grow older, we always retain symbolic thought. And, it is symbolic thought—being able to imagine layers of meaning attached to a single motif or idea—that enables us to invent, innovate, and produce original ideas, with often startling results. If the language of symbols is the mother tongue of creative life, then stories are the mother lode.

UNDERSTANDING STORY MORE DEEPLY

Stories have been interpreted since time out of mind. In mid-twentieth-century analytical psychology one amplifies all the symbols and all the events in the tale; that is, imagining all parts of a story as if all aspects belong to a single individual psyche struggling to find its way into the light of soulfulness from the darkness of the worn-out world.

This is the same theorem found in the writings of Plato, Ovid, and in ancient alchemy, wherein the metaphor of transformation is applied to stories and dreams, especially those symbolizing the struggle to find the *philosiphorum*, the philosopher's stone, in order to transform *lead* (the untaught personality) into (the refined soul) *gold*. These universal underlying themes, meant to fire the imagination to new ideas, have contributed to the thousands of metaphoric and symbolic patterns used to describe the process of coming near to and remaining close to the ineffable Self, this being one of many names for the highest power known to humankind.

Authentic *curanderismo* and other forms of indigenous *samánism* are additional arks that carry the most extensive symbolic systems, the metaphors and methods of transformation, from past generations to future generations. Arthurian legends are also based on the transformation of violent humankind into one contained within the world of courtly love. Therein, *Eros*, meaning actions of regard meant to protect the transformative moment from being flattened out by lack of feeling, remains full and flush with heart feeling and pleasure. The Arthurian legends portray a sheltering stance, which is aimed toward cherishing and protecting the Grail, another symbol of wholeness—the Self.

When we see that the flawed hero or heroine is in fact part and parcel of every single fairy tale, then we begin to see the predictable ways that the psyche often stumbles, and yet recovers. Through tales, we see we all desire and strive to develop into not just so-so ho-hum humans, but into *los humanos verdades*, true human beings, those who are able to hold heart and mind and endeavor with equanimity.

In *curanderismo*, we believe we are born as full souls, but not yet fully blossomed human beings. We develop into human beings over many years' time. We are born as true individuals, of course. But, in the mythos, it is taught that to be a true human being, *ser humano*, takes at least fifty years of living, at least fifty years of dying, without ever completely dying away. When one gathers fifty or more years, one becomes a true human being *if* one has done the work. At the very least, one now has a good chance of it, having accumulated many sufferings, many challenges, having made many mistakes, and hopefully having pulled oneself up, learned, and gone on. Just as in the oldest fairy tales, life is a world wherein one's weaknesses are often one's greatest gifts, where the world of losing and re-finding heart and soul are painful, but often the only primary and worthy point.

THE SURVIVAL OF STORIES AGAINST ALL ODDS: PURPOSEFUL OMISSIONS, ADD-ONS, AND BOWDLERIZATION OF TALES

The Grimm's Fairy Tales in this edition are now over eighty years old. This brings us to the question: Are these texts true to the original words from the speakers' mouths? Or have all translations been adulterated in small and large ways? Translation is an imperfect and beautiful art. Sometimes, if one places a period in a sentence, or does not place a period, if one misplaces even a comma, it can skew the meaning from the original speakers' timbre of voice and intents.

The question of "What is a good translation?" is very specific, but the answer must be very broad, for we cannot think there can be only one good translation, just as there cannot be only one kind of flower, only one acceptable kind of mountain, only one kind of story, one kind of storyteller, or one way of conveying story.

The people of long ago who heard and told the stories are the original translators. They heard and remembered and shaped them through the prisms of their own lives, their cultures, the zeitgeist, the spirit of their times. We know that the Brothers Grimm wrote down the stories related by the voices of their era. We know further that they added, deleted, and shaped as they wrote. In the tradition of poets and artists, this is usual.

I know from the bones of my own family's rich Eastern European fairy tales and Latino mythos, and *cuentos* (often quite rustic, all), that the Brothers Grimm left out much of what is usually found in the tales kept by a nontraditionally educated and agrarian people. The Tales of the Brothers Grimm most often omit scatological material that is common to myriad tales in the oral tradition. The chronic criticism of prelates, mayors, landlords, serfs, and the Church, are occasionally left in, but most often deleted. All material about sex, sexuality, and often sensuality too, and all material about anything elemental that might be deemed "sinful" or socially unacceptable, was left in or left out, depending on the psychology of the teller, the teller's audience, the recorder, and the translator.

So, we see the tales are shaped in many ways. In some ways, to my ear, having heard many of the same tales in the roughest and most rustic oral forms imaginable when I was a child, having heard them first in an oral tradition rather than reading them, I know too that a fine teller adds his or her own insights. The Brothers Grimm recorded and, in some cases, appeared to have inserted a Judeo-Christian version of God in some of the old tales. Even then, the tales gathered by the Brothers Grimm that have survived into our time can be considered to be in at least their third translation, the first being the *antes* one, the older one who granted the story to the teller; the second, the teller's version; the third, what was recorded on paper. The fourth, then, would be anyone who translates from the original German to any other language. To read the tales of Grimm in English is reading a fourth-version translation of the "original teller's version." The fifth translator is anyone who recites or tells from the translated manuscript of Grimm's Fairy Tales. In this way, there is a long hand-down at work in the tales that are included in this book.

Perhaps you have read about the modernist man who recently "cleaned up" *Ulysses*, the great work by James Joyce. The "cleaner-upper" punctuated all the long speeches that Joyce purposely left without punctuation. The man straightened up the Joycean words that were not spelled conventionally. He rearranged, he said, "for clarity." To what end? His idea was that one ought to be able to read *Ulysses* in two hours instead of over two years' time. Yes. Now, what is of interest to me is that there are some who may obtain this massacred text because they have always wanted to read *Ulysses* and were heretofore daunted by the time commitment. But they will hear/read a "bowdlerized" version of the breathtaking original.

Mr. Bowdler was an actual fellow who became famous for "cleaning up" various tales, removing all the parts he deemed erotic. The practice of carving up a story was named after him. Bowdlerized. Something similar also sometimes happens to fairy tales.

There have been those who, over the years, have gone through various stories of the Grimm Brothers' work, "tidying them up," so to speak, changing them, sometimes to placate their own fears. Thusly, we have a version of Baba Yaga in modern literature who no longer threatens to eat children for breakfast. This formidable Great Mother of the World Forest, now drawn in pastel tones only, has become a mere chatty wisp. We have now Bluebeards who resurrect the brides they once murdered in order not to leave justice unsatisfied in a tale. In illustrations there are now often cute, clawless cartoon witches. The greedy monsters of the forest in full horrific regalia, bulging eyes, snaggled snouts, have been turned into plush toys minus the bilge and bulge. Perhaps the greatest psychological distortion of all is the modern practice of turning characters that have depth in their purest hearts, despite their ugliness or strangeness, into nonthreatening over-sugared minimuses.

Extreme fiddling around with tales is not a new development. For a long period of time certain tales, that had originated in Perrault's collection in France, were not published in the German Grimm's Fairy Tale collection, even though they were once an integral part of the work. The reason? France and Germany were at war with one another. Only recently, in the past forty years, have they finally been added back into subsequent editions. Many of them are truly prime—"The Princess and the Pea," "Thumbelina," "Bluebeard"—and several other quite central fairy tales. Imagine fairy tales so powerful as to have been used to keep up the skirmishes of war.

American publishers often did not care to print Japanese fairy tales in the 1940s and 1950s, when, as in all wars, there was much bitterness and grief over those lost on both sides. And as for the offsprings' mothers, fathers, grandmothers, grandfathers, uncles, aunts—everyone was in a sense killed, too, in the deepest body—the heart.

It is unlikely that one country at war with another will publish or perform any stories from the opposing cultural group. Think of the wars across the world at the present. Can you imagine one people performing the most beautiful poetry of the other group? The arts carry more power than politics. Huge power. Why would one ever want to resort to banishing fairy tales, or music, or poems, for heaven's sake? Because nothing of the "enemy" culture ought to impinge on the "home" culture? No, even more so, one might fall in love with the "enemy," because the hearing of stories and poems, and the beauty of others, moves us, unites us, causes love to flower over and around all artificial barriers.

But, as in other miracles of love under duress, those that defy the machinations of war and mayhem, only *written* tales in books can be banished. The fierce spirit of the oral tradition crosses and transgresses every brand of barbed wire. Several of my elders were interred in the slave labor camps in Eastern Europe in the 1940s. There, the common languages were stories, songs, and prayers. Whether Belgian, French, Slav, Russian, Rom, Catholic, Jewish, or other Eastern European, they told fairy tales to one another. They understood the stories by animated affect, by gestures, by tone of voice, by symbols drawn in palms of hands. They would tell each other stories, sing songs, whisper prayers, seeding each others' hopes. Even the most inhumane devastations could not cause the flow of nourishing stories to cease.

Therefore, some of the tales in our family are certainly influenced in nuance here and there via the Turkish man that my uncle shared a pallet with—as he put it—in "the coldest, most freezing winter in summertime, that the world has ever known." They gestured and sang many stories about food because they were starving. They had stories about dancing oranges and talking apples and all manner of things of deepest concern to those who are both tormented and ravenous. In this good way, story is blessing taking place in the wilderness.

SYMBOLIC LANGUAGE OF FAIRY TALES

Fairy tales have a lexicon—a large group of ideas in words and images that symbolize universal thoughts. In the lexicon of depth psychology, for instance, the golden-haired princess does not represent a beautiful child who is going to grow up to be a blonde Miss America-type beauty and marry the football captain from the local high school. The fair-haired princess in the fairy tale represents a kind of beauty of the soul and spirit that, in metaphor, is golden and cannot be debased. The golden-haired princess is not your usual everyday person, but represents the essence of the soul that elevates all through its beauty, and by its honor.

The golden-haired princess can be translated again at a very mundane and base level—such as a heroine representing the ultimate physical ideal for all females. However, it is often more fruitful to understand the tale at levels that allow an individual to contemplate its symbols, and thereby to contemplate and learn about the deeper choices in life. This, by far, is the broader context of tales. The points of the tales are skewed when people say there's only one wonderful image, and that is a golden-haired princess. If you are a little girl and you have brown hair and brown eyes, to be told therefore that you are not soulful and you are not beautiful and you are just not princesslike because you have no golden hair and no pink-cheekedness, or whatever else, is purely silly. Maybe you are a lovely surly little child who is a fabulous poet and an excellent mud-pie cook, for instance. In your story, the princess will be an "original," and perhaps muddy-dressed, and funny-witted, with hair that never looks quiescent. Still, something in her and of her is golden forever—can never be degraded. This, too, is a way of understanding the symbol of golden-hair.[2]

Some argue about whether God is male or female. The fact is that God is God—a huge force that is ineffable; in other words, one cannot comprehend God's totality. But we use images to try to imagine and understand. Some believe that all stories have at their center a single irreversible sensibility that illuminates the many facets of God.

Yet others believe that if tales carry too much of a single image of God, the idea of God begins to calcify, rather than to continue to bloom as an enormous living, flowing force.

Ironically the same is true of fairy tales too. If there are too many "golden-haired princesses only" metaphors, then it gives a smaller idea of the movements of the psyche toward goodness and grace. If there are princesses and commoners, animals and saints, children and mid-age people, elders and talking trees, of all sorts and descriptions, who do all manner of odd, terrible, and fabulous things, much more can be taught and understood.

BRUTALITY IN FAIRY TALES: A SENSIBLE UNDERSTANDING

"It is more than reasonable to ask why there are such brutal episodes in fairy tales. It is a phenomenon found worldwide in mythos and folklore. The gruesome conclusion to these tales are typical of fairy tale endings wherein the spiritual protagonist is unable to complete an attempted transformation.

Psychologically, the brutal episode communicates an imperative psychic truth. This truth is so urgent—and yet so easy to disregard by saying, "Oh, um hmmmm, I do understand," and to then go traipsing off to one's doom anyway—that we are unlikely to heed the alarm if it is

stated in lesser terms.

In the modern technological world, the brutal episodes of fairy tales have been replaced by images in television commercials, such as those showing a family snapshot with one member blotted out and a trail of blood over the photograph to show what happens when a person drives while drunk. Another one attempts to dissuade people from using illegal drugs by showing an egg bubbling in a frying pan and pointing out that this is what happens to the brain on drugs. The brutal motif is an ancient way of causing the emotive [and often dismissive ego] to pay attention to a very serious message."[3]

I have many fierce stories from my own family that revolve around the character of the Baba Yaga. She is an essential figure in the life of our family, and a beloved one. In my library I also have six children's books containing different variations of the same Baba Yaga story. Two of the books tell the actual scary story. The other four are "cleaned up." Those that are cleaned up are solely so because the authors seem afraid the children hearing them will become frightened. This has been a concern about Grimm's tales, and certain other tales for a long time, and still today.

As we have known for centuries, most recently from observing the phenomena of R. L. Stine's and the Harry Potter series of popular scary works, many children (and adults) like to be held in the tension of the story in a secure way, and love to be caught unawares if they know all will be well in the end.

Often it is the parents, rather, who are frightened, and they in turn frighten the child. Usually, if the parent is not anxious, the child is not anxious either. However, there are predictable avoidances in a child's development. One can not present a five-month-old child with a stranger and expect the child not to wail. At that age, they possess a precise differentiation about who is familiar and who is not known; therefore, the child startles for a brief period. This passes after a few weeks. Then, the little one begins to treat strangers as interesting curiosities rather than as threats. What startles or intrigues a child changes as they mature.

Essentially I believe it is useful and essential for those who know and love the child best to introduce them to the more complex realities of life. For instance, we hear some parents say, "Oh well, I don't know if I should tell my child serious things. I don't know if I should say anything about death, illness, hatred, or war." Of course one ought to tell a child rough stories as well as beauteous ones. Every child must have a map to, and a training about, the great bright and dark woods of the world, both. Leaving out parts is not strengthening. Leaving out that there are violences, poor choices, great mind-bending passions loose in the world, and not giving the child knowledge about sheltering one's soul, weakens the child.

Many of us have witnessed an entire parental generation being so upset about conveying to the child at an appropriate age the mechanics and wonders of sexuality out loud, for instance—which is essentially the story of a miracle and the body's capacity for joy—that many parents hoped to spend a lifetime not talking about it at length, or at all. Then, by the time an overwhelmed parent arrived at the point of trying to say what a loving, wonderful thing human sexuality was, they flubbed it, and all concerned became totally anxiety ridden about the matter, thereby silencing one of the most beautiful stories in the world. They forgot it was a set of age-appropriate compelling stories about joy, compulsions, thoughtfulness, discipline, and wisdom.

This is why so many often learn about sexuality from peers and non-blood friends—everyone else, it often seems, except the parents. We learn from those who are more relaxed with the stories; those who find them cherished, or titillating, or intriguing. Yes, tell your child about serious life matters, or else someone else will— often unreliably and without loving guidance attached.

There is brutality in some of the tales in this book. If you are reading them to children, the best advice is to know your child and trust your own instincts. Parents do come with a full set of sound instincts. You and your child enter the forest of tales together. Your young will interpret at whatever level they are ready for, and they will understand as much as they can—sometimes more than you yourself.

Parents will interpret at whatever level they themselves live at. So, a parent who is very authoritarian, who believes that they alone rule, and no one else's opinion counts, will interpret "Red Riding Hood" a certain way. On the other hand, a parent who says "anything goes, whatever you want, however you want it to be," will interpret also at the level that he or she understands life. A parent who loves the heart and mind and soul of the little child, and who shelters and guides wisely, will interpret "Red Riding Hood" in yet another way.

If you consciously strive toward having an inner life, then you can understand the tales and respond at levels that would not be apparent to another whose viewpoint is "An apple is only an apple, and nothing more" or "If you've seen one mountain, you have seen them all."

It takes a certain kind of creative mind, a spiritual mind, a mind that wants to learn and grow and develop consciously and constantly in order to understand any idea or ideal to its depths. I suggest that by reading stories to children, your children are learning at one level, and you yourself are learning at a certain level, too. I love to imagine adults reading stories to themselves. When they're heard by children, or when they're heard by adults, or by both, stories have the effect of reinforcing and validating something they already know, a great something about goodness, deep in their hearts.

THE NEVER-ENDING STORY

Growing up, I was given many episodes of Red Riding Hood, of Cinderella, of Baba Yaga, and so on. But, to my knowledge, they are nowhere written down. With written fairy tales, as a result, people

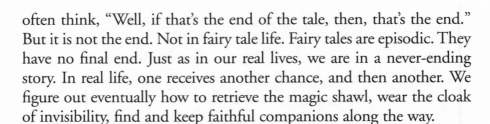

often think, "Well, if that's the end of the tale, then, that's the end." But it is not the end. Not in fairy tale life. Fairy tales are episodic. They have no final end. Just as in our real lives, we are in a never-ending story. In real life, one receives another chance, and then another. We figure out eventually how to retrieve the magic shawl, wear the cloak of invisibility, find and keep faithful companions along the way.

ILLUSTRATIONS OF FAIRY TALES

Arthur Rackham is the illustrator here, a gifted draughtsman. No computer. No Artograph—that is, a magnifying machine that projects an image onto the wall or onto the canvas so the artist can trace it. Rackham knew his anatomy, which is the absolute ground note of brilliant illustration. His figures genuinely have bones under their skins. He is also a colorist. He carries a tremendous sense of brilliant rich colors; in today's nomenclature: scarlet, vermilion, terra verde, thalocyanide blue—beautiful colors.

His work I would call fantastic in the genre of the Fabula, drawing on the fantastic images that exist in the soul's imagination. His renditions of giants, ogres, witches, kings, queens, serfs, and all the rest, are part and parcel of these fairy tales. They have a medieval tone to them, reflecting a cultured society that was divided into castes, but ones that are different than the castes that cultures are divided into today.

How do illustrations enhance the tale? Or do they?

I like to look at illustrations. They are rife with images within the images, like dreams. I especially like poster illustrations and children's book illustrations. I think children's book illustrators are God's angels. They are true voices from the soul.

At a certain age, amongst children especially, the illustrations in a book—especially in the midst of *long* fairy tales—serve to anchor the child in the story, to fasten their interest throughout.

I have been moved by the fact that so many fairy tales have been put into animation by various film companies. But I also remain ambivalent about the fact that those images, chosen by the very gifted artists, often become the sole and alpha images in a child's mind, and often in the grown-ups' minds too—and for life. We see those images only, instead of our own creative imaginings. Leaching the imagination of its many innate and continuously changing images deteriorates one's creative ability, and causes one to draw from "stock images" only.

The figure of the Hunchback of Notre Dame is a good example. In a recent animated film version, though the animation art is very lively, the hunchback appears as lovable, is very sweet in every way. Yet Victor Hugo's original hunchback was ugly, frightening, oppressed, ridiculed, beaten by others; a great moaning, horribly battered hulk. Because of his many torments, this is why it was such a miracle that the hunchback retained such a very pure heart of love for beauty. The leitmotif of the monster who has a pure heart is an ancient idea. It is found in Mary Shelley's *Frankenstein* also. The monster moves to punish wrong, and to uphold and protect beauty. Frankenstein's monster becomes angry with the doctor for manufacturing subhumans. The monster wants to protect the woman who is, to him, the heart of love, beauty, and Eros. The same leitmotif is found in the fairy tale "Beauty and the Beast."

When images are lessened into only "cute" ones, the startling impact of finding beauty and transformation in what is thought most grotesque, ugly, or ruined, is lost; the concept of redemption for all disappears. Imagination is greater than any rote material can ever be.

Some illustrators are only hacks. Their works look like they were made for a marzipan magazine. Now, imagine illustration as fine art. Rackham's illustrations *are* fine art. They are phantasmagoric; they have an ethereal quality to them; they denote hunger, distortion of scale. They offend perfection and illustrate anomalies of all kinds. They have components in them that are heavily symbolic, poetically and politically ancient.

SOULFULNESS IN FAIRY TALES

Soulfulness is not a plastic commodity, not a polymerized item to be gained "out there." But rather, it is a fierce inborn human function and drive. Through it, we can gaze upon Arthur Rackham's paintings without ever reading the stories, and yet know a great deal about the heart of the stories. Through soulfulness, we engage the stories themselves. Illustrated or not, we understand they are also a true kind of art, as elegiac, as energetic as the modernists, as ancient, as mysterious as the firelight drawings upon the chalky rock walls at Lascaux.

For all of our graceful and awkward turnings and graspings, for all of our astonished losings, and even more astounding findings of meaning in "the invisible, but palpably felt" world, it is my desire that the truths and insights of these stories truly reflect your psyche to you in some beautiful and illumined way. Certainly, they reflect all of our shiver-dreads, all of our longing-loves, and all of our incorruptible hopes.

> May such blessings be true for you;
> May they be true for me;
> May they be true for all of us.

---

[1] From *Women Who Run With the Wolves*, Clarissa Pinkola Estés, Ph.D. © 1992, 1995. Random House/Ballantine. By permission.

[2] For this reason I have always loved "The Brown-Haired Princess" by Jane Yolen.

[3] From *Women Who Run With the Wolves*, Clarissa Pinkola Estés, Ph.D. © 1992, 1995. Random House/Ballantine. By permission.

TALES
of the
BROTHERS
GRIMM

SNOWDROP

IT WAS THE MIDDLE OF WINTER, and the snowflakes were falling from the sky like feathers. Now, a Queen sat sewing at a window framed in black ebony, and as she sewed she looked out upon the snow. Suddenly she pricked her finger and three drops of blood fell on to the snow. And the red looked so lovely on the white that she thought to herself: "If only I had a child as white as snow and as red as blood, and as black as the wood of the window frame!" Soon after, she had a daughter, whose hair was black as ebony, while her cheeks were red as blood, and her skin as white as snow; so she was called Snowdrop. But when the child was born the Queen died. A year after the King took another wife. She was a handsome woman, but proud and overbearing, and could not endure that any one should surpass her in beauty. She had a magic looking-glass, and when she stood before it and looked at herself she used to say:

> "Mirror, mirror on the wall,
> Who is fairest of us all?"

then the glass answered,

> "Queen, thou 'rt fairest of them all."

Then she was content, for she knew that the looking-glass spoke the truth.

But Snowdrop grew up and became more and more beautiful, so that when she was seven years old she was as beautiful as the day, and far surpassed the Queen. Once, when she asked her glass,

> "Mirror, mirror on the wall,
> Who is fairest of us all?"

it answered—

> "Queen, thou art fairest here, I hold,
> But Snowdrop is fairer a thousandfold."

Then the Queen was horror-struck, and turned green and yellow with jealousy. From the hour that she saw Snowdrop her heart sank, and she hated the little girl.

The pride and envy of her heart grew like a weed, so that she had no rest day nor night. At last she called a huntsman, and said: "Take the child out into the wood; I will not set eyes on her again. You must kill her and bring me her lungs and liver as tokens."

The huntsman obeyed, and took Snowdrop out into the forest, but when he drew his hunting-knife and was preparing to plunge it into her innocent heart, she began to cry:

"Alas, dear huntsman, spare my life, and I will run away into the wild forest and never come back again."

And because of her beauty the huntsman had pity on her and said, "Well, run away, poor child." Wild beasts will soon devour you, he thought, but still he felt as though a weight were lifted from his heart because he had not been obliged to kill her. And as just at that moment a young fawn came leaping by, he pierced it and took the lungs and liver as tokens to the Queen. The cook was ordered to serve them up in pickle, and the wicked Queen ate them thinking that they were Snowdrop's.

Now the poor child was alone in the great wood, with no living soul near, and she was so frightened that she knew not what to do. Then she began to run, and ran over the sharp stones and through the brambles, while the animals passed her by without harming her.

She ran as far as her feet could carry her till it was nearly evening, when she saw a little house and went in to rest. Inside, everything was small, but as neat and clean as could be. A small table covered with a white cloth stood ready with seven small plates, and by every plate was a spoon, knife, fork, and cup. Seven little beds were ranged against the walls, covered with snow-white coverlets. As Snowdrop was very hungry and thirsty she ate a little bread and vegetable from each plate, and drank a little wine from each cup, for she did not want to eat up the whole of one portion. Then, being very tired, she lay down in one of the beds. She tried them all but none suited her; one was too short, another too long, all except the seventh, which was just right. She remained in it, said her prayers, and fell asleep.

When it was quite dark the masters of the house came in. They were seven dwarfs, who used to dig in the mountains for ore. They kindled their lights, and as soon as they could see they noticed that some one had been there, for everything was not in the order in which they had left it.

The first said, "Who has been sitting in my chair?"

The second said, "Who has been eating off my plate?"

The third said, "Who has been nibbling my bread?"

The fourth said, "Who has been eating my vegetables?"

The fifth said, "Who has been using my fork?"

The sixth said, "Who has been cutting with my knife?"

The seventh said, "Who has been drinking out of my cup?"

Then the first looked and saw a slight impression on his bed, and said, "Who has been treading on my bed?" The others came running up and said, "And mine, and mine." But the seventh, when he looked into his bed, saw Snowdrop who lay there asleep. He called the others, who came up and cried out with astonishment, as they held their lights and gazed at Snowdrop. "Heavens! what a beautiful child," they said, and they were so delighted that they did not wake her up but left her asleep in bed. And the seventh dwarf slept with his comrades, an hour with each all through the night.

When morning came Snowdrop woke up, and when she saw the seven dwarfs she was frightened.

But they were very kind and asked her name.

"I am called Snowdrop," she answered.

"How did you get into our house?" they asked.

Then she told them how her stepmother had wished to get rid of her, how the huntsman had spared her life, and how she had run all day till she had found the house.

Then the dwarfs said, "Will you look after our household, cook, make the beds, wash, sew and knit, and keep everything neat and clean? If so you shall stay with us and want for nothing."

"Yes," said Snowdrop, "with all my heart"; and she stayed with them and kept the house in order.

In the morning they went to the mountain and searched for copper and gold, and in the evening they came back and then their meal had to be ready. All day the maiden was alone, and the good dwarfs warned her and said, "Beware of your stepmother, who will soon learn that you are here. Don't let anyone in."

But the Queen, having, as she imagined, eaten Snowdrop's liver and lungs, and feeling certain that she was the fairest of all, stepped in front of her glass, and asked—

> "Mirror, mirror on the wall,
> Who is fairest of us all?"

the glass answered as usual—

> "Queen, thou art fairest here, I hold,
> But Snowdrop over the fells,
> Who with the seven dwarfs dwells,
> Is fairer still a thousandfold."

She was dismayed, for she knew that the glass told no lies, and she saw that the hunter had deceived her and that Snowdrop still lived. Accordingly she began to wonder afresh how she might compass her death; for as long as she was not the fairest in the land her jealous heart left her no rest. At last she thought of a plan. She dyed her face and dressed up like an old pedlar, so that she was quite unrecognizable. In this guise she crossed over the seven mountains to the home of the seven dwarfs and called out, "Wares for sale."

Snowdrop peeped out of the window and said, "Good-day, mother, what have you got to sell?"

"Good wares, fine wares," she answered, "laces of every color";

and she held out one which was made of gay plaited silk.

"I may let the honest woman in," thought Snowdrop, and she unbolted the door and bought the pretty lace.

"Child," said the old woman, "what a sight you are, I will lace you properly for once."

Snowdrop made no objection, and placed herself before the old woman to let her lace her with the new lace. But the old woman laced so quickly and tightly that she took away Snowdrop's breath and she fell down as though dead.

"Now I am the fairest," she said to herself, and hurried away.

Not long after the seven dwarfs came home, and were horror-struck when they saw their dear little Snowdrop lying on the floor without stirring, like one dead. When they saw she was laced too tight they cut the lace, whereupon she began to breathe and soon came back to life again. When the dwarfs heard what had happened, they said that the old pedlar was no other than the wicked Queen. "Take care not to let any one in when we are not here," they said.

Now the wicked Queen, as soon as she got home, went to the glass and asked—

> "Mirror, mirror on the wall,
> Who is fairest of us all?"

and it answered as usual—

> "Queen, thou art fairest here, I hold,
> But Snowdrop over the fells,
> Who with the seven dwarfs dwells,
> Is fairer still a thousandfold."

When she heard it all her blood flew to her heart, so enraged was she, for she knew that Snowdrop had come back to life again. Then she thought to herself, "I must plan something which will put an end to her." By means of witchcraft, in which she was skilled, she made a poisoned comb. Next she disguised herself and took the form of a different old woman. She crossed the mountains and came to the home of the seven dwarfs, and knocked at the door calling out, "Good wares to sell."

Snowdrop looked out of the window and said, "Go away, I must not let any one in."

"At least you may look," answered the old woman, and she took the poisoned comb and held it up.

The child was so pleased with it that she let herself be beguiled, and opened the door.

When she had made a bargain the old woman said, "Now I will comb your hair properly for once."

Poor Snowdrop, suspecting no evil, let the old woman have her way, but scarcely was the poisoned comb fixed in her hair than the poison took effect, and the maiden fell down unconscious.

"You paragon of beauty," said the wicked woman, "now it is all over with you," and she went away.

Happily it was near the time when the seven dwarfs came home. When they saw Snowdrop lying on the ground as though dead, they immediately suspected her stepmother, and searched till they found the poisoned comb. No sooner had they removed it than Snowdrop came to herself again and related what had happened. They warned her again to be on her guard, and to open the door to no one.

When she got home the Queen stood before her glass and said—

> "Mirror, mirror on the wall,
> Who is fairest of us all?"

and it answered as usual—

> "Queen, thou art fairest here, I hold,
> But Snowdrop over the fells,

Who with the seven dwarfs dwells,
Is fairer still a thousandfold."

When she heard the glass speak these words she trembled and quivered with rage, "Snowdrop shall die," she said, "even if it cost me my own life." Thereupon she went into a secret room, which no one ever entered but herself, and made a poisonous apple.

Outwardly it was beautiful to look upon, with rosy cheeks, and every one who saw it longed for it, but whoever ate of it was certain to die. When the apple was ready she dyed her face and dressed herself like an old peasant woman and so crossed the seven hills to the dwarfs' home. There she knocked.

Snowdrop put her head out of the window and said, "I must not let any one in, the seven dwarfs have forbidden me."

"It is all the same to me," said the peasant woman. "I shall soon get rid of my apples. There, I will give you one."

"No; I must not take anything."

"Are you afraid of poison?" said the woman. "See, I will cut the apple in half: you eat the red side and I will keep the other."

Now the apple was so cunningly painted that the red half alone was poisoned. Snowdrop longed for the apple, and when she saw the peasant woman eating she could hold out no longer, stretched

out her hand and took the poisoned half. Scarcely had she put a bit into her mouth than she fell dead to the ground.

The Queen looked with a fiendish glance, and laughed aloud and said, "White as snow, red as blood, and black as ebony, this time the dwarfs cannot wake you up again." And when she got home and asked the looking-glass—

"Mirror, mirror on the wall,
Who is fairest of us all?"

it answered at last—

"Queen, thou 'rt fairest of them all."

Then her jealous heart was at rest, as much at rest as a jealous heart can be. The dwarfs, when they came at evening, found Snowdrop lying on the ground and not a breath escaped her lips, and she was quite dead. They lifted her up and looked to see whether any poison was to be found, unlaced her dress, combed her hair, washed her with wine and water, but it was no use; their dear child was dead. They laid her on a bier, and all seven sat down and bewailed her and lamented over her for three whole days. Then they prepared to bury her, but she looked so fresh and living, and still had such beautiful rosy cheeks, that they said, "We cannot bury her in the dark earth." And so they had a transparent glass coffin made, so that she could be seen from every side, laid her inside and wrote on it in letters of gold her name and how she was a King's daughter. Then they set the coffin out on the mountain, and one of them always stayed by and watched it. And the birds came too and mourned for Snowdrop, first an owl, then a raven, and lastly a dove.

Now Snowdrop lay a long, long time in her coffin, looking as though she were asleep. It happened that a Prince was wandering in the wood, and came to the home of the seven dwarfs to pass the night. He saw the coffin on the mountain and lovely Snowdrop inside, and read what was written in golden letters. Then he said to the dwarfs, "Let me have the coffin; I will give you whatever you like for it."

But they said, "We will not give it up for all the gold of the world."

Then he said, "Then give it to me as a gift, for I cannot live without Snowdrop to gaze upon; and I will honor and reverence it as my dearest treasure."

When he had said these words the good dwarfs pitied him and gave him the coffin.

The Prince bade his servants carry it on their shoulders. Now it happened that they stumbled over some brushwood, and the shock dislodged the piece of apple from Snowdrop's throat. In a short time she opened her eyes, lifted the lid of the coffin, sat up and came back to life again completely.

"O heaven! where am I?" she asked.

The Prince, full of joy, said, "You are with me," and he related what had happened, and then said, "I love you better than all the world; come with me to my father's castle and be my wife."

Snowdrop agreed and went with him, and their wedding was celebrated with great magnificence. Snowdrop's wicked stepmother was invited to the feast; and when she had put on her fine clothes she stepped to her glass and asked—

> "Mirror, mirror on the wall,
> Who is fairest of us all?"

The glass answered—

> "Queen, thou art fairest here, I hold,
> The young Queen fairer a thousandfold."

Then the wicked woman uttered a curse, and was so terribly frightened that she didn't know what to do. Yet she had no rest: she felt obliged to go and see the young Queen. And when she came in she recognized Snowdrop, and stood stock still with fear and terror. But iron slippers were heated over the fire, and were soon brought in with tongs and put before her. And she had to step into the red-hot shoes and dance till she fell down dead.

THE PINK

THERE WAS ONCE A QUEEN, who had not been blessed with children. As she walked in her garden, she prayed every morning that a son or daughter might be given to her. Then one day an angel came, and said to her: "Be content: you shall have a son, and he shall be endowed with the power of wishing, so that whatsoever he wishes for shall be granted to him." She hurried to the King, and told him the joyful news; and when the time came a son was born to them, and they were filled with delight.

Every morning the Queen used to take her little son into the gardens, where the wild animals were kept, to bathe him in a clear, sparkling fountain. It happened one day, when the child was a little older, that as she sat with him on her lap she fell asleep.

The old cook, who knew that the child had the power of wishing, came by and stole it; he also killed a chicken, and dropped some of its blood on the Queen's garments. Then he took the child away to a secret place, where he placed it out to be nursed. Then he ran back to the King, and accused the Queen of having allowed her child to be carried off by a wild animal.

When the King saw the blood on the Queen's garments he believed the story, and was overwhelmed with anger. He caused a high tower to be built, into which neither the sun nor the moon could penetrate. Then he ordered his wife to be shut up in it, and the door walled up. She was to stay there for seven years, without eating or drinking, so as gradually to pine away. But two angels from heaven, in the shape of white doves, came to her, bringing food twice a day till the seven years were ended.

Meanwhile the cook thought, "If the child really has the power of wishing, and I stay here, I might easily fall into disgrace." So he left the palace, and went to the boy, who was then old enough to talk, and said to him, "Wish for a beautiful castle, with a garden, and everything belonging to it." Hardly had the words passed the boy's lips than all that he had asked for was there.

After a time the cook said, "It is not good for you to be so much alone; wish for a beautiful maiden to be your companion."

The Prince uttered the wish, and immediately a maiden stood before them, more beautiful than any painter could paint. So they grew very fond of each other, and played together, while the old cook went out hunting like any grand gentleman. But the idea came to him one day that the Prince might wish to go to his father some time, and he would thereby be placed in a very awkward position. So he took the maiden aside, and said to her, "Tonight, when the boy is asleep, go and drive this knife into his heart. Then bring me his heart and his tongue. If you fail to do it, you will lose your own life."

Then he went away; but when the next day came, the Maiden had not obeyed his command, and she said, "Why should I shed his innocent blood, when he has never done harm to any creature in his life?"

The cook again said, "If you do not obey me, you will lose your own life."

When he had gone away, she ordered a young hind to be brought and killed; then she cut out its heart and its tongue, and put them on a dish. When she saw the old man coming she said to the boy, "Get into bed, and cover yourself right over."

The old scoundrel came in and said, "Where are the tongue and the heart of the boy?"

The maiden gave him the dish; but the Prince threw off the coverings, and said, "You old sinner, why did you want to kill me? Now hear your sentence. You shall be turned into a black poodle, with a

gold chain round your neck, and you shall be made to eat live coals, so that flames of fire may come out of your mouth."

As he said the words, the old man was changed into a black poodle, with a gold chain round his neck; and the scullions brought live coals, which he had to eat till the flames poured out of his mouth.

The Prince stayed on at the castle for a time, thinking of his mother, and wondering if she were still alive. At last he said to the maiden, "I am going into my own country. If you like you can go with me; I will take you."

She answered: "Alas! it is so far off, and what should I do in a strange country where I know no one?"

As she did not wish to go, and yet they could not bear to be parted, he changed her into a beautiful pink, which he took with him.

Then he set out on his journey, and the poodle was made to run alongside till the Prince reached his own country.

Arrived there, he went straight to the tower where his mother was imprisoned, and as the tower was so high he wished for a ladder to reach the top. Then he climbed up, looked in, and cried, "Dearest Mother, lady Queen, are you still alive?"

She, thinking it was the angels who brought her food come back, said, "I have just eaten; I do not want anything more."

Then he said, "I am your own dear son whom the wild animals were supposed to have devoured; but I am still alive, and I shall soon come and rescue you."

Then he got down and went to his father. He had himself announced as a strange huntsman, anxious to take service with the King, who said, "Yes; if he was skilled in game preserving, and could procure plenty of venison, he would engage him. But there had never before been any game in the whole district."

The huntsman promised to procure as much game as the King could possibly require for the royal table.

Then he called the whole hunt together, and ordered them all to come into the forest with him. He caused a great circle to be enclosed, with only one outlet; then he took his place in the middle, and began to wish as hard as he could. Immediately over two hundred head of game came running into the enclosure; these the huntsmen had to shoot, and then they were piled on to sixty country wagons, and driven home to the King. So for once he was able to load his board with game, after having had none for many years.

The King was much pleased, and commanded his whole court to a banquet on the following day. When they were all assembled, he said to the huntsman, "You shall sit by me as you are so clever."

He answered, "My lord and King, may it please your Majesty, I am only a poor huntsman!"

The King, however, insisted, and said, "I command you to sit by me."

As he sat there, his thoughts wandered to his dear mother, and he wished one of the courtiers would speak of her. Hardly had he wished it than the Lord High Marshal said—

"Your Majesty, we are all rejoicing here, how fares it with Her Majesty the Queen? Is she still alive in the tower, or has she perished?"

But the King answered, "She allowed my beloved son to be devoured by wild animals, and I do not wish to hear anything about her."

Then the huntsman stood up and said—

"Gracious Father, she is still alive, and I am her son. He was not devoured by wild animals; he was taken away by the scoundrel of a cook. He stole me while my mother was asleep, and sprinkled her garments with the blood of a chicken." Then he brought up the black poodle with the golden chain, and said, "This is the villain."

He ordered some live coals to be brought, which he made the dog eat in the sight of all the people till the flames poured out of his mouth. Then he asked the King if he would like to see the cook in his true shape, and wished him back, and there he stood in his white apron, with his knife at his side.

The King was furious when he saw him, and ordered him to be thrown into the deepest dungeon. Then the huntsman said further—

"My father would you like to see the maiden who so tenderly saved my life when she was ordered to kill me, although by so doing she might have lost her own life?"

The King answered, "Yes, I will gladly see her."

Then his son said, "Gracious Father, I will show her to you first in the guise of a beautiful flower."

He put his hand into his pocket, and brought out the pink. It was a finer one than the King had ever seen before. Then his son said, "Now, I will show her to you in her true form."

The moment his wish was uttered, she stood before them in all her beauty, which was greater than any artist could paint.

The King sent ladies and gentlemen-in-waiting to the tower to bring the Queen back to his royal table. But when they reached the tower they found that she would no longer eat or drink, and she said, "The merciful God, who has preserved my life so long, will soon release me now."

Three days after she died. At her burial the two white doves which had brought her food during her captivity, followed and hovered over her grave.

The old King caused the wicked cook to be torn into four quarters; but his own heart was filled with grief and remorse, and he died soon after.

His son married the beautiful maiden he had brought home with him as a flower, and, for all I know, they may be living still.

BRIAR ROSE

ALONG TIME AGO THERE LIVED a King and Queen, who said every day, "If only we had a child"; but for a long time they had none.

It fell out once, as the Queen was bathing, that a frog crept out of the water on to the land, and said to her: "Your wish shall be fulfilled; before a year has passed you shall bring a daughter into the world."

The frog's words came true. The Queen had a little girl who was so beautiful that the King could not contain himself for joy, and prepared a great feast. He invited not only his relations, friends, and acquaintances, but the fairies, in order that they might be favorably and kindly disposed towards the child. There were thirteen of them in the kingdom, but as the King had only twelve golden plates for them to eat from, one of the fairies had to stay at home.

The feast was held with all splendor, and when it came to an end the fairies all presented the child with a magic gift. One gave her virtue, another beauty, a third riches, and so on, with everything in the world that she could wish for.

When eleven of the fairies had said their say, the thirteenth suddenly appeared. She wanted to revenge herself for not having been invited. Without greeting any one, or even glancing at the company, she called out in a loud voice: "The Princess shall prick herself with a distaff in her fifteenth year and shall fall down dead"; and without another word she turned and left the hall.

Every one was terror-struck, but the twelfth fairy, whose wish was still unspoken, stepped forward. She could not cancel the curse, but could only soften it, so she said: "It shall not be death, but a deep sleep lasting a hundred years, into which your daughter shall fall."

The King was so anxious to guard his dear child from the mis-

fortune, that he sent out a command that all the distaffs in the whole kingdom should be burned.

As time went on all the promises of the fairies came true. The Princess grew up so beautiful, modest, kind, and clever that every one who saw her could not but love her. Now it happened that on the very day when she was fifteen years old the King and Queen were away from home, and the Princess was left quite alone in the castle. She wandered about over the whole place, looking at rooms and halls as she pleased, and at last she came to an old tower. She ascended a narrow, winding staircase and reached a little door. A rusty key was sticking in the lock, and when she turned it the door flew open. In a little room sat an old woman with a spindle, spinning her flax busily.

"Good day, Granny," said the Princess; "what are you doing?"

"I am spinning," said the old woman, and nodded her head.

"What is the thing that whirls round so merrily?" asked the Princess; and she took the spindle and tried to spin too.

But she had scarcely touched it before the curse was fulfilled, and she pricked her finger with the spindle. The instant she felt the prick she fell upon the bed which was standing near, and lay still in a deep sleep which spread over the whole castle.

The King and Queen, who had just come home and had stepped into the hall, went to sleep, and all their courtiers with them. The horses went to sleep in the stable, the dogs in the yard, the doves on the roof, the flies on the wall; yes, even the fire flickering on the hearth grew still and went to sleep, and the roast meat stopped crackling; the cook, who was pulling the scullion's hair because he had made some mistake, let him go and went to sleep. The wind dropped, and on the trees in front of the castle not a leaf stirred.

But round the castle a hedge of briar roses began to grow up; every year it grew higher, till at last it surrounded the whole castle so that nothing could be seen of it, not even the flags on the roof.

But there was a legend in the land about the lovely sleeping Briar Rose, as the King's daughter was called, and from time to time Princes came and tried to force a way through the hedge into the castle. They found it impossible, for the thorns, as though they had hands, held them fast, and the Princes remained caught in them without being able to free themselves, and so died a miserable death.

After many, many years a Prince came again to the country and heard an old man tell of the castle which stood behind the briar hedge, in which a most beautiful maiden called Briar Rose had been asleep for the last hundred years, and with her slept the King, Queen, and all her courtiers. He knew also, from his grandfather, that many Princes had already come and sought to pierce through the briar hedge, and had remained caught in it and died a sad death.

Then the young Prince said, "I am not afraid; I am determined to go and look upon the lovely Briar Rose."

The good old man did all in his power to dissuade him, but the Prince would not listen to his words.

Now, however, the hundred years were just ended, and the day had come when Briar Rose was to wake up again. When the Prince approached the briar hedge it was in blossom, and was covered with beautiful large flowers which made way for him of their own accord and let him pass unharmed, and then closed up again into a hedge behind him.

In the courtyard he saw the horses and brindled hounds lying asleep, on the roof sat the doves with their heads under their wings: and when he went into the house the flies were asleep on the walls, and near the throne lay the King and Queen; in the kitchen was the cook, with his hand raised as though about to strike the scullion, and the maid sat with the black fowl in her lap which she was about to pluck.

He went on further, and all was so still that he could hear his own breathing. At last he reached the tower, and opened the door into the little room where Briar Rose was asleep. There she lay, looking so beautiful that he could not take his eyes off her; he bent down and gave her a kiss. As he touched her, Briar Rose opened her eyes and looked lovingly at him. Then they went down together; and the King woke up, and the Queen, and all the courtiers, and looked at each other with astonished eyes. The horses in the stable stood up and shook themselves, the hounds leaped about and wagged their tails, the doves on the roof lifted their heads from under their wings, looked round, and flew into the fields; the flies on the walls began to crawl again, the fire in the kitchen roused itself and blazed up and cooked the food, the meat began to crackle, and the cook boxed the scullion's ears so soundly that he screamed aloud, while the maid finished plucking the fowl. Then the wedding of the Prince and Briar Rose was celebrated with all splendor, and they lived happily till they died.

ASHENPUTTEL

THE WIFE OF A RICH MAN fell ill, and when she felt that she was nearing her end, she called her only daughter to her bedside, and said:

"Dear child, continue devout and good, then God will always help you, and I will look down upon you from heaven, and watch over you."

Thereupon she closed her eyes, and breathed her last.

The maiden went to her mother's grave every day and wept, and she continued to be devout and good. When the winter came, the snow spread a white covering on the grave, and when the sun of spring had unveiled it again, the husband took another wife. The new wife brought home with her two daughters, who were fair and beautiful to look upon, but base and black at heart.

Then began a sad time for the unfortunate stepchild.

"Is this stupid goose to sit with us in the parlor?" they said.

"Whoever want to eat bread must earn it; go and sit with the kitchenmaid."

They took away her pretty clothes, and made her put on an old grey frock, and gave her wooden clogs.

"Just look at the proud Princess, how well she's dressed," they laughed, as they led her to the kitchen. There, the girl was obliged to do hard work from morning till night, to get up at daybreak, carry water, light the fire, cook, and wash. Not content with that, the sisters inflicted on her every vexation they could think of; they made fun of her, and tossed the peas and lentils among the ashes,

25

so that she had to sit down and pick them out again. In the evening, when she was worn out with work, she had no bed to go to, but had to lie on the hearth among the cinders. And because, on account of that, she always looked dusty and dirty, they called her Ashenputtel.

It happened one day that the father had a mind to go to the fair. So he asked both his stepdaughters what he should bring home for them.

"Fine clothes," said one.

"Pearls and jewels," said the other.

"But you, Ashenputtel?" said he. "What will you have?"

"Father, break off for me the first twig which brushes against your hat on your way home."

Well, for his two stepdaughters he brought beautiful clothes, pearls, and jewels, and on his way home, as he was riding through a green copse, a hazel twig grazed against him and knocked his hat off. Then he broke off the branch and took it with him.

When he got home he gave his stepdaughters what they had asked for, and to Ashenputtel he gave the twig from the hazel bush.

Ashenputtel thanked him, and went to her mother's grave and planted the twig upon it; she wept so much that her tears fell and watered it. And it took root and became a fine tree.

Ashenputtel went to the grave three times every day, wept and prayed, and every time a little white bird came and perched upon the tree, and when she uttered a wish, the little bird threw down to her what she had wished for.

Now it happened that the King proclaimed a festival, which was to last three days, and to which all the beautiful maidens in the country were invited, in order that his son might choose a bride.

When the two stepdaughters heard that they were also to be present, they were in high spirits, called Ashenputtel, and said:

"Brush our hair and clean our shoes, and fasten our buckles, for we are going to the feast at the King's palace."

Ashenputtel obeyed, but wept, for she also would gladly have gone to the ball with them, and begged her stepmother to give her leave to go.

"You, Ashenputtel!" she said. "Why, you are covered with dust and dirt. You go to the festival! Besides you have no clothes or shoes, and yet you want to go to the ball."

As she, however, went on asking, her stepmother said:

"Well, I have thrown a dishful of lentils into the cinders. If you have picked them all out in two hours you shall go with us."

The girl went through the back door into the garden, and cried, "Ye gentle doves, ye turtle doves, and all ye little birds under heaven, come and help me,

"The good into a dish to throw,
The bad into your crops can go."

Then two white doves came in by the kitchen window, and were followed by the turtle doves, and finally all the little birds under heaven flocked in, chirping, and settled down among the ashes. And the doves gave a nod with their little heads, peck, peck, peck; and then the rest began also, peck, peck, peck, and collected all the good beans into the dish. Scarcely had an hour passed before they had finished, and all flown out again.

Then the girl brought the dish to her stepmother, and was delighted to think that now she would be able to go to the feast with them.

But she said, "No, Ashenputtel, you have no clothes, and cannot dance; you will only be laughed at."

But when she began to cry, the stepmother said:

"If you can pick out two whole dishes of lentils from the ashes in an hour, you shall go with us."

And she thought, "She will never be able to do that."

When her stepmother had thrown the dishes of lentils among the ashes, the girl went out through the back door, and cried, "Ye gentle doves, ye turtle doves, and all ye little birds under heaven, come and help me,

> "The good into a dish to throw,
> The bad into your crops can go."

Then two white doves came in by the kitchen window, and were followed by the turtle doves, and all the other little birds under heaven, and in less than an hour the whole had been picked up, and they had all flown away.

Then the girl carried the dish to her stepmother, and was delighted to think that she would now be able to go to the ball.

But she said, "It's not a bit of good. You can't go with us, for you've got no clothes, and you can't dance. We should be quite ashamed of you."

Thereupon she turned her back upon her, and hurried off with her two proud daughters.

As soon as every one had left the house, Ashenputtel went out to her mother's grave under the hazel-tree, and cried:

> "Shiver and shake, dear little tree,
> Gold and silver shower on me."

Then the bird threw down to her a gold and silver robe, and a pair of slippers embroidered with silk and silver. With all speed she put on the robe and went to the feast. But her stepsisters and their mother did not recognize her, and supposed that she was some foreign Princess, so beautiful did she appear in her golden dress. They never gave a thought to Ashenputtel, but imagined that she was sitting at home in the dirt picking the lentils out of the cinders.

The Prince came up to the stranger, took her by the hand, and danced with her. In fact, he would not dance with any one else, and never left go of her hand. If any one came up to ask her to dance, he said, "This is my partner."

She danced until nightfall, and then wanted to go home; but the Prince said, "I will go with you and escort you."

For he wanted to see to whom the beautiful maiden belonged. But she slipped out of his way and sprang into the pigeon-house.

Then the Prince waited till her father came, and told him that the unknown maiden had vanished into the pigeon-house.

The old man thought, "Could it be Ashenputtel?" And he had an axe brought to him, so that he might break down the pigeon-house, but there was no one inside.

When they went home, there lay Ashenputtel in her dirty clothes among the cinders, and a dismal oil lamp was burning in the chimney corner. For Ashenputtel had quietly jumped down out of the pigeon-house and ran back to the hazel-tree. There she had taken off her beautiful clothes and laid them on the grave, and the bird had taken them away again. Then she had settled herself among the ashes on the hearth in her old grey frock.

On the second day, when the festival was renewed, and her parents and stepsisters had started forth again, Ashenputtel went to the hazel-tree, and said:

> "Shiver and shake, dear little tree,
> Gold and silver shower on me."

Then the bird threw down a still more gorgeous robe than on the previous day. And when she appeared at the festival in this robe, every one was astounded by her beauty.

The King's son had waited till she came, and at once took her hand, and she danced with no one but him. When others came forward and invited her to dance, he said, "This is my partner."

At nightfall she wished to leave; but the Prince went after her, hoping to see into what house she went, but she sprang out into the garden behind the house. There stood a fine big tree on which the most delicious pears hung. She climbed up among the branches as nimbly as a squirrel, and the Prince could not make out what had become of her.

But he waited till her father came, and then said to him, "The unknown maiden has slipped away from me, and I think that she has jumped into the pear-tree."

The father thought, "Can it be Ashenputtel?" And he had the axe brought to cut down the tree, but there was no one on it. When they went home and looked into the kitchen, there lay Ashenputtel among the cinders as usual; for she had jumped down on the other side of the tree, taken back the beautiful clothes to the bird on the hazel-tree, and put on her old grey frock.

On the third day, when her parents and sisters had started, Ashenputtel went again to her mother's grave, and said:

> "Shiver and shake, dear little tree,
> Gold and silver shower on me."

Then the bird threw down a dress which was so magnificent that no one had ever seen the like before, and the slippers were entirely of gold. When she appeared at the festival in this attire, they were all speechless with astonishment. The Prince danced only with her, and if any one else asked her to dance, he said, "This is my partner."

When night fell and she wanted to leave, the Prince was more desirous than ever to accompany her, but she darted away from him so quickly that he could not keep up with her. But the Prince had used a stratagem, and had caused the steps to be covered with cobbler's wax. The consequence was, that as the maiden sprang down them, her left slipper remained sticking there. The Prince took it up. It was small and dainty, and entirely made of gold.

The next morning he went with it to Ashenputtel's father, and said to him, "No other shall become my wife but she whose foot this golden slipper fits."

The two sisters were delighted at that, for they both had beautiful feet. The eldest went into the room intending to try on the slipper, and her mother stood beside her. But her great toe prevented her getting it on, her foot was too long.

Then her mother handed her a knife, and said, "Cut off the toe; when you are Queen you won't have to walk any more."

The girl cut off her toe, forced her foot into the slipper, stifled her pain, and went out to the Prince. Then he took her up on his horse as his bride, and rode away with her.

However, they had to pass the grave on the way, and there sat the two doves on the hazel-tree, and cried:

> "Prithee, look back, prithee, look back,
> There's blood on the track,
> The shoe is too small,
> At home the true bride is waiting thy call."

Then he looked at her foot and saw how the blood was streaming from it. So he turned his horse round and carried the false bride back to her home, and said that she was not the right one; the second sister must try the shoe.

Then she went into the room, and succeeded in getting her toes into the shoe, but her heel was too big.

Then her mother handed her a knife, and said, "Cut a bit off your heel; when you are Queen you won't have to walk any more."

The maiden cut a bit off her heel, forced her foot into the shoe, stifled her pain, and went out to the Prince.

Then he took her up on his horse as his bride, and rode off with her.

As they passed the grave, the two doves were sitting on the hazel-tree, and crying:

> "Prithee, look back, prithee, look back,
> There's blood on the track,
> The shoe is too small,
> At home the true bride is waiting thy call."

He looked down at her foot and saw that it was streaming with blood, and there were deep red spots on her stockings. Then he turned his horse and brought the false bride back to her home.

"This is not the right one either," he said. "Have you no other daughter?"

"No," said the man. "There is only a daughter of my late wife's, a puny, stunted drudge, but she cannot possibly be the bride."

The Prince said that she must be sent for.

But the mother answered, "Oh no, she is much too dirty; she mustn't be seen on any account."

He was, however, absolutely determined to have his way, and they were obliged to summon Ashenputtel.

When she had washed her hands and face, she went up and curtsied to the Prince, who handed her the golden slipper.

Then she sat down on a bench, pulled off her wooden clog and put on the slipper, which fitted to a nicety.

And when she stood up and the Prince looked into her face, he recognized the beautiful maiden that he had danced with, and cried: "This is the true bride!"

The stepmother and the two sisters were dismayed and turned white with rage; but he took Ashenputtel on his horse and rode off with her.

As they rode past the hazel-tree the two white doves cried:

> "Prithee, look back, prithee, look back,
> No blood's on the track,
> The shoe's *not* too small,
> You carry the true bride home to your hall."

And when they had said this they both came flying down, and settled on Ashenputtel's shoulders, one on the right, and one on the left, and remained perched there.

When the wedding was going to take place, the two false sisters came and wanted to curry favor with her, and take part in her good fortune. As the bridal party was going to the church, the eldest was on the right side, the youngest on the left, and the doves picked out one of the eyes of each of them.

Afterwards, when they were coming out of the church, the elder was on the left, the younger on the right, and the doves picked out the other eye of each of them. And so for their wickedness and falseness they were punished with blindness for the rest of their days.

THE WOLF
AND THE SEVEN KIDS

THERE WAS ONCE AN OLD nanny goat who had seven kids, and she was just as fond of them as a mother of her children. One day she was going into the woods to fetch some food for them, so she called them all up to her, and said—

"My dear children, I am going out into the woods. Beware of the wolf! If once he gets into the house, he will eat you up, skin, and hair, and all. The rascal often disguises himself, but you will know him by his rough voice and his black feet."

The kids said, "Oh, we will be very careful, dear Mother. You may be quite happy about us."

Bleating tenderly, the old goat went off to her work. Before long, some one knocked at the door, and cried—

"Open the door, dear children! Your mother has come back and brought something for each of you."

But the kids knew quite well by the voice that it was the wolf.

"We won't open the door," they cried. "You are not our mother. She has a soft gentle voice; but yours is rough, and we are quite sure that you are the wolf."

So he went away to a shop and bought a lump of chalk, which he ate, and it made his voice quite soft. He went back, knocked at the door again, and cried—

"Open the door, dear children. Your mother has come back and brought something for each of you."

But the wolf had put one of his paws on the window sill, where the kids saw it, and cried—

"We won't open the door. Our mother has not got a black foot as you have; you are the wolf."

Then the wolf ran to a baker, and said, "I have bruised my foot; please put some dough on it." And when the baker had put some dough on his foot, he ran to the miller and said, "Strew some flour on my foot."

The miller thought, "The old wolf is going to take somebody in," and refused.

But the wolf said, "If you don't do it, I will eat you up."

So the miller was frightened, and whitened his paws. People are like that, you know.

Now the wretch went for the third time to the door, and knocked, and said—

"Open the door, children. Your dear mother has come home, and has brought something for each of you out of the wood."

The kids cried, "Show us your feet first, that we may be sure you are our mother."

He put his paws on the window sill, and when they saw that they were white, they believed all he said, and opened the door.

Alas! It was the wolf who walked in. They were terrified, and tried to hide themselves. One ran under the table, the second jumped into bed, the third into the oven, the fourth ran into the kitchen, the fifth got into the cupboard, the sixth into the washtub, and the seventh hid in the tall clock-case. But the wolf found them all but one, and made short work of them. He swallowed one after the other, except the youngest one in the clock-case, whom he did not find. When he had satisfied his appetite, he took himself off, and lay down in a meadow outside, where he soon fell asleep.

Not long after the old nanny goat came back from the woods. Oh! what a terrible sight met her eyes! The house door was wide open, table, chairs, and benches were overturned, the washing bowl was smashed to atoms, the covers and pillows torn from the bed. She searched all over the house for her children, but nowhere were they to be found. She called them by name, one by one, but no one answered. At last, when she came to the youngest, a tiny voice cried:

"I am here, dear Mother, hidden in the clock-case."

She brought him out, and he told her that the wolf had come and devoured all the others.

You may imagine how she wept over her children.

At last, in her grief, she went out, and the youngest kid ran by her side. When they went into the meadow, there lay the wolf under a tree, making the branches shake with his snores. They examined him from every side, and they could plainly see movements within his distended body.

"Ah, heavens!" thought the goat, "is it possible that my poor children whom he ate for his supper, should be still alive?"

She sent the kid running to the house to fetch scissors, needles, and thread. Then she cut a hole in the monster's side, and, hardly had she begun, when a kid popped out its head, and as soon as the hole was big enough, all six jumped out, one after the other, all alive, and without having suffered the least injury, for, in his greed, the monster had swallowed them whole. You may imagine the mother's joy. She hugged them, and skipped about like a tailor on his wedding day. At last she said:

"Go and fetch some big stones, children, and we will fill up the brute's body while he is asleep."

Then the seven kids brought a lot of stones, as fast as they could carry them, and stuffed the wolf with them till he could hold no more. The old mother quickly sewed him up, without his having noticed anything, or even moved.

At last, when the wolf had had his sleep out, he got up, and, as the stones made him feel very thirsty, he wanted to go to a spring to drink. But as soon as he moved the stones began to roll about and rattle inside him. Then he cried—

"What's the rumbling and tumbling
That sets my stomach grumbling?
I thought 'twas six kids, flesh and bones,
Now find it's nought but rolling stones."

When he reached the spring, and stooped over the water to drink, the heavy stones dragged him down, and he was drowned miserably.

When the seven kids saw what had happened, they came running up, and cried aloud—"The wolf is dead, the wolf is dead!" and they and their mother capered and danced round the spring in their joy.

THE ELVES
AND THE SHOEMAKER

THERE WAS ONCE A shoemaker who, through no fault of his own, had become so poor that at last he had only leather enough left for one pair of shoes. At evening he cut out the shoes which he intended to begin upon the next morning, and since he had a good conscience, he lay down quietly, said his prayers, and fell asleep.

In the morning when he had said his prayers, and was preparing to sit down to work, he found the pair of shoes standing finished on his table. He was amazed, and could not understand it in the least.

He took the shoes in his hand to examine them more closely. They were so neatly sewn that not a stitch was out of place, and were as good as the work of a master-hand.

Soon after a purchaser came in, and as he was much pleased with the shoes, he paid more than the ordinary price for them, so that the shoemaker was able to buy leather for two pairs of shoes with the money.

He cut them out in the evening, and next day, with fresh courage, was about to go to work; but he had no need to, for when he got up, the shoes were finished, and buyers were not lacking. These gave him so much money that he was able to buy leather for four pairs of shoes.

Early next morning he found the four pairs finished, and so it went on; what he cut out at evening was finished in the morning, so that he was soon again in comfortable circumstances, and became a well-to-do man.

Now it happened one evening, not long before Christmas, when he had cut out some shoes as usual, that he said to his wife: "How would it be if we were to sit up tonight to see who it is that lends us such a helping hand?"

The wife agreed, lighted a candle, and they hid themselves in the corner of the room behind the clothes which were hanging there.

At midnight came two little naked men who sat down at the shoemaker's table, took up the cut-out work, and began with their tiny fingers to stitch, sew, and hammer so neatly and quickly, that the shoemaker could not believe his eyes. They did not stop till everything was quite finished, and stood complete on the table; then they ran swiftly away.

The next day the wife said: "The little men have made us rich, and we ought to show our gratitude. They were running about with nothing on, and must freeze with cold. Now I will make them little shirts, coats, waistcoats, and hose, and will even knit them a pair of stockings, and you shall make them each a pair of shoes."

The husband agreed, and at evening, when they had everything ready, they laid out the presents on the table, and hid themselves to see how the little men would behave.

At midnight they came skipping in, and were about to set to work; but, instead of the leather ready cut out, they found the charming little clothes.

At first they were surprised, then excessively delighted. With the greatest speed they put on and smoothed down the pretty clothes, singing:

> "Now we're boys so fine and neat,
> Why cobble more for other's feet?"

Then they hopped and danced about, and leapt over chairs and tables and out at the door. Henceforward, they came back no more, but the shoemaker fared well as long as he lived, and had good luck in all his undertakings.

THE WOLF AND THE MAN

A FOX WAS ONE DAY TALKING to a wolf about the strength of man.

"No animals," he said, "could withstand man, and they were obliged to use cunning to hold their own against him."

The wolf answered, "If ever I happened to see a man, I should attack him all the same."

"Well, I can help you to that," said the fox. "Come to me early tomorrow, and I will show you one!"

The wolf was early astir, and the fox took him out to a road in the forest, traversed daily by a huntsman.

First came an old discharged soldier.

"Is that a man?" asked the wolf.

"No," answered the fox. "He has been a man."

After that, a little boy appeared on his way to school.

"Is that a man?"

"No; he is going to be a man."

At last the huntsman made his appearance, his gun on his back, and his hunting-knife at his side. The fox said to the wolf—

"Look! There comes a man. You may attack him, but I will make off to my hole!"

The wolf set on the man, who said to himself when he saw him, "What a pity my gun isn't loaded with ball," and fired a charge of shot in the wolf's face. The wolf made a wry face, but he was not to be so easily frightened, and attacked him again. Then the huntsman gave him the second charge. The wolf swallowed the pain, and rushed at the huntsman; but he drew his bright hunting-knife, and hit out right and left with it, so that, streaming with blood, the wolf ran back to the fox.

"Well, brother wolf," said the fox, "and how did you get on with the man?"

"Alas!" said the wolf. "I never thought the strength of man would be what it is. First, he took a stick from his shoulder, and blew into it, and something flew into my face, which tickled frightfully. Then he blew into it again, and it flew into my eyes and nose like lightning and hail. Then he drew a shining rib out of his body, and struck at me with it till I was more dead than alive."

"Now, you see," said the fox, "what a braggart you are. You throw your hatchet so far that you can't get it back again."

CLEVER HANS

W HERE ARE YOU GOING, Hans?" asked his mother.
"To see Grettel," answered Hans.
"Behave well, Hans!"
"All right, Mother. Good-bye."
"Good-bye, Hans."
Hans comes to Grettel.
"Good morning, Grettel."
"Good morning, Hans. What have you brought me?"
"I've not brought you anything. I want a present."
Grettel gives him a needle. Hans takes the needle, and sticks it
in a load of hay, and walks home behind the cart.
"Good evening, Mother."
"Good evening, Hans. Where have you been?"
"I've been to Grettel's."
"What did you give her?"
"I gave her nothing. But she made me a present."
"What did she give you?"
"She gave me a needle."
"What did you do with it?"
"Stuck it in the hay-cart."
"That was stupid, Hans. You should have stuck it in you sleeve."
"Never mind, Mother; I'll do better next time."
"Where are you going, Hans?"
"To see Grettel, Mother."
"Behave well."

"All right, Mother. Good-bye."

"Good-bye, Hans."

Hans comes to Grettel.

"Good morning, Grettel."

"Good morning, Hans. What have you brought me?"

"I've brought nothing. But I want something."

Grettel gives him a knife.

"Good-bye, Grettel."

"Good-bye, Hans."

Hans takes the knife, and sticks it in his sleeve, and goes home.

"Good evening, Mother."

"Good evening, Hans. Where have you been?"

"Been to see Grettel."

"What did she give you?"

"She gave me a knife."

"Where is the knife, Hans?"

"I stuck it in my sleeve."

"That's a stupid place, Hans. You should have put it in your pocket."

"Never mind, Mother; I'll do better next time."

"Where are you going, Hans?"

"To see Grettel, Mother."

"Behave well, then."

"All right, Mother. Good-bye."

"Good-bye, Hans."

Hans comes to Grettel.

"Good morning, Grettel."

"Good morning, Hans. Have you brought me anything nice?"

"I've brought nothing. What have you got for me?"

Grettel gives him a young kid.

"Good-bye, Grettel."

"Good-bye, Hans."

Hans takes the kid, ties its legs together, and puts it in his pocket.

When he got home, it was suffocated.

"Good evening, Mother."

"Good evening, Hans. Where have you been?

"Been to see Grettel, Mother."

"What did you give her?"

"I gave her nothing. But I brought away something."

"What did Grettel give you?"

"She gave me a young kid."

"What did you do with the kid?"

"Put it in my pocket, Mother."

"That was very stupid. You should have led it by a rope."

"Never mind, Mother; I'll manage better next time."

"Where are you going, Hans?"

"To see Grettel, Mother."

"Manage well, then."

"All right, Mother. Good-bye."

"Good-bye, Hans."

Hans comes to Grettel.

"Good morning, Grettel."

"Good morning, Hans. What have you brought me?"

"I've brought you nothing. What have you got for me?"

Grettel gives him a piece of bacon.

"Good-bye, Grettel."

"Good-bye, Hans."

Hans takes the bacon, ties a rope round it, and drags it along behind him. The dogs come after him, and eat it up. When he got home he had the rope in his hand, but there was nothing at the end of it.

"Good evening, Mother."

"Good evening, Hans. Where have you been?"

"To see Grettel, Mother."

"What did you take her?"

"I took nothing. But I brought something away."

"What did she give you?"
"She gave me a piece of bacon."
"What did you do with the bacon, Hans?"

"I tied it to a rope, and dragged it home. But the dogs ate it."
"That was a stupid business, Hans. You should have carried it on your head."
"Never mind, Mother; I'll do better next time."
"Where are you going, Hans?"
"To see Grettel, Mother."
"Behave properly then."
"All right, Mother. Good-bye."
"Good-bye, Hans.

Hans comes to Grettel.

"Good morning, Grettel."

"Good morning, Hans. What have you brought me?"

"I've brought nothing. What have you got for me?"

Grettel gives Hans a calf.

"Good-bye, Grettel."

"Good-bye, Hans."

Hans takes the calf, and puts it on his head. It kicks his face.

"Good evening, Mother."

"Good evening, Hans. Where have you been?"

"Been to see Grettel, Mother."

"What did you take her?"

"I took her nothing, Mother. She gave me something."

"What did she give you, Hans?"

"She gave me a calf, Mother."

"What did you do with the calf?"

"Put it on my head, Mother, and it kicked my face."

"That was very stupid, Hans. You should have led it by a rope, and put it in the cow-stall."

"Never mind, Mother; I'll do better next time."

"Where are you going, Hans?"

"To see Grettel, Mother."

"Mind how you behave, Hans."

"All right, Mother. Good-bye."

Hans goes to Grettel.

"Good morning, Grettel."

"Good morning, Hans. What have you brought me?"

"I've brought you nothing. I want to take away something."

"I'll go with you myself, Hans."

Hans ties Grettel to a rope, and leads her home, where he puts her in a stall, and ties her up. Then he goes into the house to his Mother.

"Good evening, Mother."

"Good evening, Hans. Where have you been?"

"To see Grettel, Mother."

"What did you take her?"

"I took nothing."

"What did Grettel give you?"

"She gave me nothing. She came with me."

"Where did you leave Grettel?"

"Tied up in the stable with a rope."

"That was stupid. You should have cast sheep's eyes at her."

"Never mind; I'll do better next time."

Hans went into the stable, plucked the eyes out of the cows and calves, and threw them in Grettel's face.

Grettel got angry, broke the rope, and ran away.

Yet she became Hans's wife.

THE THREE LANGUAGES

THERE ONCE LIVED IN Switzerland an old count, who had an only son; but he was very stupid, and could learn nothing. So his father said to him: "Listen to me, my son. I can get nothing into your head, try as hard as I may. You must go away from here, and I will hand you over to a renowned professor for a whole year." At the end of the year he came home again, and his father asked: "Now, my son, what have you learnt?"

"Father, I have learnt the language of dogs."

"Mercy on us!" cried his father, "is that all you have learnt? I will send you away again to another professor in a different town." The youth was taken there, and remained with this professor also for another year. When he came back his father asked him again: "My son, what have you learnt?"

He answered: "I have learnt bird language."

Then the father flew into a rage, and said: "Oh, you hopeless creature, have you been spending all this precious time and learnt nothing? Aren't you ashamed to come into my presence? I will send you to a third professor, but if you learn nothing this time, I won't be your father anymore."

The son stopped with the third professor in the same way for a whole year, and when he came home again and his father asked, "My son, what have you learnt?" he answered—

"My dear Father, this year I have learnt frog language."

Thereupon his father flew into a fearful passion, and said: "This creature is my son no longer. I turn him out of the house and com-

mand you to lead him into the forest and take his life."

They led him forth, but when they were about to kill him, for pity's sake they could not do it, and let him go. Then they cut out the eyes and tongue of a fawn, in order that they might take back proofs to the old count.

The youth wandered about, and at length came to a castle, where he begged a night's lodging.

"Very well," said the lord of the castle. "If you like to pass the night down there in the old tower, you may; but I warn you that it will be at the risk of your life, for it is full of savage dogs. They bark and howl without ceasing, and at certain hours they must have a man thrown to them, and they devour him at once."

The whole neighborhood was distressed by the scourge, but no one could do anything to remedy it. But the youth was not a bit afraid, and said: "Just let me go down to these barking dogs, and give me something that I can throw to them; they won't do me any harm."

As he would not have anything else, they gave him some food for the savage dogs, and took him down to the tower.

The dogs did not bark at him when he entered, but ran round him wagging their tails in a most friendly manner, ate the food he gave them, and did not so much as touch a hair of his head.

The next morning, to the surprise of every one, he made his appearance again, and said to the lord of the castle, "The dogs have revealed to me in their own language why they live there and bring mischief to the country. They are enchanted, and obliged to guard a great treasure which is hidden under the tower, and will get no rest till it has been dug up; and how that has to be done I have also learnt from them."

Every one who heard this was delighted, and the lord of the castle said he would adopt him as a son if he accomplished the task successfully. He went down to the tower again, and as he knew how to set to work he accomplished his task, and brought out a chest full of gold. The howling of the savage dogs was from that time forward heard no more. They entirely disappeared, and the country was delivered from the scourge.

After a time, he took it into his head to go to Rome. On the way he passed a swamp, in which a number of frogs were croaking. He listened, and when he heard what they were saying he became quite pensive and sad.

At last he reached Rome, at a moment when the Pope had just died, and there was great doubt among the cardinals whom they ought to name as his successor. They agreed at last that the man to whom some divine miracle should be manifested ought to be chosen as Pope. Just as they had come to this decision, the young count entered the church, and suddenly two snow-white doves flew down and alighted on his shoulders.

The clergy recognized in this the sign from heaven, and asked him on the spot whether he would be Pope.

He was undecided, and knew not whether he was worthy of the post; but the doves told him that he might accept, and at last he said "Yes."

Thereupon he was anointed and consecrated, and so was fulfilled what he had heard from the frogs on the way, which had disturbed him so much, namely, that he should become Pope.

Then he had to chant mass, and did not know one word of it. But the two doves sat upon his shoulders and whispered it to him.

THE FOUR CLEVER BROTHERS

THERE WAS ONCE A POOR man who had four sons, and when they were grown up, he said to them: "Dear children, you must go out into the world now, for I have nothing to give you. You must each learn a trade and make your own way in the world."

So the four brothers took their sticks in their hands, bid their father good-bye, and passed out of the town gate.

When they had walked some distance, they came to four cross roads, which led into four different districts. Then the eldest one said: "We must part here, but this day four years, we will meet here again, having in the meantime done our best to make our fortunes."

Then each one went his own way. The eldest met an old man, who asked him where he came from, and what he was going to do.

"I want to learn a trade," he answered.

Then the man said: "Come with me and learn to be a thief."

"No," answered he, "that is no longer considered an honest trade; and the end of that song would be that I should swing as the clapper in a bell."

"Oh," said the man, "you need not be afraid of the gallows. I will only teach you how to take things no one else wants, or knows how to get hold of, and where no one can find you out."

So he allowed himself to be persuaded, and under the man's instructions he became such an expert thief that nothing was safe from him which he had once made up his mind to have.

The second brother met a man who put the same question to him, as to what he was going to do in the world.

"I don't know yet," he answered.

"Then come with me and be a stargazer. It is the grandest thing in the world, nothing is hidden from you."

He was pleased with the idea, and became such a clever stargazer, that when he had learnt everything and wanted to go away, his master gave him a telescope, and said—

"With this you can see everything that happens in the sky and on earth, and nothing can remain hidden from you."

The third brother was taken in hand by a huntsman, who taught him everything connected with sport so well, that he became a first-rate huntsman.

On his departure his master presented him with a gun, and said: "This gun will never miss: whatever you aim at you will hit without fail."

The youngest brother also met a man who asked him what he was going to do.

"Wouldn't you like to be a tailor?" he asked.

"I don't know about that," said the young man. "I don't much fancy sitting cross-legged from morning till night, and everlastingly pulling a needle in and out, and pushing a flat iron."

"Dear, dear!" said the man, "what are you talking about? If you come to me you will learn quite a different sort of tailoring. It is a most pleasant and agreeable trade, not to say most honorable."

So he allowed himself to be talked over, and went with the man, who taught him his trade thoroughly.

On his departure, he gave him a needle, and said: "With this needle you will be able to stitch anything together, be it as soft as an egg, or as hard as steel; and it will become like a whole piece of stuff with no seam visible."

When the four years, which the brothers had agreed upon, had passed, they met at the crossroads. They embraced one another and hurried home to their father.

"Well!" said he, quite pleased to see them, "has the wind wafted you back to me again?"

They told him all that had happened to them, and that each had mastered a trade. They were sitting in front of the house under a big tree, and their father said—

"Now, I will put you to the test, and see what you can do."

Then he looked up and said to his second son—

"There is a chaffinch's nest in the topmost branch of this tree; tell me how many eggs there are in it?"

The stargazer took his glass and said: "There are five."

His father said to the eldest: "Bring the eggs down without disturbing the bird sitting on them."

The cunning thief climbed up and took the five eggs from under the bird so cleverly that it never noticed they were gone, and he gave them to his father. His father took them, and put them one on each corner of the table, and one in the middle, and said to the sportsman—

"You must shoot the five eggs through the middle at one shot."

The sportsman leveled his gun, and divided each egg in half at one shot, as his father desired. He certainly must have had some of the powder which shoots round the corner.

"Now it is your turn," said his father to the fourth son. "You will sew the eggs together again, the shells and the young birds inside them; and you will do it in such a manner that they will be none the worse for the shot."

The tailor produced his needle, and stitched away as his father ordered. When he had finished, the thief had to climb up the tree again, and put the eggs back under the bird without her noticing it. The bird spread herself over the eggs, and a few days later the fledglings crept out of the shell, and they all had a red line round their throats where the tailor had sewn them together.

"Yes," said the old man to his sons; "I can certainly praise your skill. You have learnt something worth knowing, and made the most of your time. I don't know which of you to give the palm to. I only hope you may soon have a chance of showing your skill so that it may be settled."

Not long after this there was a great alarm raised in the country: the King's only daughter had been carried off by a dragon. The King sorrowed for her day and night, and proclaimed that whoever brought her back should marry her.

The four brothers said to one another: "This would be an opportunity for us to prove what we can do." And they decided to go out together to deliver the Princess.

"I shall soon know where she is," said the stargazer, as he looked through his telescope; and then he said—

"I see her already. She is a long way from here, she is sitting on a rock in the middle of the sea, and the dragon is near, watching her."

Then he went to the King and asked for a ship for himself and his brothers to cross the sea in search of the rock.

They found the Princess still on the rock, but the dragon was asleep with his head on her lap.

The sportsman said: "I dare not shoot. I should kill the beautiful maiden."

"Then I will try my luck," said the thief, and he stole her away from beneath the dragon. He did it so gently and skillfully, that the monster never discovered it, but went snoring on.

Full of joy, they hurried away with her to the ship, and steered for the open sea. But the dragon on waking had missed the Princess, and now came after them through the air, foaming with rage.

Just as he was hovering over the ship and about to drop on them, the sportsman took aim with his gun and shot him through the heart. The monster fell down dead, but he was so huge, that in falling, he dragged the whole ship down with him. They managed to seize a few boards, on which they kept themselves afloat.

They were now in great straits, but the tailor, not to be outdone, produced his wonderful needle, and put some great stitches into the boards, seated himself on them, and collected all the floating bits of the ship. Then he stitched them all together so cleverly, that in a very short time the ship was seaworthy again, and they sailed happily home.

The King was overjoyed when he saw his daughter again, and he said to the four brothers: "One of you shall marry her, but which one, you must decide among yourselves."

An excited discussion then took place among them, for each one made a claim.

The stargazer said: "Had I not discovered the Princess, all your arts would have been in vain, therefore she is mine!"

The thief said: "What would have been the good of discovering her if I had not taken her from under the dragon? So she is mine."

The sportsman said: "You, as well as the Princess, would have been destroyed by the monster if my shot had not hit him. So she is mine."

The tailor said: "And if I had not sewn the ship together with my skill, you would all have been drowned miserably. Therefore she is mine."

The King said: "Each of you has an equal right; but, as you can't all have her, none of you shall have her. I will give every one of you half a kingdom as a reward."

The brothers were quite satisfied with this decision, and they said: "It is better so than that we should quarrel over it."

So each of them received half a kingdom, and they lived happily with their father for the rest of their days.

THE FOX AND THE HORSE

A PEASANT ONCE HAD A faithful horse, but it had grown old and could no longer do its work. Its master grudged it food, and said: "I can't use you any more, but I still feel kindly towards you, and if you show yourself strong enough to bring me a lion I will keep you to the end of your days. But away with you now, out of my stable"; and he drove it out into the open country.

The poor horse was very sad, and went into the forest to get a little shelter from the wind and weather. There he met a fox, who said: "Why do you hang your head, and wander about in this solitary fashion?"

"Alas!" answered the horse, "avarice and honesty cannot live together. My master has forgotten all the service I have done him for these many years, and because I can no longer plough he will no longer feed me, and he has driven me away."

"Without any consideration?" asked the fox.

"Only the poor consolation of telling me that if I was strong enough to bring him a lion he would keep me, but he knows well enough that the task is beyond me."

The fox said: "But I will help you. Just you lie down here, and stretch your legs out as if you were dead." The horse did as he was told, and the fox went to the lion's den, not far off, and said: "There is a dead horse out there. Come along with me, and you will have a rare meal." The lion went with him, and when they got up to the horse, the fox said: "You can't eat it in comfort here. I'll tell you what. I will tie it to you, and you can drag it away to your den, and enjoy it at your leisure."

The plan pleased the lion, and he stood quite still, close to the horse, so that the fox should fasten them together. But the fox tied the lion's legs together with the horse's tail, and twisted and knotted it so that it would be quite impossible for it to come undone.

When he had finished his work he patted the horse on the shoulder, and said: "Pull, old grey! Pull!"

Then the horse sprang up, and dragged the lion away behind him. The lion in his rage roared, so that all the birds in the forest were terrified, and flew away. But the horse let him roar, and never stopped till he stood before his master's door.

When the master saw him he was delighted, and said to him: "You shall stay with me, and have a good time as long as you live."

And he fed him well till he died.

THE GOLDEN GOOSE

T HERE WAS ONCE A MAN who had three sons. The youngest
of them was called Simpleton; he was scorned and despised
by the others, and kept in the background.

The eldest son was going into the forest to cut wood, and before
he started, his mother gave him a nice sweet cake and a bottle of
wine to take with him, so that he might not suffer from hunger or
thirst. In the wood he met a little, old, grey man, who bade him
good day, and said, "Give me a bit of the cake in your pocket, and
let me have a drop of your wine. I am so hungry and thirsty."

But the clever son said: "If I give you my cake and wine, I shan't
have enough for myself. Be off with you."

He left the little man standing there, and went on his way. But
he had not been long at work, cutting down a tree, before he made
a false stroke, and dug the axe into his own arm, and he was obliged
to go home to have it bound up.

Now, this was no accident; it was brought about by the little
grey man.

The second son now had to go into the forest to cut wood, and,
like the eldest, his mother gave him a sweet cake and a bottle of
wine. In the same way the little grey man met him, and asked for a
piece of his cake and a drop of his wine. But the second son made
the same sensible answer, "If I give you any, I shall have the less for
myself. Be off out of my way," and he went on.

His punishment, however, was not long delayed. After a few
blows at the tree, he hit his own leg, and had to be carried home.

Then Simpleton said, "Let me go to cut the wood, Father."

But his father said, "Your brothers have only come to harm by it; you had better leave it alone. You know nothing about it." But Simpleton begged so hard to be allowed to go that at last his father said, "Well, off you go then. You will be wiser when you have hurt yourself."

His mother gave him a cake which was only mixed with water and baked in the ashes, and a bottle of sour beer. When he reached the forest, like the others, he met the little grey man, who greeted him, and said, "Give me a bit of your cake and a drop of your wine. I am so hungry and thirsty."

Simpleton answered, "I only have a cake baked in the ashes, and some sour beer; but, if you like such fare, we will sit down and eat it together."

So they sat down; but when Simpleton pulled out his cake it was a sweet, nice cake, and his sour beer was turned into good wine. So they ate and drank, and the little man said, "As you have such a good heart, and are willing to share your goods, I will give you good luck. There stands an old tree; cut it down, and you will find something at the roots."

So saying he disappeared.

Simpleton cut down the tree, and when it fell, lo, and behold! a goose was sitting among the roots, and its feathers were of pure gold. He picked it up, and taking it with him, went to an inn, where he meant to stay the night. The landlord had three daughters, who saw the goose, and were very curious as to what kind of bird it could be, and wanted to get one of its golden feathers.

The eldest thought, "There will soon be some opportunity for me to pull out one of the feathers," and when Simpleton went outside, she took hold of its wing to pluck out a feather; but her hand stuck fast, and she could not get away.

Soon after, the second sister came up, meaning also to pluck out one of the golden feathers; but she had hardly touched her sister when she found herself held fast.

Lastly, the third one came, with the same intention, but the others screamed out, "Keep away! For goodness sake, keep away!"

But she, not knowing why she was to keep away, thought, "Why should I not be there, if they are there?"

So she ran up, but as soon as she touched her sisters she had to stay hanging on to them, and they all had to pass the night like this.

In the morning, Simpleton took up the goose under his arm, without noticing the three girls hanging on behind. They had to keep running behind, dodging his legs right and left.

In the middle of the fields they met the parson, who, when he saw the procession, cried out: "For shame, you bold girls! Why do

63

you run after the lad like that? Do you call that proper behavior?"

Then he took hold of the hand of the youngest girl to pull her away; but no sooner had he touched her than he felt himself held fast, and he, too, had to run behind.

Soon after the sexton came up, and, seeing his master the parson treading on the heels of the three girls, cried out in amazement, "Hullo, your reverence! Whither away so fast? Don't forget that we have a christening!"

So saying, he plucked the parson by the sleeve, and soon found that he could not get away.

As this party of five, one behind the other, tramped on, two peasants came along the road, carrying their hoes. The parson called them, and asked them to set the sexton and himself free. But as soon as ever they touched the sexton they were held fast, so now there were seven people running behind Simpleton and his goose.

By-and-by they reached a town, where a King ruled whose only daughter was so solemn that nothing and nobody could make her laugh. So the King had proclaimed that whoever could make her laugh should marry her.

When Simpleton heard this he took his goose, with all his following, before her, and when she saw these seven people running, one behind another, she burst into fits of laughter, and seemed as if she could never stop.

Thereupon Simpleton asked her in marriage. But the King did not like him for a son-in-law, and he made all sorts of conditions. First, he said Simpleton must bring him a man who could drink up a cellar full of wine.

Then Simpleton at once thought of the little grey man who might be able to help him, and he went out to the forest to look for him. On the very spot where the tree that he had cut down had stood, he saw a man sitting with a very sad face. Simpleton asked him what was the matter, and he answered—

"I am so thirsty, and I can't quench my thirst. I hate cold water, and I have already emptied a cask of wine; but what is a drop like that on a burning stone?"

"Well, there I can help you," said Simpleton. "Come with me, and you shall soon have enough to drink and to spare."

He led him to the King's cellar, and the man set to upon the great casks, and he drank and drank till his sides ached, and by the end of the day the cellar was empty.

Then again Simpleton demanded his bride. But the King was annoyed that a wretched fellow called "Simpleton" should have his daughter, and he made new conditions. He was now to find a man who could eat up a mountain of bread.

Simpleton did not reflect long, but went straight to the forest, and there in the self-same place sat a man tightening a strap round his body, and making a very miserable face. He said: "I have eaten up a whole ovenful of rolls, but what is the good of that when any one is as hungry as I am. I am never satisfied. I have to tighten my belt every day if I am not to die of hunger."

Simpleton was delighted, and said: "Get up and come with me. You shall have enough to eat."

And he took him to the court, where the King had caused all the flour in the kingdom to be brought together, and a huge mountain of bread to be baked. The man from the forest sat down before it and began to eat, and at the end of the day the whole mountain had disappeared.

Now, for the third time, Simpleton asked for his bride. But again the King tried to find an excuse, and demanded a ship which could sail on land as well as at sea.

"As soon as you sail up in it, you shall have my daughter," he said.

Simpleton went straight to the forest, and there sat the little grey man to whom he had given his cake. The little man said: "I have eaten and drunk for you, and now I will give you the ship, too. I do it all because you were merciful to me."

Then he gave him the ship which could sail on land as well as at sea, and when the King saw it he could no longer withhold his daughter. The marriage was celebrated, and, at the King's death, the Simpleton inherited the kingdom, and lived long and happily with his wife.

CLEVER GRETHEL

THERE WAS ONCE A COOK called Grethel, who wore shoes with red rosettes; and when she went out in them, she turned and twisted about gaily, and thought, "How fine I am!" After her walk she would take a draught of wine, in her light-heartedness; and as wine gives an appetite, she would then taste some of the dishes that she was cooking, saying to herself, "The cook is bound to know how the food tastes."

It so happened that one day her master said to her, "Grethel, I have a guest coming tonight; roast me two fowls in your best style."

"It shall be done, sir!" answered Grethel. So she killed the chickens, scalded and plucked them, and then put them on the spit; towards evening she put them down to the fire to roast. They got brown and crisp, but still the guest did not come. Then Grethel called to her master, "If the guest does not come I must take the fowls from the fire; but it will be a thousand pities if they are not eaten soon while they are juicy."

Her master said, "I will go and hasten the guest myself."

Hardly had her master turned his back before Grethel laid the spit with the fowls on it on one side, and said to herself, "It's a thirsty work standing over the fire so long. Who knows when he will come. I'll go down into the cellar in the meantime and take a drop of wine."

She ran down and held a jug to the tap, then said, "Here's to your health, Grethel," and took a good pull. "Drinking leads to drinking," she said, "and it's not easy to give it up," and again she took a good pull. Then she went upstairs and put the fowls to the fire again, poured some butter over them, and turned the spit round with a will. It smelt so good that she thought, "There may be something wanting, I must have a taste." And she passed her finger over the fowls and put it in her mouth. "Ah, how good they are; it's a sin and a shame that there's nobody to eat them." She ran to the window to see if her master was coming with the guest, but she saw nobody. Then she went back to the fowls again, and thought, "One wing is catching a little, better to eat it—and eat it I will." So she cut it off and ate it with much enjoyment. When it was finished, she thought, "The other must follow, or the master will notice that something is wanting." When the wings were consumed she went back to the window again to look for her master, but no one was in sight.

"Who knows," she thought. "I dare say they won't come at all; they must have dropped in somewhere else." Then she said to herself, "Now, Grethel, don't be afraid, eat it all up: why should the good food be wasted? When it's all gone you can rest; run and have another drink and then finish it up." So she went down to the cellar, took a good drink, and contentedly ate up the rest of the fowl. When it had all disappeared and still no master came, Grethel looked at the other fowl and said, "Where one is gone the other must follow. What is good for one is right for the other. If I have a drink first I shall be none the worse." So she took another hearty pull at the jug, and then she sent the other fowl after the first one.

In the height of her enjoyment, her master came back, and cried, "Hurry, Grethel, the guest is just coming."

"Very well, sir, I'll soon have it ready," answered Grethel.

Her master went to see if the table was properly laid, and took the big carving-knife with which he meant to cut up the fowls, to sharpen it. In the meantime the guest came and knocked politely at the door. Grethel ran to see who was there, and, seeing the guest, she put her finger to her lips and said, "Be quiet, and get away quickly; if my master catches you it will be the worse for you. He certainly invited you to supper, but only with the intention of cutting off both your ears. You can hear him sharpening his knife now."

The guest heard the knife being sharpened, and hurried off down the steps as fast as he could.

Grethel ran with great agility to her master, shrieking, "A fine guest you have invited, indeed!"

"Why, what's the matter, Grethel? What do you mean?"

"Well," she said, "he has taken the two fowls that I had just put upon the dish, and run off with them."

"That's a clever trick!" said her master, regretting his fine fowls. "If he had only left me one so that I had something to eat."

He called out to him to stop, but the guest pretended not to hear. Then he ran after him, still holding the carving-knife, and cried, "Only one, only one!"—meaning that the guest should leave him one fowl; but the guest only thought that he meant he was to give him one ear, and he ran as if he was pursued by fire, and so took both his ears safely home.

THE KING OF
THE GOLDEN MOUNTAIN

THERE WAS ONCE A merchant who had two children, a boy and a girl. They were both small, and not old enough to run about. He had also two richly-laden ships at sea, and just as he was expecting to make a great deal of money by the merchandise, news came that they had both been lost. So now instead of being a rich man he was quite poor, and had nothing left but one field near the town.

To turn his thoughts from his misfortune, he went out into this field, and as he was walking up and down a little black mannikin suddenly appeared before him, and asked why he was so sad. The merchant said, "I would tell you at once, if you could help me."

"Who knows," answered the little mannikin. "Perhaps I could help you."

Then the merchant told him that all his wealth had been lost in a wreck, and that now he had nothing left but this field.

"Don't worry yourself," said the mannikin. "If you will promise to bring me in twelve years' time the first thing which rubs against your legs when you go home, you shall have as much gold as you want."

The merchant thought, "What could it be but my dog?" He never thought of his boy, but said yes, and gave the mannikin his bond signed and sealed, and went home.

When he reached the house his little son, delighted to hold on to the benches and totter towards his father, seized him by the leg to steady himself.

The merchant was horror-stricken, for his vow came into his head, and now he knew what he had promised to give away. But as he still found no gold in his chests, he thought it must only have been a joke of the mannikin's. A month later he went up into the loft to gather together some old tin to sell it, and there he found a great heap of gold on the floor. So he was soon up in the world again, bought and sold, became a richer merchant than ever, and was altogether contented.

In the meantime the boy had grown up, and he was both clever and wise. But the nearer the end of the twelve years came, the more sorrowful the merchant grew; you could even see his misery in his face. One day his son asked him what was the matter, but his father would not tell him. The boy, however, persisted so long that at last he told him that, without knowing what he was doing, he had promised to give him up at the end of twelve years to a little black mannikin, in return for a quantity of gold. He had given his hand and seal on it, and the time was now near for him to go.

Then his son said, "O father, don't be frightened, it will be all right. The little black mannikin has no power over me."

When the time came, the son asked a blessing of the priest, and he and his father went to the field together; and the son made a circle within which they took their places.

When the little black mannikin appeared, he said to the father, "Have you brought what you promised me?"

The man was silent, but his son said, "What do you want?"

The mannikin said, "My business is with your father, and not with you."

The son answered, "You deceived and cheated my father. Give me back his bond."

"Oh, no!" said the little man; "I won't give up my rights."

They talked to each other for a long time, and at last they decided that, as the son no longer belonged to his father, and declined to belong to his foe, he should get into a boat on a flowing stream, and

his father should push it off himself, thus giving him up to the stream.

So the youth took leave of his father, got into the boat, and his father pushed it off. Then, thinking that his son was lost to him for ever, he went home and sorrowed for him. The little boat, however, did not sink, it drifted quietly down the stream, and the youth sat in it in perfect safety. It drifted for a long time, till at last it stuck fast on an unknown shore. The youth landed, and seeing a beautiful castle near, walked towards it. As he passed under the doorway, however, a spell fell upon him. He went through all the rooms, but found them empty, till he came to the very last one, where a serpent lay coiling and uncoiling itself. The serpent was really an enchanted maiden, who was delighted when she saw the youth, and said, "Have you come at last, my preserver? I have been waiting twelve years for you. This whole kingdom is bewitched, and you must break the spell."

"How am I to do that?" he asked.

She said, "Tonight, twelve black men hung with chains will appear, and they will ask what you are doing here. But do not speak a word, whatever they do or say to you. They will torment you, strike, and pinch you, but don't say a word. At twelve o'clock they will have to go away. On the second night twelve more will come, and on the third twenty-four. These will cut off your head. But at twelve o'clock their power goes, and if you have borne it, and not spoken a word, I shall be saved. Then I will come to you, and bring a little flask containing the Water of Life, with which I will sprinkle you, and you will be brought to life again, as sound and well as ever you were."

Then he said, "I will gladly save you!"

Everything happened just as she had said. The black men could not force a word out of him; and on the third night the serpent became a beautiful Princess, who brought the Water of Life as she had promised, and restored the youth to life. Then she fell on his neck and kissed him, and there were great rejoicings all over the castle.

Their marriage was celebrated, and he became King of the Golden Mountain.

They lived happily together, and in course of time a beautiful boy was born to them.

When eight years had passed, the King's heart grew tender within him as he thought of his father, and he wanted to go home to see him. But the Queen did not want him to go. She said, "I know it will be to my misfortune." However, he gave her no peace till she agreed to let him go. On his departure she gave him a wishing-ring, and said, "Take this ring, and put it on your finger, and you will at once be at the place where you wish to be. Only, you must promise never to use it to wish me away from here to be with you at your father's."

He made the promise, and put the ring on his finger; he then wished himself before the town where his father lived, and at the same moment found himself at the gate. But the sentry would not let him in because his clothes, though of rich material, were of such strange cut. So he went up a mountain, where a shepherd lived, and, exchanging clothing with him, put on his old smock, and passed into the town unnoticed.

When he had reached his father he began making himself known; but his father, never thinking that it was his son, said that it was true he had once had a son, but he had long been dead. But, he added, seeing that he was a poor shepherd, he would give him a plate of food.

The supposed shepherd said to his parents, "I am indeed your son. Is there no mark on my body by which you may know me?"

His mother said, "Yes, our son has a strawberry mark under his right arm."

He pushed up his shirt sleeve, and there was the strawberry mark; so they no longer doubted that he was their son. He told them that he was the King of the Golden Mountain, his wife was a Princess, and they had a little son seven years old.

"That can't be true," said his father. "You are a fine sort of King to come home in a tattered shepherd's smock."

His son grew angry, and, without stopping to reflect, turned his ring round and wished his wife and son to appear. In a moment they both stood before him; but his wife did nothing but weep and lament, and said that he had broken his promise, and by so doing had made her very unhappy. He said, "I have acted incautiously, but from no bad motive," and he tried to soothe her.

She appeared to be calmed, but really she nourished evil intentions towards him in her heart.

Shortly after he took her outside the town to the field, and showed her the stream down which he had drifted in the little boat. Then he said, "I am tired; I want to rest a little."

So she sat down, and he rested his head upon her lap, and soon fell fast asleep. As soon as he was asleep, she drew the ring from his finger, and drew herself gently away from him, leaving only her slipper behind. Last of all, taking her child in her arms, she wished herself back in her own kingdom. When he woke up, he found himself quite deserted; wife and child were gone, the ring had disappeared from his finger, and only her slipper remained as a token.

"I can certainly never go home to my parents," he said. "They would say I was a sorcerer. I must go away and walk till I reach my own kingdom again."

So he went away, and at last he came to a mountain, where three giants were quarreling about the division of their father's property. When they saw him passing, they called him up, and said, "Little people have sharp wits," and asked him to divide their inheritance for them.

It consisted, first, of a sword, with which in one's hand, if one said, "All heads off, mine alone remain," every head fell to the ground. Secondly, of a mantle which rendered any one putting it on invisible. Thirdly, of a pair of boots which transported the wearer to whatever place he wished.

He said, "Give me the three articles so that I may see if they are all in good condition."

So they gave him the mantle, and he at once became invisible. He took his own shape again, and said, "The mantle is good; now give me the sword."

But they said, "No, we can't give you the sword. If you were to say, 'All heads off, mine alone remain,' all our heads would fall, and yours would be the only one left."

At last, however, they gave it to him, on condition that he was to try it on a tree. He did as they wished, and the sword went through the tree trunk as if it had been a straw. Then he wanted the boots, but they said, "No, we won't give them away. If you were to put them on and wish yourself on the top of the mountain, we should be left standing here without anything."

"No," said he; "I won't do that."

So they gave him the boots too; but when he had all three he could think of nothing but his wife and child, and said to himself, "Oh, if only I were on the Golden Mountain again!" and immediately he disappeared from the sight of the giants, and there was an end of their inheritance.

When he approached his castle he heard sounds of music, fiddles and flutes, and shouts of joy. People told him that his wife was celebrating her marriage with another husband. He was filled with rage, and said, "The false creature! She deceived me, and deserted me when I was asleep."

Then he put on his mantle, and went to the castle, invisible to all. When he went into the hall, where a great feast was spread with the richest foods and the costliest wines, the guests were joking and laughing while they ate and drank. The Queen sat on her throne in their midst in gorgeous clothing, and no one saw him. Whenever the Queen put a piece of meat on her plate, he took it away and ate it, and when her glass was filled he took it away and drank it. Her

plate and her glass were constantly refilled, but she never had anything, got up, and went to her room in tears, but he followed her
there too. She said to herself, "Am I still in the power of the demon?
Did my preserver never come?"

He struck her in the face, and said, "Did your preserver never come?
He is with you now, deceiver that you are. Did I deserve such treatment
at your hands?" Then he made himself visible, and went into the
hall, and cried, "The wedding is stopped, the real King has come."

The Kings, Princes, and nobles who were present laughed him
to scorn. But he only said, "Will you go, or will you not?" They
tried to seize him, but he drew his sword and said,

"All heads off, mine alone remain."

Then all their heads fell to the ground, and he remained sole
King and Lord of the Golden Mountain.

DOCTOR KNOW-ALL

O NCE UPON A TIME a poor peasant, named Crabb, was taking a load of wood drawn by two oxen to the town for sale. He sold it to a doctor for four thalers. When the money was being paid to him, it so happened that the doctor was sitting at dinner. When the peasant saw how daintily the doctor was eating and drinking, he felt a great desire to become a doctor too. He remained standing and looking on for a time, and then asked if he could not be a doctor.

"Oh yes!" said the doctor; "that is easily managed."

"What must I do?" asked the peasant.

"First buy an ABC book; you can get one with a cock as a frontispiece. Secondly, turn your wagon and oxen into money, and buy with it clothes and other things suitable for a doctor. Thirdly, have a sign painted with the words, 'I am Doctor Know-All,' and have it nailed over your door."

The peasant did everything that he was told to do.

Now when he had been doctoring for a while, not very long though, a rich nobleman had some money stolen from him. He was told about Doctor Know-All, who lived in such and such a village, who would be sure to know what had become of it. So the gentleman ordered his carriage and drove to the village.

He stopped at the doctor's house, and asked Crabb if he were Doctor Know-All.

"Yes, I am."

"Then you must go with me to get my stolen money back."

"Yes, certainly; but Grethe, my wife, must come too."

The nobleman agreed, and gave both of them seats in his carriage, and they all drove off together.

When they reached the nobleman's castle the dinner was ready, and Crabb was invited to sit down to table.

"Yes; but Grethe, my wife, must dine too"; and he seated himself with her.

When the first servant brought in a dish of choice food, the peasant nudged his wife, and said: "Grethe, that was the first"—meaning that the servant was handing the first dish. But the servant thought he meant, "That was the first thief." As he really was the thief, he became much alarmed, and said to his comrades outside—

"That doctor knows everything, we shan't get out of this hole; he said I was the first."

The second servant did not want to go in at all, but he had to go, and when he offered his dish to the peasant he nudged his wife, and said—"Grethe, that is the second."

This servant also was frightened and hurried out.

The third one fared no better. The peasant said again: "Grethe, that is the third."

The fourth one brought in a covered dish, and the master told the doctor that he must show his powers and guess what was under the cover. Now it was a dish of crabs.

The peasant looked at the dish and did not know what to do, so he said: "Wretched Crabb that I am."

When the master heard him he cried: "There, he knows it! Then he knows where the money is too."

Then the servant grew terribly frightened, and signed to the doctor to come outside.

When he went out, they all four confessed to him that they had stolen the money; they would gladly give it to him and a large sum in addition, if only he would not betray them to their master, or their necks would be in peril. They also showed him where the money was hidden. Then the doctor was satisfied, went back to the table, and said—

"Now, sir, I will look in my book to see where the money is hidden."

The fifth, in the meantime, had crept into the stove to hear if the doctor knew still more. But he sat there turning over the pages of his ABC book looking for the cock, and as he could not find it at once, he said: "I know you are there, and out you must come."

The man in the stove thought it was meant for him, and sprang out in a fright, crying: "The man knows everything."

Then Doctor Know-All showed the nobleman where the money was hidden, but he did not betray the servants; and he received much money from both sides as a reward, and became a very celebrated man.

THE YOUTH
WHO COULD NOT SHUDDER

THERE WAS ONCE A FATHER who had two sons. One was clever and sensible, and always knew how to get on. But the younger one was stupid, and could not learn anything, and he had no imagination.

When people saw him, they said: "His father will have plenty of trouble with him."

Whenever there was anything to be done, the eldest one always had to do it. But if his father sent him to fetch anything late in the evening, or at night, and the way lay through the churchyard, or any other dreary place, he would answer: "Oh no, Father, not there; it makes me shudder!" For he was afraid.

In the evening, when stories were being told round the fire which made one's flesh creep, and the listeners said: "Oh, you make me shudder!" the youngest son, sitting in the corner listening, could not imagine what they meant. "They always say 'It makes me shudder. It makes me shudder!' And it doesn't make me shudder a bit. It must be some art which I can't understand."

Now it happened one day that his father said to him: "I say, you in the corner there, you are growing big and strong. You must learn something by which you can make a living. See what pains your brother takes, but you are not worth your salt."

"Well, Father," he answered, "I am quite ready to learn something; nay, I should very much like to learn how to shudder, for I know nothing about that."

The elder son laughed when he heard him, and thought: "Good

heavens! what a fool my brother is; he will never do any good as long as he lives."

But his father sighed, and answered: "You will easily enough learn how to shudder, but you won't make your bread by it."

Soon after, the sexton came to the house on a visit, and the father confided his troubles about his son to him. He told him how stupid he was, and how he never could learn anything. "Would you believe that when I asked him how he was going to make his living, he said he would like to learn how to shudder?"

"If that's all," said the sexton, "he may learn that from me. Just let me have him, and I'll soon put the polish on him."

The father was pleased, for he thought: "Anyhow, the lad will gain something by it."

So the sexton took him home with him, and he had to ring the church bells.

A few days after, the sexton woke him at midnight, and told him to get up and ring the bells. "You shall soon be taught how to shudder!" he thought, as he crept stealthily up the stairs beforehand.

When the lad got up into the tower, and turned round to catch hold of the bell rope, he saw a white figure standing on the steps opposite the belfry window.

"Who is there?" he cried; but the figure neither moved nor answered.

"Answer," cried the lad, "or get out of the way. You have no business here in the night."

But so that the lad should think he was a ghost, the sexton did not stir.

The lad cried for the second time: "What do you want here? Speak if you are an honest fellow, or I'll throw you down the stairs."

The sexton did not think he would go to such lengths, so he made no sound, and stood as still as if he were made of stone.

Then the lad called to him the third time, and, as he had no answer, he took a run and threw the ghost down the stairs. It fell down ten steps, and remained lying in a corner.

Then he rang the bells, went home, and, without saying a word to anybody, went to bed and was soon fast asleep.

The sexton's wife waited a long time for her husband, but, as he never came back, she got frightened, and woke up the lad.

"Don't you know what has become of my husband?" she asked. "He went up into the church tower before you."

"No," answered the lad. "There was somebody standing on the stairs opposite the belfry window, and, as he would neither answer me nor go away, I took him to be a rogue and threw him downstairs. Go and see if it was your husband; I should be sorry if it were."

The woman hurried away and found her husband lying in the corner, moaning, with a broken leg. She carried him down, and then hastened with loud cries to the lad's father.

"You son has brought about a great misfortune; he has thrown my husband downstairs and broken his leg. Take the good-for-nothing fellow away, out of our house."

The father was horrified, and, going back with her, gave the lad a good scolding.

"What is the meaning of this inhuman prank? The evil one must have put it into your head."

"Father," answered the lad, "just listen to me. I am quite innocent. He stood there in the dark, like a man with some wicked design. I did not know who it was, and I warned him three times to speak, or to go away!"

"Alas!" said his father, "you bring me nothing but disaster. Go away out of my sight. I will have nothing more to do with you."

"Gladly, Father. Only wait till daylight; then I will go away, and learn to shudder. Then, at least, I shall have one art to make my living by."

"Learn what you like," said his father. "It's all the same to me. Here are fifty thalers for you. Go out into the world, and don't tell a creature where you come from, or who your father is, for you will only bring me to shame."

"Just as you please, Father. If that is all you want, I can easily fulfill your desire."

At daybreak, the lad put his fifty thalers into his pocket, and went out along the high road, repeating over and over to himself as he went: "If only I could shudder, if only I could shudder."

A man came by and overheard the words the lad was saying to himself, and when they had gone a little further, and came within sight of the gallows, he said: "See, there is the tree where those seven have been wedded to the ropemaker's daughter, and are now learning to fly. Sit down below them, and when night comes you will soon learn to shudder."

"If nothing more than that is needed," said the lad, "it is easily done. And if I learn to shudder as easily as that, you shall have my fifty thalers. Come back to me early tomorrow morning."

Then the lad went up to the gallows, and sat down under them to wait till night came.

As he was cold he lighted a fire, but at midnight the wind grew so cold that he did not know how to keep himself warm.

The wind blew the men on the gallows backwards and forwards, and swung them against each other, so he thought: "Here am I freezing by the fire, how much colder they must be up there."

And as he was very compassionate, he mounted the ladder, undid them, and brought all seven down one by one.

Then he blew up the fire, and placed them round it to warm themselves.

They sat there and never moved, even when the fire caught their clothing.

"Take care, or I will hang you all up again."

The dead men, of course, could not hear, and remained silent while their few rags were burnt up.

Then he grew angry, and said: "If you won't take care of yourselves, I can't help you, and I won't be burnt with you."

So he hung them all up again in a row, and sat down by the fire and went to sleep again.

Next morning, the man, wanting to get his fifty thalers, came to him and said: "Now do you know what shuddering means?"

"No," he said; "how should I have learnt it? Those fellows up there never opened their mouths, and they were so stupid that they let the few poor rags they had about them burn."

Then the man saw that no thalers would be his that day, and he went away, saying: "Never in my life have I seen such a fellow as this."

The lad also went on his way, and again began saying to himself: "Oh, if only I could learn to shudder, if only I could learn to shudder."

A carter, walking behind him, heard this, and asked: "Who are you?"

"I don't know," answered the youth.

"Who is your father?"

"That I must not say."

"What are you always mumbling in your beard?"

"Ah," answered the youth, "I want to learn to shudder, but no one can teach me."

"Stop your silly chatter," said the carter. "Just you come with me, and I'll see that you have what you want."

The youth went with the carter, and in the evening they reached an inn, where they meant to pass the night. He said quite loud, as they entered: "Oh, if only I could learn to shudder, if only I could learn to shudder."

The landlord, who heard him, laughed, and said: "If that's what you want, there should be plenty of opportunity for you here."

"I will have nothing to say to it," said the landlady. "So many a prying fellow has already paid the penalty with his life. It would be a sin and a shame if those bright eyes should not see the light of day again."

But the youth said: "I will learn it somehow, however hard it may be. I have been driven out for not knowing it."

He gave the landlord no peace till he told him that there was an enchanted castle a little way off, where any one could be made to shudder, if he would pass three nights in it.

The King had promised his daughter to become wife to any one who dared to do it, and she was the prettiest maiden the sun had ever shone on.

There were also great treasures hidden in the castle, watched over by evil spirits, enough to make any poor man rich who could break the spell.

Already many had gone in, but none had ever come out.

Next morning the youth went to the King, and said: "By your

leave, I should like to pass three nights in the enchanted castle."

The King looked at him, and, as he took a fancy to him, he said: "You may ask three things to take into the castle with you, but they must be lifeless things."

He answered: "Then I ask for a fire, a turning-lathe, and a cooper's bench with the knife."

The King had all three carried into the castle for him.

When night fell, the youth went up to the castle and made a bright fire in one of the rooms. He put the cooper's bench with the knife near the fire, and seated himself on the turning-lathe.

"Oh, if only I could shudder," he said; "but I shan't learn it here either."

Towards midnight he wanted to make up the fire, and, as he was blowing it up, something in one corner began to shriek: "Miau, miau, how cold we are!"

"You fools!" he cried. "What do you shriek for? If you are cold, come and warm yourselves by the fire."

As he spoke, two big black cats bounded up and sat down, one on each side of him, and stared at him with wild, fiery eyes.

After a time, when they had warmed themselves, they said: "Comrade, shall we have a game of cards?"

"Why not?" he answered; "but show me your paws first."

Then they stretched out their claws.

"Why," he said, "what long nails you've got. Wait a bit; I must cut them for you."

He seized them by the scruff of their necks, lifted them on to the cooper's bench, and screwed their paws firmly to it.

"I have looked at your fingers, and the desire to play cards with you has passed."

Then he killed them and threw them out into the moat.

But no sooner had he got rid of these two cats, and was about to sit down by his fire again, than crowds of black cats and dogs swarmed out of every corner, more and more of them.

They howled horribly, and trampled on his fire, and tried to put it out.

For a time he looked quietly on, but when it grew too bad he seized his cooper's knife, and cried: "Away with you, you rascally pack," and let fly among them right and left. Some of them sprang away, the others he killed, and threw them out into the water.

When he came back he scraped the embers of his fire together again, and warmed himself. He could hardly keep his eyes open, and felt the greatest desire to go to sleep. He looked round, and in one corner he saw a big bed.

"That's the very thing," he said, and lay down in it. As soon as he closed his eyes, the bed began to move, and soon it was tearing round and round the castle. "Very good!" he said. "The faster the better!" The bed rolled on as if it were dragged by six horses; over thresholds and stairs, up and down.

Suddenly it went hop, hop, hop, and turned topsy-turvy, so that it lay upon him like a mountain. But he pitched the pillows and blankets into the air, slipped out of it, and said: "Now any one may ride who likes."

Then he lay down by his fire and slept till daylight.

In the morning the King came, and when he saw him lying on the floor, he thought the ghosts had killed him, and he was dead. So he said: "It's a sad pity, for such a handsome fellow."

But the youth heard him, and sat up, saying: "It has not come to that yet."

The King was surprised and delighted, and asked him how he had got on.

"Pretty well!" he answered. "One night is gone, I suppose I shall get through the others too."

When the landlord saw him he opened his eyes, and said: "I never thought I should see you alive again. Have you learnt how to shudder now?"

"No," he answered; "it's all in vain. If only some one would tell me how."

The second night came, and up he went again and sat down by the fire, and began his old song: "Oh, if only I could learn to shudder."

In the middle of the night a great noise and uproar began, first soft, and then growing louder; then for a short time there would be silence.

At last, with a loud scream, half the body of a man fell down the chimney in front of him.

"Hullo!" he said, "another half is wanting here; this is too little."

The noise began again, and, amidst shrieks and howls, the other half fell down.

"Wait a bit," he said; "I'll blow up the fire."

When this was done, and he looked round, the two halves had come together, and a hideous man sat in his place.

"We didn't bargain for that," said the youth. "The bench is mine."

The man wanted to push him out of the way, but the youth would not have it, flung him aside, and took his own seat.

Then more men fell down the chimney, one after the other, and they fetched nine human shinbones and two skulls, and began to play skittles.

The youth felt inclined to join them, and cried: "I say, can I play too?"

"Yes, if you've got any money."

"Money enough," he answered, "but your balls aren't quite round."

Then he took the skulls and turned them on the lathe till they were quite round. "Now they will roll better," he said. "Here goes! The more, the merrier!"

So he played with them, and lost some money, but when it struck twelve everything disappeared. He lay down, and was soon fast asleep.

Next morning the King came again to look after him, and said:

"Well, how did you get on this time?"

"I played skittles," he answered, "and lost a few coins."

"Didn't you learn to shudder?"

"Not I. I only made merry. Oh, if I could but find out how to shudder."

On the third night he again sat down on his bench, and said quite savagely: "If only I could shudder!"

When it grew late, six tall men came in, carrying a bier, and he said: "Hullo there! That must be my cousin who died a few days ago." And he beckoned and said: "Come along, cousin, come along."

The men put the coffin on the floor, and he went up and took the lid off, and there lay a dead man. He felt the face, and it was as cold as ice. "Wait," he said; "I will warm him."

Then he went to the fire and warmed his hand, and laid it on his face, but the dead man remained cold. He took him out of the coffin, sat down by the fire, and took him on his knees, and rubbed his arms to make the blood circulate.

But it was all no good. Next, it came into his head that if two people were in bed together, they warmed each other. So he put the dead man in the bed, covered him up, and lay down beside him.

After a time the dead man grew warm, and began to move.

Then the youth said: "There, you see, cousin mine, have I not warmed you?"

But the man rose up, and cried: "Now, I will strangle you!"

"What!" said he, "are those all the thanks I get. Back you go into your coffin then." So saying, he lifted him up, threw him in, and fastened down the lid. Then the six men came back and carried the coffin away.

"I cannot shudder," he said; "and I shall never learn it here."

Just then a huge man appeared. He was frightful to look at, old, and with a long white beard.

"Oh, you miserable wight!" he cried. "You shall soon learn what shuddering is, for you shall die."

"Not so fast," said the youth. "If I am to die, I must be present."

"I will make short work of you," said the old monster.

"Softly! softly! don't you boast. I am as strong as you, and very likely much stronger."

"We shall see about that," said the old man. "If you are the stronger, I will let you go. Come; we will try."

Then he led him through numberless dark passages to a smithy, took an axe, and with one blow struck one of the anvils into the earth.

"I can better that," said the youth, and went to the other anvil. The old man placed himself near to see, and his white beard hung over.

Then the youth took the axe and split the anvil with one blow, catching in the old man's beard at the same time.

"Now, I have you fast," said the youth, "and you will be the one to die."

Then he seized an iron rod, and belabored the old man with it, till he shrieked for mercy, and promised him great riches if he would stop.

Then the youth pulled out the axe and released him, and the old man led him back into the castle, and showed him three chests of gold in a cellar.

"One is for the poor," he said, "one for the King, and one for you."

The clock struck twelve, and the ghost disappeared, leaving the youth in the dark.

"I must manage to get out somehow," he said, and groped about till he found his way back to his room, where he lay down by the fire and went to sleep.

Next morning the King came and said: "Now you must have learnt how to shudder."

"No," said he. "What can it be? My dead cousin was there, and an old man with a beard came and showed me a lot of gold. But what shuddering is, that no man can tell me."

Then said the King: "You have broken the spell on the castle, and you shall marry my daughter."

"That is all very well," he said; "but still I don't know what shuddering is."

The gold was got out of the castle, and the marriage was celebrated, but, happy as the young King was, and much as he loved his wife, he was always saying: "Oh, if only I could learn to shudder, if only I could learn to shudder."

At last his wife was vexed by it, and her waiting-woman said: "I can help you; he shall be taught the meaning of shuddering."

And she went out to the brook which ran through the garden and got a pail full of cold water and little fishes.

At night, when the young King was asleep, his wife took the coverings off and poured the cold water over him, and all the little fishes flopped about him.

Then he woke up, and cried: "Oh, how I am shuddering, dear wife, how I am shuddering! Now I know what shuddering is!"

KING THRUSHBEARD

THERE WAS ONCE A KING who had a daughter. She was more beautiful than words can tell, but at the same time so proud and haughty that no man who came to woo her was good enough for her. She turned away one after another, and even mocked them.

One day her father ordered a great feast to be given, and invited to it all the marriageable young men from far and near.

They were all placed in a row, according to their rank and position. First came Kings, then Princes, then Dukes, Earls, and Barons.

The Princess was led through the ranks, but she had some fault to find with all of them.

One was too stout. "That barrel!" she said. The next was too tall. "Long and lean is no good!" The third was too short. "Short and stout, can't turn about!" The fourth was too white. "Pale as death!" The fifth was too red. "Turkey-cock!" The sixth was not straight. "Oven-dried!"

So there was something against each of them. But she made specially merry over one good King, who stood quite at the head of the row, and whose chin was a little hooked.

"Why!" she cried, "he has a chin like the beak of a thrush."

After that, he was always called "King Thrushbeard."

When the old King saw that his daughter only made fun of them, and despised all the suitors who were assembled, he was very angry, and swore that the first beggar who came to the door should be her husband.

A few days after, a wandering musician began to sing at the window, hoping to receive charity.

When the King heard him, he said: "Let him be brought in."

The musician came in, dressed in dirty rags, and sang to the King and his daughter, and when he had finished, he begged alms of them.

The King said: "Your song has pleased me so much, that I will give you my daughter to be your wife."

The Princess was horror-stricken. But the King said: "I have sworn an oath to give you to the first beggar who came; and I will keep my word."

No entreaties were of any avail. A parson was brought, and she had to marry the musician there and then.

When the marriage was completed, the King said: "Now you are a beggar-woman, you can't stay in my castle any longer. You must go away with your husband."

The beggar took her by the hand and led her away, and she was obliged to go with him on foot.

When they came to a big wood, she asked:

> "Ah! who is the lord of this forest so fine?"
> "It belongs to King Thrushbeard. It might have
> been thine,
> If his Queen you had been."
> "Ah! sad must I sing!
> I would I'd accepted the love of the King."

After that they reached a great meadow, and she asked again:

> "Ah! who is the lord of these meadows so fine?"
> "They belong to King Thrushbeard, and would have
> been thine.
> If his Queen you had been."

"Ah! sad must I sing!
I would I'd accepted the love of the King."

Then they passed through a large town, and again she asked:

"Ah! who is the lord of this city so fine?"
"It belongs to King Thrushbeard, and it might have
        been thine,
If his Queen you had been."
"Ah! sad must I sing!
I would I'd accepted the love of the King."

"It doesn't please me at all," said the musician, "that you are always wishing for another husband. Am I not good enough for you?"

At last they came to a miserable little hovel, and she said:

"Ah, heavens! what's this house, so mean and small?
This wretched little hut's no house at all."

The musician answered: "This is my house, and yours; where we are to live together."

The door was so low that she had to stoop to get in.

"Where are the servants?" asked the Princess.

"Servants indeed!" answered the beggar. "Whatever you want done, you must do for yourself. Light the fire, and put the kettle on to make my supper. I am very tired."

But the Princess knew nothing about lighting fires or cooking, and to get it done at all, the beggar had to do it himself.

When they had finished their humble fare, they went to bed. But in the morning the man made her get up very early to do the housework.

They lived like this for a few days, till they had eaten up all their store of food.

Then the man said: "Wife, this won't do any longer; we can't live here without working. You shall make baskets."

So he went out and cut some osiers, and brought them home. She began to weave them, but the hard osiers bruised her tender hands.

"I see that won't do," said the beggar. "You had better spin; perhaps you can manage that."

So she sat down and tried to spin, but the harsh yarn soon cut her delicate fingers and made them bleed.

"Now you see," said the man, "what a good-for-nothing you are. I have made a bad bargain in you. But I will try to start a trade in earthenware. You must sit in the market and offer your goods for sale."

"Alas!" she thought, "if any of the people from my father's kingdom come and see me sitting in the marketplace, offering goods for sale, they will scoff at me." But it was no good. She had to obey, unless she meant to die of hunger.

All went well the first time. The people willingly bought her wares because she was so handsome, and they paid what she asked them—nay, some even gave her the money and left her the pots as well.

They lived on the gains as long as they lasted, and then the man laid in a new stock of wares.

She took her seat in a corner of the market, set out her crockery about her, and began to cry her wares.

Suddenly, a drunken hussar came galloping up, and rode right in among the pots, breaking them into thousands of bits.

She began to cry, and was so frightened that she did not know what to do. "Oh! what will become of me?" she cried. "What will my husband say to me?" She ran home, and told him her misfortune.

"Who would ever think of sitting at the corner of the market with crockery?" he said. "Stop that crying. I see you are no manner of use for any decent kind of work. I have been to our King's palace, and asked if they do not want a kitchen wench, and they have promised to try you. You will get your victuals free, at any rate."

So the Princess became a kitchen wench, and had to wait upon the cook and do all the dirty work. She fixed a pot into each of her pockets, and in them took home her share of the scraps and leavings, and upon these they lived.

It so happened that the marriage of the eldest Princess just then took place, and the poor woman went upstairs and stood behind the door to peep at all the splendor.

When the rooms were lighted up, and she saw the guests streaming in, one more beautiful than the other, and the scene grew more and more brilliant, she thought, with a heavy heart, of her sad fate. She cursed the pride and haughtiness which had been the cause of her humiliation, and of her being brought to such depths.

Every now and then the servants would throw her bits from the savory dishes they were carrying away from the feast, and these she put into her pots to take home with her.

All at once the King's son came in. He was dressed in silk and velvet, and he had a golden chain round his neck.

When he saw the beautiful woman standing at the door, he seized her by the hand, and wanted to dance with her.

But she shrank and refused, because she saw that it was King Thrushbeard, who had been one of the suitors for her hand, and whom she had most scornfully driven away.

Her resistance was no use, and he dragged her into the hall. The string by which her pockets were suspended broke. Down fell the pots, and the soup and savory morsels were spilt all over the floor.

When the guests saw it, they burst into shouts of mocking laughter.

She was so ashamed, that she would gladly have sunk into the earth. She rushed to the door, and tried to escape, but on the stairs a man stopped her and brought her back.

When she looked at him, it was no other than King

Thrushbeard again.

He spoke kindly to her, and said: "Do not be afraid. I and the beggar-man, who lived in the poor little hovel with you, are one and the same. For love of you I disguised myself; and I was also the hussar who rode among your pots. All this I did to bend your proud spirit, and to punish you for the haughtiness with which you mocked me."

She wept bitterly, and said: "I was very wicked, and I am not worthy to be your wife."

But he said: "Be happy! Those evil days are over. Now we will celebrate our true wedding."

The waiting-women came and put rich clothing upon her, and her father, with all his court, came and wished her joy on her marriage with King Thrushbeard.

Then, in truth, her happiness began. I wish we had been there to see it, you and I.

IRON HANS

THERE WAS ONCE A KING whose castle was surrounded by a forest full of game. One day he sent a huntsman out to shoot a deer, but he never came back.

"Perhaps an accident has happened to him," said the King.

Next day he sent out two more huntsmen to look for him, but they did not return either. On the third day he sent for all his huntsmen, and said to them, "Search the whole forest without ceasing, until you have found all three."

But not a single man of all these, or one of the pack of hounds they took with them, ever came back. From this time forth no one would venture into the forest; so there it lay, wrapped in silence and solitude, with only an occasional eagle or hawk circling over it.

This continued for several years, and then one day a strange huntsman sought an audience of the King, and offered to penetrate into the dangerous wood. The King, however, would not give him permission, and said, "It's not safe, and I am afraid if you go in that you will never come out again, any more than all the others."

The huntsman answered, "Sire, I will take the risk upon myself. I do not know fear."

So the huntsman went into the wood with his dog. Before long the dog put up some game, and wanted to chase it; but hardly had he taken a few steps when he came to a deep pool, and could go no further. A naked arm appeared out of the water, seized him, and drew him down.

When the huntsman saw this, he went back and fetched three

men with pails to empty the pool. When they got to the bottom they found a wild man, whose body was as brown as rusty iron, and his hair hanging down over his face to his knees. They bound him with cords, and carried him away to the castle. There was great excitement over the wild man, and the King had an iron cage made for him in the courtyard. He forbade any one to open the door of the cage on pain of death, and the Queen had to keep the key in her own charge.

After this, anybody could walk in the forest with safety.

The King had a little son eight years old, and one day he was playing in the courtyard. In his play his golden ball fell into the cage. The boy ran up, and said, "Give me back my ball."

"Not until you have opened the door," said the wild man.

"No; I can't do that," said the boy. "My father has forbidden it," and then he ran away.

Next day he came again, and asked for his ball. The man said, "Open my door"; but he would not.

On the third day the King went out hunting, and the boy came again, and said, "Even if I would, I could not open the door. I have not got the key."

Then the wild man said, "It is lying under your mother's pillow. You can easily get it."

The boy, who was very anxious to have his ball back, threw his scruples to the winds, and fetched the key. The door was very stiff, and he pinched his fingers in opening it. As soon as it was open the wild man came out, gave the boy his ball, and hurried away. The boy was now very frightened, and cried out, "O wild man, don't go away, or I shall be beaten!"

The wild man turned back, picked up the boy, put him on his shoulder, and walked hurriedly off into the wood.

When the King came home he saw at once the cage was empty, and asked the Queen how it had come about. She knew nothing about it, and went to look for the key, which was of course gone.

They called the boy, but there was no answer. The King sent people out into the fields to look for him, but all in vain; he was gone. The King easily guessed what had happened, and great grief fell on the royal household.

When the wild man got back into the depths of the dark forest he took the boy down off his shoulder, and said, "You will never see your father and mother again; but I will keep you here with me, because you had pity on me and set me free. If you do as you are told, you will be well treated. I have treasures and gold enough and to spare, more than anybody in the world."

He made a bed of moss for the boy, on which he went to sleep. Next morning the man led him to a spring, and said, "You see this golden well is bright and clear as crystal? You must sit by it, and take care that nothing falls into it, or it will be contaminated. I shall come every evening to see if you have obeyed my orders."

The boy sat down on the edge of the spring to watch it; sometimes he would see a gold fish or a golden snake darting through it, and he guarded it well, so that nothing should fall into it. One day as he was sitting like this his finger pained him so much that involuntarily he dipped it into the water. He drew it out very quickly, but saw that it was golden, and although he tried hard to clean it, it remained golden. In the evening Iron Hans came back, looked at the boy, and said, "What has happened to the well today?"

"Nothing, nothing!" he answered, keeping his finger behind his back, so that Iron Hans should not see it.

But he said, "You have dipped your finger into the water. It does not matter this time, but take care that nothing of the kind occurs again."

Early next morning the boy took his seat by the spring again to watch. His finger still hurt very much, and he put his hand up above his head; but, unfortunately, in so doing he brushed a hair into the well. He quickly took it out, but it was already gilded. When Iron Hans came in the evening, he knew very well what had happened.

"You have let a hair fall into the well," he said. "I will overlook it once more, but if it happens for the third time, the well will be polluted, and you can no longer stay with me."

On the third day the boy again sat by the well; but he took good care not to move a finger, however much it might hurt. The time seemed very long to him as he looked at his face reflected in the water. As he bent over further and further to look into his eyes, his long hair fell over his shoulder right into the water. He started up at once, but not before his whole head of hair had become golden, and glittered like the sun. You may imagine how frightened the poor boy was. He took his pocket-handkerchief and tied it over his head, so that Iron Hans should not see it. But he knew all about it before he came, and at once said, "Take that handkerchief off your head," and then all the golden hair tumbled out. All the poor boy's excuses were no good. "You have not stood the test, and you can no longer stay here. You must go out into the world, and there you will learn the meaning of poverty. But as your heart is not bad, and as I wish you well, I will grant you one thing. When you are in great need, go to the forest and cry 'Iron Hans,' and I will come and help you. My power is great, greater than you think, and I have gold and silver in abundance."

So the King's son left the forest, and wandered over trodden and untrodden paths till he reached a great city. He tried to get work, but he could not find any; besides, he knew no trade by which to make a living. At last he went to the castle and asked if they would employ him. The courtiers did not know what use they could make of him, but they were taken with his appearance, and said he might stay. At last the cook took him into his service, and said he might carry wood and water for him, and sweep up the ashes.

One day, as there was no one else at hand, the cook ordered him to carry the food up to the royal table. As he did not want his golden hair to be seen, he kept his cap on. Nothing of the sort had ever happened in the presence of the King before, and he said, "When

you come into the royal presence, you must take your cap off."

"Alas, sire," he said, "I cannot take it off, I have a bad wound on my head."

Then the King ordered the cook to be called, and asked how he could take such a boy into his service, and ordered him to be sent away at once. But the cook was sorry for him, and exchanged him with the gardener's boy.

Now the boy had to dig and hoe, plant and water, in every kind of weather. One day in the summer, when he was working alone in the garden, it was very hot, and he took off his cap for the fresh air to cool his head. When the sun shone on his hair it glittered so that the beams penetrated right into the Princess's bedroom, and she sprang up to see what it was. She discovered the youth, and called to him, "Bring me a nosegay, young man."

He hurriedly put on his cap, picked a lot of wild flowers, and tied them up. On his way up to the Princess, the gardener met him, and said, "How can you take such poor flowers to the Princess? Quickly cut another bouquet, and mind they are the choicest and rarest flowers."

"Oh no," said the youth. "The wild flowers have a sweeter scent, and will please her better."

As soon as he went into the room the Princess said, "Take off your cap; it is not proper for you to wear it before me."

He answered again, "I may not take it off, because I have a wound on my head."

But she took hold of the cap, and pulled it off, and all his golden hair tumbled over his shoulders in a shower. It was quite a sight. He tried to get away, but she took hold of his arm, and gave him a handful of ducats. He took them, but he cared nothing for the gold, and gave it to the gardener for his children to play with.

Next day the Princess again called him to bring her a bunch of wild flowers, and when he brought it she immediately clutched at his cap to pull it off; but he held it on with both hands. Again she gave him a handful of ducats, but he would not keep them, and gave them to the gardener's children. The third day the same thing happened, but she could not take off his cap, and he would not keep the gold.

Not long after this the kingdom was invaded. The King assembled his warriors. He did not know whether they would be able to conquer his enemies or not, as they were very powerful, and had a mighty army. Then the gardener's assistant said, "I have been brought up to fight; give me a horse, and I will go too."

The others laughed and said, "When we are gone, find one for yourself. We will leave one behind in the stable for you."

When they were gone, he went and got the horse out; it was lame in one leg, and hobbled along, humpety-hump, humpety-hump. Nevertheless, he mounted it and rode away to the dark forest. When he came to the edge of it, he called three times, "Iron Hans," as loud as he could, till the trees resounded with it.

The wild man appeared immediately, and said, "What do you want?"

"I want a strong horse to go to the war."

"You shall have it, and more besides."

The wild man went back into the wood, and before long a groom came out, leading a fiery charger with snorting nostrils. Behind him followed a great body of warriors, all in armor, and their swords gleaming in the sun. The youth handed over his three-legged steed to the groom, mounted the other, and rode away at the head of the troop.

When he approached the battlefield a great many of the King's men had already fallen, and before long the rest must have given in. Then the youth, at the head of his iron troop, charged, and bore down the enemy like a mighty wind, smiting everything which came in their way. They tried to fly, but the youth fell upon them, and did not stop while one remained alive.

Instead of joining the King, he led his troop straight back to the wood and called Iron Hans again.

"What do you want?" asked the wild man.

"Take back your charger and your troop, and give me back my three-legged steed."

His request was granted, and he rode his three-legged steed home.

When the King returned to the castle his daughter met him and congratulated him on his victory.

"It was not I who won it," he said; "but a strange knight, who came to my assistance with his troop." His daughter asked who the strange knight was, but the King did not know, and said, "He pursued the enemy, and I have not seen him since."

She asked the gardener about his assistant, but he laughed, and said, "He has just come home on his three-legged horse, and the others made fun of him, and said, 'Here comes our hobbler back again,' and asked which hedge he had been sleeping under. He answered, 'I did my best, and without me things would have gone badly.' Then they laughed at him more than ever."

The King said to his daughter, "I will give a great feast lasting three days, and you shall throw a golden apple. Perhaps the unknown knight will come among the others to try and catch it."

When notice was given of the feast, the youth went to the wood and called Iron Hans.

"What do you want?" he asked.

"I want to secure the King's golden apple," he said.

"It is as good as yours already," answered Iron Hans. "You shall have a tawny suit, and ride a proud chestnut."

When the day arrived the youth took his place among the other knights, but no one knew him. The Princess stepped forward and threw the apple among the knights, and he was the only one who could catch it. As soon as he had it he rode away.

On the second day Iron Hans fitted him out as a white knight, riding a gallant grey. Again he caught the apple; but he did not stay a minute, and, as before, hurried away.

The King now grew angry, and said, "This must not be; he must come before me and give me his name."

He gave an order that if the knight made off again he was to be pursued and brought back.

On the third day the youth received from Iron Hans a black outfit, and a fiery black charger.

Again he caught the apple; but as he was riding off with it the King's people chased him, and one came so near that he wounded him in the leg. Still he escaped, but his horse galloped so fast that his helmet fell off, and they all saw that he had golden hair. So they rode back, and told the King what they had seen.

Next day the Princess asked the gardener about his assistant.

"He is working in the garden. The queer fellow went to the feast, and he only came back last night. He has shown my children three golden apples which he won."

The King ordered him to be brought before him. When he appeared he still wore his cap. But the Princess went up to him and took it off; then all his golden hair fell over his shoulders, and it was so beautiful that they were all amazed by it.

"Are you the knight who came to the feast every day in a different color, and who caught the three golden apples?" asked the King.

"Yes," he answered, "and here are the apples," bringing them out of his pocket, and giving them to the King. "If you want further proof, here is the wound in my leg given me by your people when they pursued me. But I am also the knight who helped you to conquer the enemy."

"If you can do such deeds you are no gardener's boy. Tell me who is your father?"

"My father is a powerful King, and I have plenty of gold—as much as ever I want."

"I see very well," said the King, "that we owe you many thanks. Can I do anything to please you?"

"Yes," he answered; "indeed, you can. Give me your daughter to be my wife!"

The maiden laughed, and said, "He does not beat about the bush; but I saw long ago that he was no gardener's boy."

Then she went up to him and kissed him.

His father and mother came to the wedding, and they were full of joy, for they had long given up all hope of ever seeing their dear son again. As they were all sitting at the wedding feast, the music suddenly stopped, the doors flew open, and a proud King walked in at the head of a great following. He went up to the bridegroom, embraced him, and said, "I am Irons Hans, who was bewitched and changed into a wild man; but you have broken the spell and set me free. All the treasure that I have is now your own."

SNOW-WHITE AND ROSE-RED

THERE WAS ONCE A POOR widow who lived in a lonely cottage. In front of the cottage was a garden where stood two rose-trees, one a white rose and the other red. She had two children who were like the two rose-trees, and one was called Snow-White, and the other Rose-Red. They were as good and happy, and as busy and cheerful as ever were any two children in the world, only Snow-White was more quiet and gentle than Rose-Red. Rose-Red liked better to run about in the meadows and fields picking flowers and chasing butterflies. But Snow-White sat at home with her mother, and helped her with her housework, or read to her when there was nothing to do.

The two children were so fond of each other that they always held each other by the hand when they went out together, and when Snow-White said, "We will not leave each other," Rose-Red answered, "Never so long as we live," and their mother would add, "What one has, she must share with the other."

They often ran about the forest alone and gathered red berries, and no wild animals did them any harm, but came close to them trustfully. The little hare would eat a cabbage-leaf out of their hands, the roe grazed by their side, the stag leapt merrily by them, and the birds sat still upon the boughs, and sang all the songs they knew.

No mishap ever overtook them. If they had stayed too late in the forest, and night came on, they just laid themselves down near one another upon the moss, and slept until morning came, and their mother knew this and had no distress on their account.

Once when they had spent the night in the wood and the dawn had roused them, they saw a beautiful child in a shining white dress sitting near their bed of moss. He rose up and looked kindly at them, but said nothing and went away into the forest. And when they looked round they found that they had been sleeping quite close to a precipice, and would certainly have fallen over it in the darkness if they had gone only a few paces further. And their mother told them that it must have been the angel who watches over good children.

Snow-White and Rose-Red kept their mother's little cottage so neat that it was a pleasure to look inside it. In the summer Rose-Red took care of the house, and every morning laid a nosegay by her mother's bed before she awoke, and in it was a rose from each tree. In the winter Snow-White lit the fire and hung the kettle over it on the hook. The kettle was of copper and shone like gold, so brightly was it polished.

In the evening, when the snowflakes fell, the mother said, "Go, Snow-White, and bolt the door," and then they sat round the hearth, and the mother took her spectacles and read aloud out of a large book, and the two girls listened as they sat and span. And close by them lay a lamb upon the floor, and behind them upon a perch sat a white dove with its head tucked under its wing.

One evening, as they were sitting cozily together, there was a knock at the door as if some one wished to be let in.

The mother said, "Quick, Rose-Red, open the door, it must be a traveler who is seeking shelter."

Rose-Red went and pushed back the bolt, thinking that it was some poor man, but it was not. It was a bear that pushed his broad black head in at the door.

Rose-Red screamed and sprang back, the lamb bleated, and the dove fluttered, and Snow-White hid herself behind her mother's bed. But the bear began to speak and said, "Do not be afraid, I will do you no harm! I am half-frozen, and only want to warm myself a little beside your fire."

"Poor bear," said the mother, "lie down by the fire, only take care that you do not burn your coat." Then she cried, "Snow-White, Rose-Red, come out, the bear will do you no harm, he means kindly."

So they both came out again, and by and by the lamb and dove came nearer, and ceased to be afraid of him.

The bear said, "Here, children, knock the snow out of my coat a little."

So they brought the broom and swept the bear's hide clean, and he stretched himself by the fire and growled contentedly. It was not long before they grew quite at home, and began to play tricks with their clumsy guest. They tugged his hair with their hands, put their feet upon his back and rolled him about, or they took a hazel-switch and beat him, and when he growled they laughed. But the bear took it all in good part, only when they were too rough he called out, "Children, children, leave me my life!"

> "Snow-White, Rose-Red,
> Will you beat your lover dead?"

When it was bedtime, and the others went to bed, the mother said to the bear, "You can lie there by the hearth, and then you will be safe from the cold and the bad weather." As soon as day dawned the two children let him out, and he trotted across the snow into the forest.

Henceforth the bear came every evening at the same time, laid himself down by the hearth, and let the children amuse themselves with him as much as they liked, and they got so used to him that the doors were never fastened until their black friend had arrived.

When spring had come and all outside was green, the bear said one morning to Snow-White, "Now I must go away, and cannot come back for the whole summer."

"Where are you going, then, dear bear?" asked Snow-White.

"I must go into the forest and guard my treasures from the wicked dwarfs. In the winter, when the earth is frozen hard, they are obliged to stay below and cannot work their way through. But now, when the sun has thawed and warmed the earth, they break through it, and come out to pry and steal, and what once gets into their hands, and in their caves, does not easily see daylight again."

Snow-White was quite sorry for his going away, and as she unbolted the door for him, and the bear was hurrying out, he caught against the bolt and a piece of his hairy coat was torn off, and it seemed to Snow-White as if she had seen gold shining through it, but she was not sure about it. The bear ran away quickly, and was soon out of sight among the trees.

A short time afterwards the mother sent her children into the forest to get firewood. There they came to a big fallen tree which lay on the ground, and close by the trunk something was jumping backwards and forwards in the grass, but they could not make out what it was. When they got nearer they found it was a dwarf with an old withered face and a snow-white beard a yard long. The end of his beard was caught in a crack in the tree, and the little fellow was jumping backwards and forwards like a dog tied to a rope, and did not know what to do.

He glared at the girls with his fiery red eyes and cried, "Why do you stand there? Can you not come here and help me?"

"Why, little man, what are you about there?" asked Rose-Red.

"You stupid prying goose!" answered the dwarf; "I was going to split the tree, of course, to get a little wood to cook with. The little bit of food that one of us wants gets burnt up directly with thick logs. We do not swallow so much as you coarse greedy folks do. I had just driven the wedge safely in, and everything was going as I wished, but the wretched wood was too smooth and suddenly out jumped the wedge, and the tree closed so quickly that I could not pull out my beautiful white beard. So now it is tight in and I cannot get away, and the silly, sleek, milk-faced things laugh! Ugh! how odious you are!"

The children tried very hard, but they could not pull the beard out, it was caught too fast.

"I will run and fetch some one," said Rose-Red.

"You senseless goose!" snarled the dwarf; "why should you fetch some one? You are already two too many for me. Can you not think of something better?"

"Don't be impatient," said Snow-White, "I will help you," and she pulled her scissors out of her pocket, and cut off the end of his beard.

As soon as the dwarf felt himself free he laid hold of a bag which lay among the roots of the tree, and which was full of gold, and lifted it up, grumbling to himself, "Clumsy people, cutting off a piece of my fine beard. Bad luck to you!" And then he swung the bag upon his back, and went off without even once looking at the children.

Some time after that Snow-White and Rose-Red went to catch a dish of fish. As they came near the brook, they saw something like a large grasshopper jumping towards the water, as if it were going to leap in. They ran up and found it was the dwarf.

"Where are you going?" asked Rose-Red; "you surely don't want to go into the water?"

"I am not such a fool!" cried the dwarf; "don't you see it's that wretched fish wants to pull me in?" The little man had been sitting there fishing, and unluckily the wind twisted his beard in the fishing-line, at the very moment that a big fish took the bait. The little weakling had not strength to pull it out, and the fish had the better of it, and was pulling the dwarf nearer the edge. He held on to all the reeds and rushes, but it was little good, he was forced to follow the movements of the fish, and was in urgent danger of being dragged into the water.

The girls came just in time. They held him fast and tried to free his beard from the line, but all in vain; beard and line were entangled fast together. Nothing was left but to bring out the scissors and cut the beard, whereby a little bit of it was lost. When the dwarf saw that he screamed out:

"Do you call that civil, you toadstool, disfiguring one's face like that? Was it not enough to clip off the end of my beard? Now you have cut off the best part of it. I cannot let myself be seen by my people. I wish you had been made to run the soles off your shoes!" Then he took out a sack of pearls which lay in the rushes, and without saying a word more he dragged it away and disappeared behind a stone.

It happened that soon afterwards the mother sent the two children to the town to buy needles and thread, and laces and ribbons. The road led them across a heath upon which huge rocks lay strewn here and there. Soon they noticed a great bird hovering in the air, flying slowly round and round above them. It sank lower and lower, and at last settled near a rock not far off. Directly afterwards they heard a loud cry of terror. They ran up and saw with horror that the eagle had seized their old friend the dwarf, and was going to carry him off.

The children, full of pity, at once caught tight hold of the little man, and pulled against the eagle so long that at last he let his booty go.

As soon as the dwarf had recovered from his first fright he cried with his shrill voice, "Could you not have done it more carefully! You dragged at my brown coat so that it is all torn and full of holes, you helpless clumsy creatures!" Then he took up a sack full of precious stones, and slipped away again under the rock into his hole. The girls, who by this time were used to his thanklessness, went on their way and did their business in the town.

As they crossed the heath again on their way home they surprised the dwarf, who had emptied out his bag of precious stones in a clean spot, and had not thought that any one would come there so late. The evening sun shone upon the brilliant stones. They glittered and sparkled with all colors so beautifully that the children stood still and looked at them.

"Why do you stand gaping there?" cried the dwarf, and his ashen-grey face became copper-red with rage.

He was going on with his bad words when a loud growling was heard, and a black bear came trotting towards them out of the forest. The dwarf sprang up in a fright, but he could not get to his cave, for the bear was already close.

Then in the dread of his heart he cried, "Dear Mr. Bear, spare me, I will give you all my treasures. Look, the beautiful jewels lying there! Grant me my life. What do you want with such a skinny little fellow as I am? You would not feel me between your teeth. Come, take these two wicked girls, they are tender morsels for you, fat as young quails. For mercy's sake eat them!"

The bear took no heed of his words, but gave the scoundrel just one blow with his paw, and he did not move again.

The girls had run away, but the bear called to them. "Snow-White and Rose-Red, do not be afraid. Wait, I will come with you." Then they knew his voice and waited, and when he came up to them suddenly his bearskin fell off, and he stood there a handsome youth, clothed all in gold. "I am a King's son," he said, "and I was bewitched by that wicked dwarf, who had stolen my treasures. I have had to run about the forest as a savage bear until I was freed by his death. Now he has got his well-deserved punishment."

Snow-White was married to him, and Rose-Red to his brother, and they divided between them the great treasure which the dwarf had gathered together in his cave. The old mother lived peacefully and happily with her children for many years. She took the two rose-trees with her, and they stood before her window, and every year bore the most beautiful roses, white and red.

THUMBLING'S TRAVELS

A CERTAIN TAILOR HAD A SON, who was so tiny that he was no bigger than a thumb, and because of this he was always called Thumbling. He had, however, plenty of courage, and said to his father, "Father, I must and will go out into the world."

"That's right, my son," said the old man, and took a long darning needle and made a knob of sealing wax on it at the candle, "and there is a sword for you to take with you on the way."

Then the little tailor wanted to have just one more meal with them, and skipped into the kitchen to see what his lady mother had cooked for the last time. It was just dished up, and the dish stood on the hearth. Then said he, "Mother, what's there for dinner today?"

"See for yourself," said his mother.

So Thumbling jumped on to the hearth, and peeped into the dish, but as he stretched his neck too far in, the steam from the food caught him and carried him up the chimney. He rode about in the air on the steam for a while, until at length he sank down to the ground again. Now the little tailor was out in the wide world, and he traveled about, and went to work with a master in his craft, but the food was not good enough for him. "Mistress, if you don't feed us better, I shall go," said Thumbling, "and early tomorrow morning I'll chalk on the door of your house, 'Too many potatoes, too little meat! Farewell, Mr. Potato-King.'"

"What would you have forsooth, grasshopper?" said the mistress, growing angry, and she seized a dishcloth, and was just going to strike him. But my little tailor crept nimbly under a thimble, and peeped out from beneath it, and put his tongue out at her. She took up the thimble to catch him, but little Thumbling hopped into the cloth, and while the mistress was opening it out and searching for him, he got into a crack in the table. "Ho, ho, lady mistress," cried he, and thrust his head out, and when she hit at him he leapt down into the drawer. At last, however, she caught him and drove him out of the house.

The little tailor journeyed on and came to a great forest, where he fell in with a band of robbers who were planning to steal the King's treasure. When they saw the little tailor, they thought, "That's the little fellow for us! He can creep through the keyhole and pick the lock."

"Hi!" cried one of them, "you giant Goliath, will you go to the treasure-chamber with us? You can slip in and throw out the money."

Thumbling thought for a moment, and then said "yes," and he went with them to the treasure-chamber. He began by searching the doors from top to bottom to see if he could find a crack in them. It was not long before he espied one broad enough to let him in. He was just about to slip in at once, when one of the two sentries who stood before the door, caught sight of him, and said to the other, "Eh! what an ugly spider is creeping there; I will kill it."

"Let the poor creature alone," said the other, "it has done you no harm." So Thumbling got safely through the crack into the treasure-chamber, opened the window beneath which the robbers were standing, and threw out to them one dollar after another. While the little tailor was hard at work, he heard the King coming to inspect his treasure-chamber, and crept hastily into hiding. The King noticed that several solid silver pieces were missing, but could not conceive who could have stolen them, for locks, bars, and bolts were all in order, and well guarded. Then he went away again, saying to the sentries, "Be on the watch, some one is after the money."

When therefore Thumbling began again, they heard the chink, chink of moving coins. They ran in swiftly to seize the thief, but the little tailor, who heard them coming, was still swifter, and leapt into a corner and covered himself with a dollar, so that nothing could be seen of him, and at the same time he mocked the sentries and cried, "Here am I!" Thither ran the sentries, but by the time they got there, he had already hidden in another corner and was crying, "Ho, ho, here am I!" The watchmen dashed there at top speed, but Thumbling had long ago hopped into a third corner, and was crying, "Ho, ho, here am I!" And thus he made fools of them, and drove them so long round about the treasure-chamber that they were tired out and went away. So, one by one, he threw out all the money. He flung out the last coin with all his might, hopping nimbly on to it as it flew down through the window. The robbers paid him great compliments. "You are a valiant hero indeed," said they; "will you be our captain?"

Thumbling, however, said he wouldn't, as he wanted to see the world first. They now divided the booty, but the little tailor asked for one groat only because he could not carry more.

Then he buckled on his sword again, bade the robbers good-bye, and took to the road. First, he went to work under some masters, but he had no liking for that, and at last he hired himself as man-servant in an inn. The maids, however, could not endure him, for he saw secretly all that they did without their seeing him, and he told their master and mistress what they had helped themselves to off the plates, and carried off out of the cellar. Then they said, "Wait! We'll pay you off!" and arranged with each other to play him a trick.

Soon afterwards one of the maids was mowing in the garden, and saw Thumbling jumping and creeping up and down in the long grass. Quickly she mowed him up with the grass, made it all into a bundle, and took it and threw it to the cattle. Now among them there was a great black cow, who swallowed him down whole without hurting him. But down below it pleased him ill, for it was quite dark, and there wasn't any candle burning either. So while the cow was being milked he cried,

> "Strip, strap, strull,
> Will the pail soon be full?"

But the noise of the milking kept him from being heard. After this the master of the house came into the cowshed and said, "That cow shall be killed tomorrow."

Then Thumbling was so alarmed that he cried out in a clear voice, "Let me out first, for I am shut up inside her."

The master heard that quite well, but did not know from whence the voice came. "Where are you?" asked he.

"In the black one," answered Thumbling, but the master did not understand what that meant, and went out.

Next morning the cow was killed. Happily Thumbling did not meet with one blow at the killing and quartering, and he got among the sausage-meat. And when the butcher came in and began his work, he cried out with all his might, "Don't chop too deep, don't chop too deep, for I am here." But no one heard this because of the noise of the chopping-knife. Now, indeed, poor Thumbling was in trouble, but trouble sharpens the wits, and he dodged about so cleverly between the blows that none of them touched him, and he got off with a whole skin. But still he could not get away, there was nothing for it, and he had to let himself be thrust into a black-pudding with the bits of bacon. He found himself in rather close quarters, and besides that he was hung up in the chimney to be smoked, and there the time did hang terribly heavy on his hands.

At length in winter he was taken down again, as the black-pudding was to be set before a guest. And while the hostess was cutting it in slices, he took care not to stretch out his head too far, I can tell you, lest a bit of it should be sliced off; at last he saw his opportunity, cleared a way for himself, and jumped out.

The little tailor, however, would not stay any longer in a house where he fared so ill, and at once set out on his journey again. But his liberty did not last long. In the open country he met with a fox who snapped him up without thinking.

"Hullo, Mr. Fox," cried the little tailor. "Set me free, set me free! It's me here, sticking in your throat!"

"You are right," answered the fox. "And it's little or nothing you are to me too. So if you shall promise me the fowls in your father's yard I'll let you go."

"With all my heart," replied Thumbling. "You shall have all the cocks and hens, that I promise you."

Then the fox let him go again, and himself carried him home. When the father once more saw his dear son, he willingly gave the fox all the fowls he had. "For this I bring you a handsome bit of money too," said Thumbling, and gave his father the silver groat which he had earned on his travels.

THE SKILLFUL HUNTER

THERE WAS ONCE A YOUNG fellow who had learned the trade of locksmith, and told his father he would now go out into the world and seek his fortune.

"Very well," said the father, "I am quite content with that," and gave him some money for his journey.

So he traveled about and looked for work. After a time he resolved not to follow the trade of locksmith any more, for he no longer liked it, but he took a fancy for hunting. Then there met him in his rambles a hunger dressed in green, who asked whence he came and where he was going? The youth said he was a locksmith's apprentice, but that the trade no longer pleased him, and he had a liking for woodcraft, would he teach it to him?

"Oh, yes," said the hunter, "if you will go with me."

Then the young fellow went with him, bound himself to him for some years, and learned the art of hunting. After this he wished to try his luck elsewhere, and the hunter gave him nothing in the way of payment but an air-gun, which had, however, this property, that it hit its mark without fail whenever he shot with it. Then he set out and found himself in a very large forest, which he could not get to the end of in one day. When evening came he seated himself in a high tree in order to escape the wild beasts. Towards midnight, it seemed to him as if a tiny little light glimmered in the distance. He looked down through the branches towards it, and kept well in his mind where it was. But in the first place he took off his hat and threw it down in the direction of the light, so that he might go to the hat as a mark when he had descended. Then he climbed down and went to his hat, put it on again and went straight forward. The farther he went, the larger the light grew, and when he got close to it he saw that it was an enormous fire, and that three giants were sitting by it, who had an ox on the spit and were roasting it.

Presently one of them said, "I must just taste if the meat will soon be fit to eat," and he pulled a scrap off, and was about to put it in his mouth when the hunter shot it out of his hand.

"Well, really," said the giant, "if the wind has not blown the bit out of my hand!" and helped himself to another. But when he was just about to taste it, the hunter again shot it away from him.

On this the giant gave the one who was sitting next to him a box on the ear, and cried angrily, "Why are you snatching my piece away from me?"

"I have not snatched it away," said the other; "a sharpshooter must have shot it away from you."

The giant took another piece, but he could not keep it in his hand, for the hunter shot it out.

Then the giant said, "That must be a good shot to shoot the bit out of one's very mouth. Such a one would be useful to us." And he cried out loud, "Come here, you sharpshooter. Seat yourself at the fire beside us and eat your fill, we will not hurt you. But if you will not come, and we have to bring you by force, you are a lost man!"

When he heard this, the youth went up to them and told them he was a skilled hunter, and that whatever he aimed at with his gun, he was certain to hit. Then they said if he would go with them he should be well treated, and they told him that outside the forest there was a great lake, behind which stood a tower, and in the tower was imprisoned a lovely Princess, whom they wished very much to carry off.

"Good," said he, "I will soon get her for you."

Then they added, "But there is still something else; there is a tiny little dog, which begins to bark directly when any one goes near, and as soon as it barks every one in the royal palace wakes up, and for this reason we cannot get there. Can you undertake to shoot it dead?"

"Yes," said he, "that will be a little bit of fun for me."

After this he got into a boat and rowed over the lake, and as soon as he landed, the little dog came running out, and was about to bark, but the hunter took his air-gun and shot it dead. When the giants saw that, they rejoiced, and thought they already had the King's daughter safe, but the hunter wished first to see how matters stood, and told them that they must stay outside until he called them. Then he went into the castle, and all was perfectly quiet within, and every one was asleep. When he opened the door of the first room, a sword was hanging on the wall which was made of pure silver, and there was a golden star on it, and the name of the King, and on a table near it lay a sealed letter which he broke open, and inside it was written that whoever had the sword could kill any one who opposed him. So he took the sword from the wall, hung it at his side and went on. Next he entered the room where the King's daughter was lying asleep, and she was so beautiful that he stood still and held his breath to look at her. He thought to himself, "How can I give an innocent maiden into the power of the wild giants, who have evil in their minds?" He looked about further, and under the bed stood a pair of slippers, on the right one of which was her father's name with a star, and on the left her own name with a star. She wore also a great neckerchief of silk embroidered with gold, and on the right side was her father's name, and on the left her own, all in golden letters. Then the hunter took a pair of scissors and cut the right corner off and put it in his knapsack, and then he took the right slipper with the King's name, and thrust that in too. The maiden still lay sleeping, and he cut a little piece from her nightgown, and thrust it in with the rest, but he did it all without touching her. Then he went out and left her lying asleep undis-

turbed, and when he came to the gate again, the giants were still standing outside waiting for him, and expecting that he was bringing the Princess. But he cried out to them that they were to come in, for the maiden was already in their power, and that he could not open the gate to them, but that there was a hole through which they must creep. As the first began to creep through, the hunter wound the giant's hair round his hand, pulled his head in, and cut it off at one stroke with his sword, and then he drew the rest of him in. He called to the second to come on and cut his head off in the same way, and then he killed the third also, and he was well pleased that he had freed the beautiful maiden from her enemies. Before he went he cut out their tongues and put them too in his knapsack. Then he thought, "I will go home to my father and let him see what I have already done, and afterwards I will travel about the world. The luck which God is pleased to grant me will easily find me."

But when the King in the castle awoke, he saw the three giants lying there dead. So he went into his daughter's bedroom, woke her up, and asked her who could have killed the giants?

Then said she, "Dear Father, I know not, I have been asleep."

But when she rose and would have put on her slippers, the right one was gone, and when she looked at her neckerchief it was cut, and the right corner was missing, and when she looked at her nightdress a piece was cut out of it. The King summoned his whole court together, soldiers and every one else who was there, and asked who had set his daughter at liberty, and killed the giants? Now it happened that he had a captain, who was one-eyed and hideous, and he said that he had done it. Then the old King said that as he had accomplished this, he should marry his daughter.

But the maiden said, "Rather than marry him, dear Father, I will go away into the world as far as my legs can carry me."

But the King said that if she would not marry him she should take off her royal garments and wear peasant's clothing, and out she should go, and that she should go to a potter, and begin to sell earthen vessels. So she put off her royal apparel, and went to a potter and borrowed crockery enough for a stall, and she promised him also that if she had sold it by the evening, she would pay for it. Then the King said she was to seat herself in a corner with it and sell it, and he arranged with some peasants to drive over it with their carts, so that everything should be broken into a thousand pieces. So when the King's daughter had set up her stall in the street, by came the carts and smashed all she had into fragments.

She began to weep and said, "Alas, how shall I ever pay for the pots now?"

The King had, however, wished by this to force her to marry the captain, but instead of that, she went again to the potter, and asked him if he would lend her some more pots and pans. He said no, she must first pay for the things she had already had.

Then she went to her father and cried and lamented, and said she would go out into the world.

Then said he, "I will have a little hut built for you in the forest outside, and in it you will stay all your life long and cook for every one, but you shall take no money for it."

When the hut was ready, a sign was hung on the door on which was written, "For nothing today, tomorrow for pay." There she remained a long time, and it was rumored about the world that a maiden was there who cooked without asking for payment, and that this was set forth on a sign outside her door.

The hunter heard it too, and thought to himself, "That would suit you. You are poor, and have no money."

So he took his air-gun and his knapsack, with all the things in it that he had formerly carried away with him from the castle as tokens of his truthfulness, and he went into the forest, and found the hut with the sign, "For nothing today, tomorrow for pay." He had put on the sword with which he had cut off the heads of the three giants, and so prepared, he entered the hut, and ordered something to eat to be given to him. He was charmed with the beautiful maiden, who was indeed as lovely as any picture.

She asked him where he came from and where he was going, and he said, "I am roaming about the world."

Then she asked him where he had got the sword, for that in truth her father's name was on it. He asked her if she were the King's daughter?

"Yes," answered she.

"With this sword," said he, "did I cut off the heads of three giants." And he took their tongues out of his knapsack in proof. Then he also showed her the slipper, and the corner of the neckerchief, and the bit of the nightdress. Hereupon she was overjoyed, and said that he was the one who had delivered her. On this they went together to the old King and brought him to the hut, and she led him into her room, and told him that the hunter was the man who had really set her free from the giants. And when the aged King saw all the proofs of this, he could no longer doubt, and said that he was very glad he knew how everything had happened, and that the hunter should marry her, at which the maiden was glad at heart.

Then she dressed the hunter as if he were a foreign nobleman, and the King ordered a feast to be prepared. When they went to table, the captain sat on the left side of the King's daughter, but the hunter was on the right, and the captain thought he was a foreign lord who had come on a visit. When they had eaten and drunk, the old King said to the captain that he would set before him something which he must guess.

"Supposing any one said that he had killed the three giants and he was asked where the giants' tongues were, and was forced to go and look, and there were none in their heads, how could that happen?"

The captain said, "Then they cannot have had any."

"Not so," said the King. "Every animal has a tongue," and then he asked what any one would deserve who made such an answer.

The captain replied, "He ought to be torn to pieces." Then the King said he had pronounced his own sentence, and the captain was put in prison and then torn into four pieces. But the King's daughter was married to the hunter. Afterwards he sent for his father and mother, and they lived with their son in happiness, and when the old King died the kingdom came to him.

THE STAR-MONEY

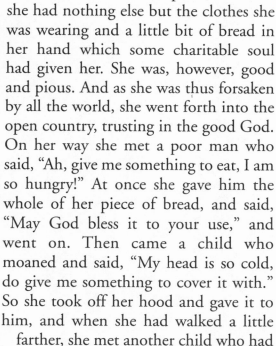

ONCE UPON A TIME there was a little girl whose father and mother were dead, and she was so poor that she no longer had any little room to live in or bed to sleep in, and at last she had nothing else but the clothes she was wearing and a little bit of bread in her hand which some charitable soul had given her. She was, however, good and pious. And as she was thus forsaken by all the world, she went forth into the open country, trusting in the good God. On her way she met a poor man who said, "Ah, give me something to eat, I am so hungry!" At once she gave him the whole of her piece of bread, and said, "May God bless it to your use," and went on. Then came a child who moaned and said, "My head is so cold, do give me something to cover it with." So she took off her hood and gave it to him, and when she had walked a little farther, she met another child who had no jacket and was frozen with cold. So she gave it her own jacket, and a little farther on another one begged for a frock, and she gave away that also. At length she came to a forest and it had already become dark, and there came yet another child, and asked for a little shirt, and the good little girl thought to herself, "It is a dark night and no one sees you, you can very well give your little smock away," and took it off, and gave away that also. And as she stood there without one single thing left to call her own, suddenly some stars from heaven fell down, and they were nothing else but hard smooth pieces of money, and although she had just given her little shirt away, she had a new one of the very finest linen. Then she gathered the money into this, and was rich all the days of her life.

ONE-EYE, TWO-EYES, AND THREE-EYES

THERE WAS ONCE A WOMAN who had three daughters, the eldest of whom was called One-Eye, because she had only one eye in the middle of her forehead, and the second, Two-Eyes, because she had two eyes like other folks, and the youngest, Three-Eyes, because she had three eyes. And her third eye, also, was in the middle of her forehead. However, as Two-Eyes saw just as other human beings did, her sisters and her mother could not endure her.

They said to her, "You, with your two eyes, are no better than the common people. You do not belong to us!" They pushed her about, and threw old clothes to her, and gave her nothing to eat but what they left, and did everything that they could to make her unhappy.

It came to pass that Two-Eyes had to go out into the fields and tend the goat, but she was still quite hungry, because her sisters had given her so little to eat. So she sat down on a bank and began to weep, and she wept so bitterly that two streams ran down from her eyes. And once in the midst of her grief she looked up and there stood a woman beside her, who said, "Why are you weeping, little Two-Eyes?"

Two-Eyes answered, "Have I not reason to weep, when I have two eyes like other people, and my sisters and mother hate me for it, and push me from one corner to another, and throw old clothes at me, and give me nothing to eat but the scraps they leave? Today they have given me so little that I am still very hungry."

Then the wise woman said, "Wipe away your tears, Two-Eyes, and I will tell you something to stop you suffering from hunger ever again. Just say to your goat,

> "Little goat, bleat!
> Little table, spread!

and then a clean well-spread little table will stand before you, with the most delicious food upon it of which you may eat as much as ever you wish, and when you have had enough, and have no more need of the little table, just say,

> "Little goat, bleat!
> Little table, go!

and then it will vanish again from your sight." Hereupon the wise woman departed.

But Two-Eyes thought, "I must try this at once, and see if what she said is true, for I am too hungry to bear it," so she said,

> "Little goat, bleat!
> Little table, spread!"

and scarcely had she spoken the words than a little table covered with a white cloth was standing there, and on it was a plate with a knife and fork and a silver spoon, and the most delicious food was there also, warm and smoking as if it had just come out of the kitchen. Then Two-Eyes said the shortest prayer she knew, "Lord God, be with us always, Amen," and helped herself, and enjoyed it very much. And when she was satisfied, she said, as the wise woman had taught her,

> "Little goat, bleat!
> Little table, go!"

and immediately the little table and everything on it was gone again. "That is a delightful way of keeping house!" thought Two-Eyes, and was quite glad and happy.

In the evening, when she went home with her goat, she found a small earthenware dish with something to eat, which her sisters had set ready for her, but she did not touch it. Next day again she went out with her goat, and the few crusts of bread which had been given her, she left untouched. The first and second time that she did this, her sisters did not notice it at all, but as it happened every time, they soon did observe it, and said, "There is something wrong about Two-Eyes, she always leaves her food untasted, and she used to eat up everything that was given her. She must have found other ways of getting her food."

In order that they might learn the truth, they resolved to send One-Eye with Two-Eyes when she went to drive her goat to the pasture, to watch what Two-Eyes did when she was there, and whether any one brought her anything to eat and drink. So when Two-Eyes set out the next time, One-Eye went to her and said, "I will go with you to the pasture, and see that the goat is well taken care of, and driven where there is food." But Two-Eyes knew what was in One-Eye's mind, and after she had driven the goat into long grass, she said, "Come, One-Eye, we will sit down, and I will sing something to you." One-Eye sat down, tired with the unaccustomed walk and the heat of the sun, and Two-Eyes sang constantly,

> "One-Eye, wakest thou?
> One-Eye, sleepest thou?"

until One-Eye shut her one eye, and fell asleep, and as soon as Two-Eyes saw that One-Eye was fast asleep, and could discover nothing, she said,

> "Little goat, bleat!
> Little table, spread!"

137

and seated herself at her table, and ate and drank until she had had enough, and then she said,

> "Little goat, bleat!
> Little table, go!"

and in an instant all was gone. Two-Eyes now awakened One-Eye, and said, "One-Eye, you set out to take care of the goat, and go to sleep while you are doing it. In the meantime the goat might run all over the world. Come, let us go home again." So they went home, and again Two-Eyes let her little dish stand untouched, and One-

Eye could not tell her mother why she would not eat it, and to excuse herself said, "I fell asleep when I was out."

Next day the mother said to Three-Eyes, "This time you shall go and watch if Two-Eyes eats anything when she is out, and if any one fetches her food and drink, for she must eat and drink in secret." So Three-Eyes went to Two-Eyes, and said, "I will go with you and see if the goat is taken proper care of, and driven where there is food." But Two-Eyes knew what was in Three-Eyes's mind, and drove the goat into long grass, and said, "We will sit down, and I will sing something to you, Three-Eyes."

Three-Eyes sat down, tired with the walk and the heat of the sun, and Two-Eyes began the same song as before, and sang,

> "Three-Eyes, are you waking?"

but then, instead of singing,

> "Three-Eyes, are you sleeping?"

as she ought to have done, she thoughtlessly sang,

> "Two-Eyes, are you sleeping?"

and sang all the time,

> "Three-Eyes, are you waking?
> "Two-Eyes, are you sleeping?"

Then two of the eyes which Three-Eyes had, shut and fell asleep, but the third, as it had not been named in the song, did not sleep. It is true that Three-Eyes shut it, but only in her cunning, to pretend it was asleep too, but it blinked and could see everything very well. And when Two-Eyes thought that Three-Eyes was fast asleep, she used her little charm,

> "Little goat, bleat!
> Little table, spread!"

and ate and drank as much as her heart desired, and then ordered the table to go away again,

> "Little goat, bleat!
> Little table, go!"

and Three-Eyes had seen everything. Then Two-Eyes came to her, waked her and said, "Have you been asleep, Three-Eyes? You are a good caretaker! Come, we will go home." And when they got home, Two-Eyes again did not eat, and Three-Eyes said to the mother, "Now I know why that stuck-up thing there does not eat. When she is out, she says to the goat,

> "Little goat, bleat!
> Little table, spread!

and then a little table appears before her covered with the best of food, much better than any we have here, and when she has eaten all she wants, she says,

> "Little goat, bleat!
> Little table, go!

and all disappears. I watched everything closely. She put two of my eyes to sleep by using a certain form of words, but luckily the one in my forehead kept awake." Then the envious mother cried, "Do you want to fare better than we do? The desire shall pass away," and she took a butcher's knife, and thrust it into the heart of the goat, and it fell down dead.

When Two-Eyes saw that, she went out full of trouble, seated herself on the grass bank at the edge of the field, and wept bitter tears. Suddenly the wise woman once more stood by her side, and said, "Two-Eyes, why are you weeping?"

"Have I not reason to weep?" she answered. "The goat that spread the table for me every day when I spoke your charm has been killed by my mother, and now I shall again have to bear hunger and want."

The wise woman said, "Two-Eyes, I will give you a piece of good advice. Ask your sisters to give you the entrails of the slaughtered goat, and bury them in the ground in front of the house, and your fortune will be made."

Then she vanished, and Two-Eyes went home and said to her sisters, "Dear sisters, do give me some part of my goat. I don't wish for what is good, but give me the entrails."

Then they laughed and said, "If that's all you want, you can have it."

So Two-Eyes took the entrails and buried them quietly in the evening, in front of the house-door, as the wise woman had counseled her to do.

Next morning, when they all woke, and went to the house-door, there stood a strange and beautiful tree with leaves of silver, and fruit of gold hanging among them, so that in all the wide world there was nothing more beautiful or precious. They did not know how the tree could have come there during the night, but Two-Eyes saw that it had grown up out of the entrails of the goat, for it was standing on the exact spot where she had buried them.

Then the mother said to One-Eye, "Climb up, my child, and gather some of the fruit of the tree for us."

One-Eye climbed up, but just when she was about to take hold of one of the golden apples, the branch escaped from her hands, and that happened each time, so that she could not pluck a single apple, do what she might.

Then said the mother, "Three-Eyes, do you climb up; you with your three eyes can look about you better than One-Eye."

One-Eye slipped down, and Three-Eyes climbed up. Three-Eyes was not more skillful, and might try as she liked, but the golden apples always escaped her. At length the mother grew impatient, and climbed up herself, but could get hold of the fruit no better than One-Eye and Three-Eyes, for she always clutched empty air.

Then said Two-Eyes, "I will just go up, perhaps I may succeed better."

The sisters cried, "You indeed, with your two eyes, what can you do?"

But Two-Eyes climbed up, and the golden apples did not get out of her way, but came into her hand of their own accord, so that she could pick them one after the other, and brought a whole apronful down with her. The mother took them away from her, and instead of treating poor Two-Eyes any better for this, she and One-Eye and Three-Eyes were only envious, because Two-Eyes alone had been able to get the fruit, and so they treated her still more cruelly.

It so befell that once when they were all standing together by the tree, a young knight came along.

"Quick, Two-Eyes," cried the two sisters, "creep under this, and don't disgrace us!" and with all speed they turned an empty barrel which was standing close by the tree over poor Two-Eyes, and they pushed the golden apples that she had been gathering under it too. When the knight came nearer it could be seen that he was a fine lord, and handsome too, and he stopped to admire the magnificent gold and silver tree, and said to the two sisters, "To whom does this fine tree belong? Any one who would give a branch of it to me might in return ask whatever he desired."

Then One-Eye and Three-Eyes replied that the tree belonged to them, and that they would give him a branch. And they both tried hard, but they were not able to do it, for the branches and fruit slipped away from them every time.

Then said the knight, "It is very strange that the tree should belong to you, and yet you are not able to break a branch off."

Again they asserted that the tree was theirs. And whilst they were saying so, Two-Eyes rolled out a couple of golden apples from under the barrel to the feet of the knight, for she was vexed with One-Eye and Three-Eyes for not speaking the truth. When the knight saw the apples he was astonished, and asked where they came from. One-Eye and Three-Eyes answered that they had another sister, who was not allowed to show herself, for she had only two eyes like any common person. But the knight desired to see her, and cried, "Two-Eyes, come forth."

Then Two-Eyes, quite comforted, came from beneath the barrel, and the knight was surprised at her great beauty, and said, "You, Two-Eyes, can certainly break off a branch from the tree for me."

"Yes," replied Two-Eyes, "that I certainly shall be able to do, for the tree belongs to me."

And she climbed up, and with the greatest ease broke off a branch with beautiful silver leaves and golden fruit, and gave it to the knight.

Then said the knight, "Two-Eyes, what shall I give you for it?"

"Alas!" answered Two-Eyes, "I suffer from hunger and thirst, grief and want, from early morning till late night. If only you would take me with you, and deliver me from these things, I should be very happy."

So the knight lifted Two-Eyes on to his horse, and took her

home with him to his father's castle, and there he gave her beautiful clothes, and meat and drink to her heart's content, and as he loved her so much he married her, and their wedding took place with great rejoicing.

When Two-Eyes was carried away by the handsome knight, her two sisters grudged her her good fortune in real earnest.

"The wonderful tree, however, still remains with us," thought they, "and even if we can gather no fruit from it, still every one will stand still and look at it, and come to us and admire it. Who knows what good things may not be in store for us?" But next morning the tree had vanished, and all their hopes were at an end. And when Two-Eyes looked out of the window of her own little room, to her great delight it was standing in front of it, and so it had followed her.

Two-Eyes lived a long time in happiness. Once two poor women came to her in her castle, and begged for alms. She looked in their faces, and recognized her sisters, One-Eye and Three-Eyes, who had fallen into such poverty that they had to wander about and beg their bread from door to door. Two-Eyes, however, made them welcome, and was kind to them, and took care of them, so that they both with all their hearts repented the evil that they had done their sister in their youth.

THE WISHING-TABLE,
THE GOLD-ASS, AND THE
CUDGEL IN THE KNAPSACK

O NCE UPON A TIME there was a tailor who had three sons, and only one goat. But as the goat supported the whole of them with her milk, she was obliged to have good food, and had to be taken every day to pasture. So the sons did this in turn. Once the eldest took her to the churchyard, where the finest grass was to be found, and let her eat and run about there. At night when it was time to go home he asked, "Goat, have you had enough?" The goat answered,

> "I have eaten so much,
> Not a leaf more I'll touch, meh! meh!"

"Come along home, then," said the youth, and took hold of the cord round her neck, led her back to the stable and tied her up for the night.

"Well," said the tailor, "has the goat had as much food as she ought?"

"Oh," answered the son, "she has eaten so much, not a leaf more she'll touch."

But the father wished to satisfy himself, so he went down to the stable, stroked the dear animal and asked, "Nannie, are you full?" The goat answered,

> "And how should I be full?
> Among the graves I leapt about,
> But found no food, so went without, maa! maa!"

145

"What's this I hear?" cried the tailor, and ran upstairs and said to the youth, "Hullo, you liar; you said the goat had had enough, and have let her starve!" and in his anger he took the yard-measure from the wall, and beat him out of the house.

Next day it was the turn of the second son, who looked out for a place near the fence of the garden, where nothing but good herbs grew, and the goat cleared them all off. At night when he wanted to go home, he asked, "Goat, are you full?" The goat answered,

> "I have eaten so much,
> Not a leaf more I'll touch, meh! meh!"

"Come along home, then," said the youth, and led her home, and tied her up in the stable.

"Well," said the old tailor, "has the goat had as much food as she ought?"

"Oh," answered the son, "she has eaten so much, not a leaf more she'll touch."

The tailor would not rely on this, but went down to the stable and said, "Nannie, have you had enough?" The goat answered,

> "And how should I be full?
> Among the graves I leapt about,
> But found no food, so went without, maa! maa!"

"The wicked rascal!" cried the tailor, "to let such a good animal hunger," and he ran up and drove the youth out of doors with the yard-measure.

Now came the turn of the third son, who was determined to do his best, and sought out the bushes with the finest leaves, and let the goat browse there. In the evening when he wanted to go home, he asked, "Goat, have you had enough?" The goat answered,

> "I have eaten so much,
> Not a leaf more I'll touch, meh! meh!"

"Come along home, then," said the youth, and led her back to the stable, and tied her up.

"Well," said the old tailor, "has the goat really had enough this time?"

"She has eaten so much, not a leaf more she'll touch."

The tailor did not trust to that, but went down and asked, "Nannie, have you had enough?" The wicked beast answered,

> "And how should I have had enough?
> Among the graves I leapt about,
> But found no leaves, so went without, maa! maa!"

"Oh, what a pack of liars!" cried the tailor, "each as wicked and forgetful as the other! They shall no longer make a fool of me," and, quite beside himself with anger, he ran upstairs and belabored the poor young fellow so vigorously with the yard-measure that he darted out of the house and away.

The old tailor was now alone with his goat. Next morning he went down into the stable, caressed the goat and said, "Come, my dear little animal, I will take you to feed myself." He took her by the rope and conducted her where there were green hedges, and clover, and whatever else goats like to eat. "There you may for once eat to your heart's content," said he to her, and let her browse till evening. Then he asked, "Goat, are you full?" She replied,

> "I have eaten so much,
> Not a leaf more I'll touch, meh! meh!"

"Come along home, then," said the tailor, and led her into the stable, and tied her fast. When he was going away, he turned round again and said, "Well, are you full for once?" But the goat did not

behave any better to him, and cried,

> "And how should I be full?
> Among the graves I leapt about,
> But found no leaves, so went without, maa! maa!"

When the tailor heard that, he was shocked, and saw clearly that he had driven away his three sons without cause. "Wait, you ungrateful creature!" cried he. "It is not enough to drive you forth; I will mark you so that you will no more dare to show yourself among honest tailors." In great haste he ran upstairs, fetched his razor, lathered the goat's head, and shaved her as clean as the palm of his hand. And as the yard-measure would have been too good for her, he went and fetched to her the horsewhip, and gave her such a thrashing that she ran away as fast as she could go.

When the tailor was thus left quite alone in his house he fell into great grief, and would gladly have had his sons back again, but no one knew where they were gone.

Now the eldest had apprenticed himself to a joiner, and learned industriously and untiringly, and when the time came for him to go traveling, his master presented him with a little table which was in no way remarkable to look at, and was made of common wood, but it had one good property; if any one set it down anywhere and said, "Little table, spread thyself," the good little table was at once covered with a clean little cloth, and a plate was there, and a knife and fork beside it, and dishes with boiled meat, and roasted meat, as many as there was room for, and a great bumper of red wine shone so that it made the heart glad. The young journeyman thought, "With this you have enough for your whole life," and wandered joyously about the world never troubling himself whether an inn was good or bad, or if anything was to be had there or not. When it suited him he did not enter an inn at all, but either in the open country, or in a wood, or a meadow, or wherever he fancied, he took his little table off his back, set it down before him, and said, "Cover thyself," and everything appeared that his heart desired. At length he took it into his head to go back to his father, whose anger would now be appeased, and who would now willingly receive him with his wishing-table.

It came to pass that on his way home, he came one evening to an inn which was filled with guests. They bade him welcome, and invited him to sit and eat with them, for otherwise he would have had difficulty in getting anything.

"No indeed," answered the joiner, "I wouldn't rob you of a mouthful; rather than that, you shall do me the honor of being my guests."

They laughed, and thought he was jesting with them; but he placed his wooden table in the middle of the room, and said, "Little table, cover thyself." Instantly it was covered with good things, better far than the host could have provided, and the smell alone would have been too tempting to resist. "Fall to, dear friends," said the joiner; and the guests when they saw that he meant it, did not need to be asked twice, but drew their chairs up, pulled out their knives and attacked it valiantly. And what surprised them the most was that when a dish became empty, a full one instantly took its place of its own accord. The innkeeper stood in a corner and watched; he did not know at all what to say, but he thought, "You could easily find a use for such a cook as that in your kitchen." The joiner and his comrades made merry until late into the night. At length they all lay down to sleep, the young apprentice setting his magic table against the wall before he went to bed. The host's thoughts, however, let him have no rest; it occurred to him that there was a little old table in his lumber-room, which looked just like the apprentice's, and he brought it out quite softly, and exchanged it for the wishing-table. Next morning, the joiner paid for his bed, took up his table, never thinking that he had got a false one, and went his way. At midday he reached the house of his father, who received him with great joy.

"Well, my dear son, what have you learned?" said he to him.

"Father, I have become a joiner."

"A good trade," replied the old man; "but what have you brought back with you from your apprenticeship?"

"Father, the best thing that I have brought back with me is this little table."

The tailor inspected it on all sides and said, "You did not make a masterpiece when you made that; it is a wretched old table that."

"But it is a table which furnishes itself," replied the son. "When I set it down, and tell it to cover itself, the most beautiful dishes stand on it, and a wine also, which gladdens the heart. Just invite all our relations and friends; they shall refresh and enjoy themselves for once, for the table will give them all they can desire."

When the company was assembled, he put his table in the middle of the room and said, "Little table, cover thyself," but the little table did not bestir itself, and remained just as bare as any other table which did not understand when it was spoken to. Then the poor apprentice became aware that his table had been changed, and was ashamed at having to stand there like a liar. And his relations all mocked him, and were forced to go home without having eaten or drunk. His father brought out his patches again, and went on tailoring, but the son went off to find a new master.

The second son had gone to a miller and had apprenticed himself to him. When his years were over, the master said, "As you have conducted yourself so well, I give you this ass of a very unusual kind, which neither draws a cart nor carries a sack."

"To what use is he put, then?" asked the young apprentice.

"He lets gold drop from his mouth," answered the miller. "Set him on a cloth and say, 'Bricklebrit' to him and the good animal will drop gold pieces for you."

"That is a fine thing," said the apprentice, and thanked the master, and went out into the world. When he had need of gold, he had only to say "Bricklebrit" to his ass, and it rained gold pieces, and he had nothing to do but to pick them up from the ground. Wherever he went, the best of everything was good enough for him, and the dearer the better, for he had always a full purse. When he had looked about the world for some time, he thought to himself, "You must seek out your father; if you go to him with the gold-ass he will forget his anger, and receive you well."

It came to pass that he came to the same public-house in which his brother's table had been exchanged. He led his ass by the bridle, and the host was about to take the animal from him and tie him up, but the young apprentice said, "Don't trouble yourself, I will take my grey horse into the stable, and tie him up myself too, for I must know just where he is." This struck the host as odd, and he thought that a man who was forced to look after his ass himself could not have much to spend; but when the stranger put his hand in his pocket and brought out two gold pieces, and said he was to provide something good for him, the host opened his eyes wide, and ran and sought out the best he could muster. After dinner the guest asked what he owed. The host did not see why he should not double the reckoning, and said the apprentice must give two more gold pieces. He felt in his pocket, but his gold had just come to an end.

"Wait an instant, sir host," said he, "I will go and fetch some money," and he took the tablecloth with him. The host could not imagine what this could mean, and being curious, he stole after him, and as the guest bolted the stable door, he peeped through a hole left by a knot in the wood. The stranger spread out the cloth under the animal and cried, "Bricklebrit," and immediately the beast began to let gold pieces fall, so that it fairly rained down money on the ground.

"Eh, my word," thought the host, "ducats are quickly coined there! A purse like that is not amiss." The guest paid his score, and went to bed, but in the night the host stole down into the stable, led away the master of the mint, and tied up another ass in his place.

Early next morning the apprentice traveled away with the ass, thinking all the time that he had his gold-ass. At midday he reached the house of his father, who rejoiced to see him again, and gladly took him in.

"What have you made of yourself, my son?" asked the old man.

"A miller, dear Father," he answered.

"What have you brought back with you from your travels?"

"Nothing else but an ass."

"There are asses enough here," said the father; "I would rather have had a good goat."

"Yes," replied the son, "but mine is no common ass, but a gold-ass. When I say 'Bricklebrit,' the good beast opens its mouth and drops a whole sheetful of gold pieces. Just summon all our relations hither, and I will make them rich people."

"That suits me well," said the tailor, "for then I shall have no need to torment myself any longer with the needle," and ran out himself and called the relations together.

As soon as they were assembled, the miller bade them make way, spread out his cloth, and brought the ass into the room. "Now watch," said he, and cried, "Bricklebrit," but no gold pieces fell, and it was clear that the animal knew nothing of the art, for every ass does not attain such perfection. Then the poor miller pulled a long face, saw that he was betrayed, and begged pardon of the relatives, who went home as poor as they came. There was no help for it, the old man had to betake him to his needle once more, and the youth hired himself to a miller.

The third brother had apprenticed himself to a turner, and as that is skilled labor, he was the longest in learning. His brothers, however, told him in a letter how badly things had gone with them, and how the innkeeper had cheated them of their wonderful wishing-gifts on the last evening before they reached home. When the turner had served his time, and had to set out on his travels, as he had conducted himself so well, his master presented him with a knapsack and said, "There is a cudgel in it."

"I can put on the knapsack," said he, "and it may be of good service to me, but why should the cudgel be in it? It only makes it heavy."

"I will tell you why," replied the master; "if any one has done anything to injure you, do but say, 'Out of the sack, cudgel!' and the cudgel will lap forth among the people, and play such a dance on their backs that they will not be able to stir or move for a week, and it will not leave off until you say, 'Into the sack, cudgel!'"

The apprentice thanked him, put the sack on his back, and

when any one came too near him, and threatened to attack him, he said, "Out of the sack, cudgel!" and instantly the cudgel sprang out, and gave the coat of the evil-doer such a dusting that he soon wished that he had never tried to interfere. In the evening the young turner reached the inn where his brothers had been cheated. He laid his knapsack on the table before him, and began to talk of all the wonderful things which he had seen in the world.

"Yes," said he, "people may easily find a table which will cover itself, a gold-ass, and things of that kind—extremely good things which I by no means despise—but these are nothing in comparison with the treasure which I have won for myself, and am carrying about with me in my knapsack there."

The innkeeper pricked up his ears. "What in the world can that be?" thought he. "The knapsack must be filled with nothing but jewels; I ought to get them cheap too, for all good things go in threes." When it was time for sleep, the guest stretched himself on the bench, and laid his knapsack beneath him for a pillow. When the innkeeper thought his guest was lying in a sound sleep, he went to him and pushed and pulled quite gently and carefully at the knapsack to see if he could possibly draw it away and lay another in its place. The turner, had, however, been waiting for this for a long time, and now just as the innkeeper was about to give a hearty tug, he cried, "Out of the sack, cudgel!" Instantly the little cudgel came forth, and fell on the innkeeper, and gave him a sound thrashing.

The host cried for mercy; but the louder he cried, the heavier the cudgel beat the time on his back, until at length he fell to the ground exhausted. Then the turner said, "If you do not give back the table which covers itself, and the gold-ass too, the dance shall begin afresh."

"Oh no," cried the host in terror, "I will gladly produce everything, only make that dreadful little goblin creep back into the sack."

Then said the apprentice, "I will have mercy instead of giving you your deserts, but beware of getting into mischief again!" So he cried, "Into the sack, cudgel!" and let him have rest.

Next morning the turner went home to his father with the wishing-table and the gold-ass. The tailor rejoiced when he saw him once more, and asked him likewise what he had learned in foreign parts.

"Dear Father," said he, "I have become a turner."

"A skilled trade," said the father. "What have you brought back with you from your travels?"

"A precious thing, dear Father," replied the son, "a cudgel in the knapsack."

"What!" cried the father, "a cudgel! That's worth your trouble, indeed! From every tree you can cut yourself one."

"But not one like this, dear Father. If I say, 'Out of the sack, cudgel!' the cudgel springs out and leads any one who means ill with me such a dance, I can tell you, and never stops until he lies on the ground and prays for fair weather. Look you, with this cudgel I have got back the wishing-table and the gold-ass which the thievish innkeeper stole from my brothers. Now let them both be sent for, and invite all our kinsmen. I will give them the best to eat and to drink, and will fill their pockets with gold into the bargain." The old tailor would not quite believe, but nevertheless got the relatives together. Then the turner spread a cloth in the room and led in the gold-ass, and said to his brother, "Now, dear brother, speak to him." The miller said, "Bricklebrit," and instantly the gold pieces fell down on the cloth like a thundershower, and the ass did not stop until every one of them had so much that he could carry no more. (I can see in your face that you also would have liked to be there.)

Then the turner brought the little table, and said, "Now, dear brother, speak to it." And scarcely had the carpenter said, "Table, cover thyself," than it was spread and amply covered with the most savory dishes.

Then such a meal took place as the good tailor had never yet known in his house, and the whole party of kinsmen stayed till far into the night, and were all merry and glad together. The tailor locked away in a cupboard needle and thread, yard-measure and goose, and lived with his three sons in plenty and happiness.

What, however, has become of the goat who was to blame for the tailor driving out his three sons? That I will tell you. She was ashamed that she had a bald head, and ran to a fox's hole and crept into it. When the fox came home, he was met by two great eyes shining out of the darkness, and he was terrified and ran away.

A bear met him, and as the fox looked upset, he said, "What is the matter with you, brother fox? Why do you look like that?"

"Ah," answered Redskin, "a fierce beast is in my cave and stared at me with its fiery eyes."

"We will soon drive him out," said the bear, and went with him to the cave and looked in, but when he saw the fiery eyes, fear seized on him too; he would have nothing to do with the fearful beast, and took to his heels.

The bee met him, and as she saw that he was ill at ease, she said, "Bear, you are really pulling a very pitiful face; what has become of all your gaiety?"

"It is all very well for you to talk," replied the bear; "a furious beast with staring eyes is in Redskin's house, and we can't drive him out."

The bee said, "Bear, I pity you. I am a poor weak creature whom you would not turn aside to look at, but still I believe I can help you." And she flew into the fox's cave, settled on the goat's shaven head, and stung her so sharply that she sprang up, crying "Meh, meh," and ran forth into the world like mad, and to this hour no one knows where she has gone.

THE WONDERFUL MUSICIAN

THERE WAS ONCE A wonderful musician, who was going all alone through a forest thinking of all manner of things, and when nothing was left for him to think about, he said to himself, "Time is beginning to pass heavily with me here in the forest. I'll call hither some one to keep me company." Then he took his fiddle from his back, and played so that it echoed through the trees. It was not long before a wolf came trotting through the thicket towards him.

"Ah, here's a wolf coming! I've no desire for him!" said the musician.

But the wolf came nearer and said to him, "Ah, dear musician, how beautifully you do play! I should like to learn that, too."

"It is soon learned," the musician replied; "you have only to do all that I bid you."

"O musician," said the wolf, "I will obey you as a scholar obeys his master."

The musician bade him follow him, and when they had gone a little way together, they came to an old oak-tree which was hollow, and cleft in the middle.

"Look," said the musician, "if you will learn to fiddle, put your forepaws into this crack."

The wolf obeyed, but the musician quickly picked up a stone and with one blow wedged his two paws so fast that he was forced to stay there prisoner.

"Stay there until I come back again," said the musician, and went his way.

After a while he said to himself again, "Time is beginning to pass heavily with me here in the forest. I will call hither another companion," and he took his fiddle again and played a tune. It was not long before a fox came creeping through the trees towards him.

"Ah, there's a fox coming!" said the musician. "I have no desire for him."

The fox came up to him and said, "Oh, dear musician, how beautifully you do play! I should like to learn that, too."

"That is soon learned," said the musician; "you have only to do everything that I bid you."

"Oh, musician," then said the fox, "I will obey you as a scholar obeys his master."

"Follow me," said the musician; and when they had walked a little way, they came to a footpath, with high bushes on both sides of it. There the musician stopped, and from one side bent a young hazel down to the ground, and put his foot on it, then he bent down a sapling from the other side as well, and said, "Now, little fox, if you will learn something, give me your left forepaw." The fox obeyed, and the musician fastened his paw to the left bough.

"Little fox," said he, "now give me your right paw," and he tied it to the right bough. He made sure they were safely tied, and then he let go; the bushes sprang up again, and up jerked the little fox, so that he hung struggling in the air.

"Wait there till I come back again," said the musician, and went his way.

Again he said to himself, "Time is beginning to pass heavily with me here in the forest. I will call hither another companion." So he took his fiddle, and the sound echoed through the forest. This time a little hare came leaping towards him.

"Why, here's a hare coming," said he. "I don't want her."

"Ah, dear musician," said the hare, "how beautifully you do fiddle! I, too, should like to learn that."

"That's soon learned," said the musician; "you have only to do everything I bid you."

"Oh, musician," replied the little hare, "I will obey you as a scholar obeys his master." They went on a little way together until they came to an open space in the forest, where stood an aspen. The musician tied a long string round the little hare's neck, the other end of which he fastened to the tree.

"Now, briskly, little hare, run twenty times round the tree!" cried the musician, and the little hare obeyed, and when she had run round twenty times, she had twisted the string twenty times round the trunk of the tree, and the little hare was caught, and let her pull and tug as she liked, it only made the string cut into her tender neck.

"Wait there till I come back," said the musician, and on he went.

The wolf, in the meantime, had pushed and tugged and bitten at the stone, until at last he had set his feet at liberty and had dragged them out of the cleft. Full of rage and fury he rushed after the musician and wanted to tear him to pieces.

When the fox saw him running past, he began to yelp and howl with all his might, "Brother wolf, come to my help; the musician has betrayed me!" So the wolf drew down the little trees, bit the cords in two, and freed the fox, who went on with him to take revenge on the musician. They found the hare tied up too and delivered her, and then they all sought the enemy together.

Once more the musician had played his fiddle as he went on his way, and this time he had been more fortunate. The sound reached the ears of a poor woodcutter, who instantly had to give up his work, willy-nilly, and came with his hatchet under his arm to listen to the music.

"At last comes the right companion," said the musician, "for I was seeking a human being, not a wild beast." And he began to play so sweetly and enchantingly that the poor man stood there as if bewitched, and his heart leaped with gladness. And as he stood thus, the wolf, the fox, and the hare came up, and he saw well that they meant no good. So he raised his glittering axe and placed himself before the musician, as if to say, "Whoever wishes to touch him let him beware, for he will have to do with me!" And that frightened the beasts and they ran back into the forest. The musician, however, played once more to the man out of gratitude, and then went on.

THE CUNNING LITTLE TAILOR

ONCE UPON A TIME there was a Princess who was extremely proud. If a wooer came she gave him a riddle to guess, and if he could not find it out, he was made fun of and turned out. She had it made known also that he who solved her riddle should marry her, whoever he might be.

In time three tailors fell in with each other, the two eldest of whom thought they had done so many neat jobs before that they could not fail to succeed in this also. The third was a little useless vagrant, who did not even know his trade, but thought he might have some luck in this venture, for heaven knows where else it was to come from. The two others told him to stay at home. What could he do, said they, with the little sense he possessed. The little tailor, however, did not let himself be discouraged, and said he had set his head to work about this for once, and he'd do well enough, and out he went as if the whole world were his.

They all three presented themselves before the Princess, and said she was to propound her riddle to them, for at last the right persons had come, who had wits so fine that they could be threaded in a needle.

Then the Princess said, "I have two kinds of hair on my head, of what color is it?"

"If that's all," said the first, "it must be black and white, like the cloth which is called pepper and salt."

"Wrong," said the Princess. "Let the second answer."

Then said the second, "If it isn't black and white, then it's brown

163

and red, like my father's best Sunday coat."

"Wrong," said the Princess. "Let the third give the answer, for I see very well he knows it for certain."

Then the little tailor stepped boldly forth and said, "The Princess has a silver and a golden hair on her head, and those are the two different colors."

When the Princess heard that, she turned pale and nearly fell down with terror, for the little tailor had guessed her riddle, and she had firmly believed that no man on earth could discover it. When her courage returned she said, "But you have not won me yet, there is still something else that you must do. Below, in the stable, is a bear with which you shall pass the night, and when I get up in the morning if you are still alive, you shall marry me." And she was quite sure she would thus get rid of the tailor, for the bear had never yet left any one alive who had fallen into his clutches.

The little tailor did not let himself be frightened away, but was quite delighted, and said, "Boldly ventured is half won."

So, when evening came, our little tailor was taken down to the bear. The bear was about to make for the little fellow at once, and give him a hearty welcome with his paws, but "Softly, softly," said the little tailor, "I will soon make you quiet."

Then quite coolly, and as if he hadn't a care in the world, he took some nuts out of his pocket and cracked them, and ate the kernels. When the bear saw that, he was seized with a desire to have some nuts too. The tailor felt in his pockets, and held him out a handful. Really, however, they were not nuts at all, but pebbles. The bear put them in his mouth, but could make nothing of them, let him bite as he would.

"Eh!" thought he, "what a stupid blockhead I am! I cannot even crack a nut!" And then he said to the tailor, "Here, crack me the nuts."

"There, see what a stupid fellow you are!" said the little tailor, "with such a great mouth, and not able to crack a little nut!" And he took the pebble and quickly put a nut in his mouth in the place of it, and crack, it was in two!

"I must try the thing again," said the bear; "when I watch you, it makes me think I ought to be able to do it too."

So the tailor once more gave him a pebble, and the bear tried and tried to get his teeth into it with all his might. But no one will imagine that he did it.

When that was over, the tailor took out a violin from under his coat, and played a tune on it to himself. When the bear heard the music he could not help beginning to dance, and when he had danced a while, it pleased him so well that he said to the little tailor, "Hark you, is the fiddle heavy?"

"Light enough for a child. Look, with the left hand I lay my fingers on it, and with the right I stroke it with the bow, and then it goes merrily, hop sa sa vivallalera!"

"So," said the bear; "fiddling is a thing I should like to master too, that I might dance whenever I had a fancy. What do you think of that? Will you give me lessons?"

"With all my heart," said the tailor, "if you have a talent for it. But just let me see your claws, they are terribly long. I must cut your nails a little." Then a vice was brought, and the bear put his claws in it, and the little tailor screwed it tight, and said, "Now wait until I come with the scissors." And the bear might growl as he liked, but the tailor lay down in the corner on a bundle of straw, and fell asleep.

When the Princess heard the bear growling so fiercely during the night, she thought all the time that he was growling for joy, and had made an end of the tailor. In the morning she arose careless and happy, but when she peeped into the stable, the tailor stood gaily before her, as spry as a fish in the water. Now she could not say another word against the wedding because she had given her promise before every one, and the King ordered a carriage to be brought for her to drive to church with the tailor, and there she was to be married.

When they had got into the carriage, the two other tailors, who had false hearts and envied him his good fortune, went into the stable and set free the bear again. The bear in great fury ran after the carriage. The Princess heard him snorting and growling; she was terrified, and she cried, "Oh, oh, the bear is coming after us and wants to get thee!" The tailor was quick and stood on his head, stuck his legs out of the window, and cried, "Do you see the vice? If you do not be off you shall be put into it again." When the bear saw that, he turned round and ran away. The tailor drove quietly to church, and the Princess was married to him at once, and he lived with her as happy as a woodlark. Whoever does not believe this must pay a thaler.

HANS THE HEDGEHOG

THERE WAS ONCE A COUNTRYMAN who had money and land in plenty, but however rich he might be, there was still one thing wanting to his happiness, for he had no children. Often when he went into the town with the other peasants they mocked him, asking him why he had no children. At last one day he became angry, and when he got home he said, "Wife, I will have a child, even if it be but a hedgehog."

And in time they did have a child, and it was like a hedgehog in the upper part of his body, and a boy in the lower, and when the wife saw the child, she was terrified, and said, "See there, you have brought ill-luck on us."

Then said the man, "What can be done now? The boy must be christened, but we shall never be able to find a godfather for him."

And the woman said, "Nor can we call him anything else but Hans the Hedgehog."

When he was christened, the parson said, "You cannot put him into any ordinary bed because of his spikes." So a little straw was placed behind the stove, and Hans the Hedgehog was laid on it. His mother could not nurse him, for his quills would have pricked her. So he lay there behind the stove for eight years, and his father grew tired of him and wished, "If he would but die!" He did not die, however, but went on lying there.

Now it happened that there was a fair in the town, and the peasant was about to go to it, and he asked his wife what he should bring back for her.

"A little meat and a couple of white rolls that are wanted for the house," said she.

Then he asked the servant, and she wanted a pair of slippers and some stockings with clocks.

Last of all he said, "And what will you have, Hans my Hedgehog?"

"Dear Father," he said, "do bring me some bagpipes."

When the father came home again, he gave his wife what he had brought for her, meat and white rolls. And then he gave the maid the slippers, and the stockings with clocks. And lastly he went behind the stove, and gave Hans the Hedgehog the bagpipes.

And when Hans the Hedgehog had the bagpipes, he said, "Dear Father, do go to the forge and get the cock shod, and then I'll ride away, and never come back again." On hearing this, the father was delighted to think that he was going to get rid of him, and he had the cock shod for him, and when it was done, Hans the Hedgehog got on its back, and rode away, and he took some swine and asses with him which he intended to keep in the forest. When they got there he made the cock fly on to a high tree with him, and there he sat for many a long year, and watched his asses and swine until the herd was quite large. And all this time his father knew nothing about him. While he was sitting in the tree, however, he learned to play his bagpipes, and made music that was very beautiful.

Once a King came wandering by who had lost his way and he heard the music. He was astonished by it, and sent his servant to look about and find out where this music came from. He spied about, but saw nothing but a little animal sitting up aloft on the tree, which looked like a cock with a hedgehog on it making music. The King told the servant to ask why he sat there, and if he knew the road that led to his kingdom. So Hans the Hedgehog came down from the tree, and said he would show him the way if the King would write a bond and promise him whatever he first met in the royal courtyard as soon as he arrived at home. Then the King

thought, "I can do that without any fear. Hans the Hedgehog can understand nothing, and I can write what I like." So the King took pen and ink and wrote, and when he had done, Hans the Hedgehog showed him the way, and he got safely home. But his daughter, when she saw him from afar, was so overjoyed that she ran to meet him and kissed him. Then he remembered Hans the Hedgehog and told her what had happened, and that he had been forced to promise whatever first met him when he got home to a very strange animal that sat on a cock as if it were a horse, and made beautiful music, but that instead of writing that he should have what he wanted, he had written that he should not have it. Thereupon the princess was glad, and said he had done well, for she never would have gone away with the hedgehog.

Hans the Hedgehog, however, looked after his asses and pigs, and was always merry and sat on the tree and played his bagpipes. Now it came to pass that another King came journeying by with his servants and footmen, and he also had lost his way, and did not know how to get home again because the forest was so large. He too heard the beautiful music from a distance, and asked his footman what that could be, and told him to go and see. Then the footman went under the tree, and saw the cock sitting at the top of it, and Hans the Hedgehog on the cock. The footman asked him what he was about up there?

"I am keeping my asses and my pigs, but what is it you want?"

The messenger said that they had lost their way, and could not get back into their own kingdom, and asked if he would not show them the way. Then Hans the Hedgehog climbed down the tree with the cock, and told the old King that he would show him the way, if he would give him for his own whatsoever first met him in front of his royal palace.

The King said, "Yes," and wrote a promise to Hans the Hedgehog that he should have this.

That done, Hans rode on before him on the cock, and pointed out the way, and the King reached his kingdom again in safety. When he reached the courtyard, there were great rejoicings. Now he had an only daughter who was very beautiful. And she ran to meet him, threw her arms round his neck, and was delighted to have her old father back again. She asked him where in the world he had been so long. So he told her how he had lost his way, and had very nearly not come back at all, but that as he was traveling through a great forest, a creature half-hedgehog half-man, who was sitting astride a cock in a high tree and making music, had shown him the way and helped him to get out, but that in return he had promised him whatsoever first met him in the royal courtyard, and how that was she herself, which made him unhappy now. But she promised at once, that for love of her father, she would willingly go with this Hans if he came.

Hans the Hedgehog, however, took care of his pigs, and the pigs multiplied until they became so many that the whole forest was full of them. Then Hans the Hedgehog resolved not to live in the forest any longer, and sent word to his father to have every sty in the village emptied, for he was coming with such a great herd that all might kill pigs who wished to do so. When his father heard that he was troubled, for he thought Hans the Hedgehog had died long ago. But Hans the Hedgehog seated himself on the cock, drove the pigs before him into the village, and ordered the slaughter to begin. Ho!—but then there was a killing and a chopping that might have been heard two miles off!

After this Hans the Hedgehog said, "Father, let me have the cock shod once more at the forge, and then I will ride away and never come back as long as I live." Then the father had the cock shod once more, and was pleased that Hans the Hedgehog would never return again.

Hans the Hedgehog rode away to the first kingdom. There the King had commanded that whosoever came mounted on a cock and had bagpipes with him should be shot at or cut down, or stabbed by every one, so that he might not enter the palace. When, therefore, Hans the Hedgehog came riding up, all came running to stop him with their pikes, but he spurred the cock and it flew up over the gate in front of the King's window and lighted there, and Hans cried that the King must give him what he had promised, or he would take both his life and his daughter's. At that the King began to speak his daughter fair, and beg her to go away with Hans in order to save her own life and her father's. So she dressed herself in white, and her father gave her a carriage with six horses and magnificent attendants together with gold and possessions. She seated herself in the carriage, and placed Hans the Hedgehog beside her with the cock and the bagpipes, and then they took leave and drove away, and the King thought he should never see her again. He was, however, deceived in his expectation, for when they were a short distance from the town, Hans the Hedgehog tore her pretty clothes off and scratched her with his hedgehog's prickles until she was covered in blood.

"That's the reward for your falseness," said he. "Go, get you gone, I won't have you!" and he chased her back home, and she was disgraced for the rest of her life.

Hans the Hedgehog rode on further on the cock, with his bagpipes, till he got to the dominions of the second King to whom he had shown the way. This one, however, had arranged that if any one like Hans the Hedgehog should come, they were to present arms, bring him safely in, cry long life to him, and lead him to the royal palace.

But when the King's daughter saw him she was terrified, for he looked quite too extraordinary. Still she remembered that she could not change her mind, for she had given her promise to her father. So Hans the Hedgehog was welcomed by her, and married to her, and had to go with her to the royal table, and she seated herself by his side, and they ate and drank.

When the evening came and they wanted to go to sleep, she was afraid of his quills, but he told her she was not to fear, for no harm would befall her, and he told the old King that he was to appoint four men to watch by the door of the chamber, and light a great fire, and when he entered the room and was about to get into bed, he would creep out of his hedgehog's skin and leave it lying there by the bedside, and that the men were to spring swiftly to it, throw it in the fire, and stay by until it was consumed. When the clock struck eleven, he went into the chamber, stripped off the hedgehog's skin, and left it lying by the bed. In came the men and seized it instantly, and threw it in the fire. And when the fire had consumed it, he was delivered, and lay there in bed in human form, but he was coal-black as if he had been burnt. The King sent for his physician who washed him with precious salves, and anointed him, and he became white, and was a handsome young man. When the King's daughter saw that she was glad, and the next morning they arose joyfully, ate and drank, and then the marriage was properly solemnized, and Hans the Hedgehog received the kingdom from the aged King.

When several years had passed he went with his wife to his father, and said that he was his son. The father, however, declared he had no son—he had never had but one, and he had been born like a hedgehog with spikes, and had gone out into the world. Then Hans made himself known, and the old father rejoiced and went with him to his kingdom.

THE NOSE TREE

ALONG TIME AGO there were three old soldiers who, when they were no longer able to fight for the King, were dismissed from the army without a penny in their pockets, and they had to beg their bread from door to door.

Their way once led through a great forest where night overtook them. And two of them lay down to rest while the third kept watch lest they should be seized in their sleep by wild beasts.

As he stood there in the dark, watching, a little red dwarf came up. "Who's there?" cried the dwarf.

"We are three poor old discharged soldiers with scarcely a tooth among us, and yet teeth too many for the fare that has fallen to us this day." And he told the dwarf how hardly they had been treated.

The dwarf in pity produced a queer old cloak, which looked as if it was fit for nothing but the rag-bag. This he gave to the soldier telling him that he must keep it secret from the others till morning, for it was a wishing-cloak, and whatever its wearer might wish, his wish was instantly fulfilled.

The next watch was kept by the second soldier. And he, too, received a visit from the little red man, who gave him a wonderful purse that was always full of money.

During the last watch of the night when the third soldier was on guard, the little man came yet again, and this time his gift was of a horn at whose sound all men near and far were bound to come running to follow its magic music.

At sunrise each showed his wonderful possession to the others, and you may be sure they wasted no time before they were living in comfort and riches, with a coach and three white horses when they wished to travel and a splendid great castle to live in.

After a time, so fine had they become, that they felt the need to pay the King a visit. And they were welcomed and entertained as befitted the great lords they now appeared to be.

The King had an only daughter, and once, while she was playing cards with one of the soldiers, she discovered that it mattered not to him whether he won or lost, for his purse never failed to have money in it, no matter how much he had to pay. It was not long before she guessed that it could only be a wishing-purse. This she must have. So, waiting her opportunity, she slyly mixed a sleeping-draught in a cup of wine that she gave him, and while he slept she changed his purse for another one which was just the same to look at.

Next morning their visit came to an end, and the soldiers drove away. And they soon found out the trick that had been played upon them.

"Alas!" cried one, "now we are beggars again."

"Oh! don't be in such a hurry about that," said the first. "I'll warrant we've no cause yet to grow grey with trouble. I'll soon have it back again." And throwing on his magic old cloak, he wished himself in the Princess's room.

There he was at once. And there she sat at her table counting out gold from the purse as fast as she could count.

"Help! Help!" screamed the Princess at the top of her voice. "Robbers! Robbers! Help!"

In an instant the alarm was raised, and the guard rushed into the room followed by the whole court.

Startled out of his wits, the soldier forgot the magic power of his cloak, dashed for the window and escaped. But he left the cloak behind him, caught fast to the curtain hook as he leaped.

And then he, too, had lost the little red dwarf's gift!

Now they had nothing left but the horn. And this time they would indeed be wise. So they agreed upon a plan to recover the cloak and the purse.

They marched through the country blowing the horn, till they had raised an enormous army. And then they went to the King's city and demanded that the lost gifts should be given back to them or else not one stone of the King's palace would they leave standing on another.

The King consulted his daughter, but she wasn't going to give up her treasures as readily as all that. And she disguised herself as a poor girl, selling drinks to the soldiers of the camp, whither she went with a basket on her arm.

When she was there she began to sing. And so beautifully, that the whole army ran out of their tents and gathered round to hear her, the soldier who had the horn among them. At this her waiting-maid, who had also been disguised, stole into his tent, hid the horn under her apron and ran away with it to the palace.

And now the King's daughter had all three wishing-gifts. For, of course, with the help of the horn she had easily been able to overcome the three soldiers and their men.

Once more the old soldiers found themselves in poverty.

"We must separate," one said. "You two go that way and I'll go this." And with that he went off alone, lying down beneath a tree in the forest when night came. At daybreak he saw that he was under an apple-tree covered with beautiful ripe fruit and he was so hungry that he picked one apple after another and ate them. What then did he find but that his nose was growing longer and longer and longer! And it grew, and grew, until it reached the ground!

There was nothing he could do to stop it, and so there he sat, while his nose kept on growing along the ground till it went right out of sight among the trees, miles away.

By this time, however, his companions had decided to rejoin him and were wandering through the forest in search. Suddenly one of them stumbled against something soft that was lying across the path.

"What the mischief is this?" cried he. And as he looked at it, it moved a little. "A nose? Upon my word it's a nose, neither more nor less!"

"We'll follow this nose," said they, and up and down through the wood they went, through bushes and briars, till they came at last to their poor old friend, lying on the ground where he had slept, unable to stir a step.

Try as they could, the great long nose was too heavy for them to lift. So they hunted about till they found a donkey, and put their friend upon it, with his nose wound round a couple of poles that they helped to carry. But even the ass could bear the weight only a very short way, so they set him down again in despair.

But it happened that they had stopped by a pear-tree, and who should step from behind it but their little friend, the red dwarf.

Said he to Brother Long-Nose, "Eat just one of these pears, and your nose will fall off."

And so it came about. The long nose fell right off, leaving exactly the same amount as the man had had before.

Again the little man spoke and said, "Prepare a powder from the apples, and prepare another powder from the pears. Then if any one eats of the first his nose will grow, and if he eats the pear-powder, it will fall off again."

"With these two powders," he went on, "go back to the Princess and give her, first, two of the apples. Then give her some of the powder made from the apples, and her nose will grown even twenty times as long as yours. But be firm." With these words he vanished.

The soldier followed the dwarf's advice, and went in the guise of a costermonger to the King's palace, saying he came with apples to sell, sweeter and finer than had ever been seen there before. The Princess bought some, and she ate two with very great pleasure.

And now her nose began to grow! And it grew so quickly that

she couldn't lift herself out of her chair. And it grew round and round the table, and round and round the wardrobe, and out of the window, and round the castle, and down the street, and out about the town till there were twenty miles or so of Princess's nose in the kingdom.

Rich for life the King said he would make him who eased the Princess of her terrible burden. And he caused a proclamation to be made throughout the land.

After a while, the old soldier presented himself dressed like a learned doctor, and he gave her some of the apple-powder, as the dwarf had advised. And her nose grew more and more and more, twenty times more. He waited until she could bear her distress no longer and then he gave her a little pear-powder, but not very much, and her nose perceptibly shortened. But he wasn't going to let her off yet, so next morning he gave her another dose of apple-powder, so that her nose started growing again and gained more than it had lost the day before.

At that he told her she must have something on her conscience. She must have robbed some one. No, she said, she hadn't. "Well," said he, "you'll lose your life then. There's nothing I can do to save you." And he went out of the room.

This added to her terror, and after the King had urged her to give up the purse, the horn, and the cloak to be restored to their rightful owners, she sent after the physician and told him all. Then she bade her waiting-maid get all three things out of the cupboard and handed them over to him.

When he had them all safe, he measured out to the Princess the right quantity of pear-powder, the nose fell off immediately, to the great delight of every one, and two hundred and fifty men had to come and cut it in pieces before it could be cleared away.

As for the old soldier, he joyfully went back home to his two friends, and they spent the rest of their lives together in the enjoyment of their three magic possessions.

THE THREE FEATHERS

THERE WAS ONCE ON A TIME a King who had three sons, of whom two were clever and wise, but the third did not talk much, and was simple, and was called the Duffer. When the King had become old and weak, and began to think of his end, he did not know which of his sons ought to inherit the kingdom after him.

So he said to them, "Go forth, and he who brings me the most beautiful carpet shall be King after my death." And that there should be no dispute among them, he took them outside his castle, blew three feathers in the air, and said, "You shall go as they fly."

One feather flew to the east, the other to the west, but the third flew straight up and did not fly far, but soon fell to the ground. So one brother went to the right, and the other to the left, mocking at the Duffer who was forced to stay where the third feather had fallen. He sat down feeling very sad, when all at once he saw that there was a trapdoor in the ground close by the feather. He lifted it up, and found some steps, which he went down. Then he came to a door, and knocked at it, and heard somebody inside call out,

> "Little green maiden,
> Hop, hop about!
> Hop to the door,
> And see who's without."

The door opened, and there he saw a great fat toad sitting surrounded by a crowd of little toads. The fat toad asked what he wanted? He answered, "I should like to have the prettiest and finest carpet in the world." Then she called one of the little ones and said,

"Little green maiden,
Hopping all about,
Hop quick and get me
My great box out."

The young toad brought the box, and the fat toad opened it, and gave the Duffer a carpet, so beautiful and so fine, that on the earth above none could have been woven like it. Then he thanked her, and climbed the stairs again.

The two others, however, had looked on their youngest brother as so stupid that they never believed he would find or bring anything at all. "Why should we give ourselves a great deal of trouble searching about?" said they, and they got some coarse kerchiefs from the first shepherds' wives they met, and carried them home to the King. At the same time also the Duffer came back, and brought his beautiful carpet, and when the King saw it he was astonished, and said, "If justice be done, the kingdom must belong to the youngest." But the two others let their father have no peace, saying that it was impossible that the Duffer, who lacked understanding in everything, should be King, and entreating him to make another trial.

"Then," said the father, "he who brings me the most beautiful ring shall inherit the kingdom," and he led the three brothers out and blew into the air the three feathers that they were to follow.

Those of the two eldest again went east and west, and the Duffer's feather flew straight up, and fell down near the trapdoor into the ground. Then he went down again to the fat toad, and told her that he wanted the most beautiful ring. She at once ordered her great box to be brought, and gave him a ring out of it, which sparkled with jewels, and was so beautiful that no goldsmith on earth would have been able to make it. The two eldest laughed at the idea of the Duffer seeking a golden ring. So they gave themselves no trouble, but picked up an old harness-ring, and took it to the King; but when the Duffer produced his golden ring, his father again said, "The kingdom belongs to him." The two eldest did not cease from tormenting the King until he made a third condition, and declared that the one who brought the most beautiful woman home should have the kingdom. He again blew the three feathers into the air, and they flew as before.

The Duffer without more ado went down to the fat toad, and said, "I am to take home the most beautiful woman!"

"Oh," answered the toad, "the most beautiful woman! She is not at hand at the moment, but still you shall have her." She gave him a yellow turnip that had been hollowed out, to which six mice were harnessed. Then the Duffer said quite mournfully, "What am I to do with that?" The toad answered, "Just put one of my little toads into it." Then he seized one at random out of the circle, and put her into the yellow coach, but hardly was she seated inside it than she turned into the most beautiful maiden, and the turnip into a coach, and the six mice into horses. So he kissed her, and drove off quickly back home to the King. His brothers came in soon afterwards. They had given themselves no trouble at all to seek beautiful girls, but had brought with them the first peasant women they chanced to meet.

When the King saw them he said, "After my death the kingdom shall belong to my youngest son."

But the two eldest deafened the King's ears afresh with their clamor. "We cannot consent to the Duffer being King," and demanded that the one whose wife could leap through a hoop which hung in the center of the hall should have the preference. They thought, "Our peasant women can do that easily; they are strong enough, but this delicate maiden will kill herself in the attempt." The aged King agreed to this plan too. Then the two peasant women jumped, and jumped through the hoop, but were so stout and heavy that they fell and broke their coarse arms and legs. And then the pretty maiden whom the Duffer had brought with him took her turn and skipped through the hoop as lightly as a deer, and then there was no more to be said. So the Duffer received the crown, and has ruled wisely and well for many a long year.

THE THREE
ARMY SURGEONS

THREE ARMY SURGEONS, who considered they were perfect masters of their art, were traveling about the world, and they came to an inn where they wanted to pass the night. The host asked whence they came, and where they were going to?

"We are roaming about the world and practicing our art."

"Just show me for once in a way what you can do," said the host.

Then the first said he would cut off his hand, and put it on again early next morning. The second said he would tear out his heart, and replace it next morning. The third said he would cut out his eyes and put them back again next morning.

"Well," said the innkeeper, "if you can do that, you have learned everything."

They, however, had a salve, with which they rubbed themselves, which joined parts together, and they carried the little bottle containing the salve constantly with them. Then they cut the hand, heart and eyes from their bodies as they had said they would, and laid them all together on a plate, and gave it to the innkeeper. The innkeeper gave it to a servant who was to put it in the cupboard, and take good care of it. The girl, however, had a lover in secret, who was a soldier. So when the innkeeper, the three army surgeons, and every one else in the house had gone to bed, in came the soldier and wanted something to eat. The girl opened the cupboard and brought him some food, and in her love forgot to shut the cupboard-door again. She seated herself at the table by her lover, and they chattered away together. While she sat there so contentedly thinking of no ill luck, the cat came creeping in, found the cupboard open, took the hand and heart and eyes of the three army surgeons, and ran off with them. When the soldier had finished his supper, and the girl was taking away the things and going to shut the cupboard she saw that the plate that the innkeeper had given her to take care of, was empty. Then she said in a fright to her lover, "Oh, miserable girl that I am, what shall I do? The hand is gone, and the heart and the eyes are gone too! What will become of me in the morning?"

"Be easy," said he, "I will help you out of your trouble. There is a thief hanging outside on the gallows, and I will cut off his hand. Which hand was it?"

"The right one."

Then the girl gave him a sharp knife, and he went and cut the dead robber's right hand off, and brought it to her. After this he caught the cat and cut its eyes out, and now nothing but the heart was wanting. "Have you not just been killing, and are not the dead pigs in the cellar?" said he.

"Yes," said the girl.

"That's well," said the soldier, and he went down and fetched a pig's heart. The girl placed them all together on the plate, and put it in the cupboard, and when after this her lover took leave of her, she went quietly to bed.

In the morning when the three army surgeons got up, they told the girl to bring them the plate on which the hand, heart and eyes were lying. Then she brought it out of the cupboard, and the first fixed the thief's hand on and smeared it with his salve, and it grew on to his arm at once. The second took the cat's eyes and put them in his own head. The third fixed the pig's heart firm in the place where his own had been, and the innkeeper stood by, admired their skill, and said he had never yet seen such a thing as that done, and would sing their praises and recommend them to every one. Then they paid their bill, and traveled farther.

As they were on their way, the one with the pig's heart could never keep with them at all, but wherever there was a corner he ran to it, and rooted about in it with his nose as pigs do. The others wanted to hold him back by the tail of his coat, but that did no good, he tore himself loose, and ran wherever the dirt was thickest. The second also behaved very strangely. He rubbed his eyes, and said to the other, "Comrades, what is the matter? I can't see at all. Will one of you lead me, so that I don't fall." With difficulty they traveled on till evening, when they reached another inn. They went into the bar together, and there at a table in the corner sat a rich man counting his money. The one with the thief's hand walked round about him, made a sudden movement twice with his arm, and at last when the stranger turned away, he snatched at the pile of money, and took a handful from it. One of the others saw this, and said, "Comrade, what are you about? You must not steal! Shame on you!" "Eh," said he, "but how can I stop myself? My hand twitches, and I am forced to snatch things whether I will or not."

After this, they lay down to sleep and as they were lying there it was so dark that no one could see his own hand. All at once the one with the cat's eyes awoke, aroused the others, and said, "Brothers,

185

look up! Do you see the white mice running about there?" The two sat up, but could see nothing. Then said he, "Things are not right with us, we have not got back again what is ours. We must return to the innkeeper, he has deceived us." So they went back next morning, and told the host they had not got what was their own again. That the first had a thief's hand, the second cat's eyes, and the third a pig's heart. The innkeeper said that the girl must be to blame for that, and was going to call her, but she had seen the three coming, and had run out by the back door and not come back. Then the three said he must give them a great deal of money, or they would set his house on fire. He gave them all he had, and all he could get together, and the three went away with it. It was enough for the rest of their lives, but they would rather have had their own proper organs.

THE YOUNG GIANT

ONCE UPON A TIME a countryman had a son who was as big as a thumb, and did not become any bigger; even during several years he did not grow one hairbreadth.

Once when the father was going out to plough, the little one said, "Father, I'll go with you."

"You would go out with me?" said his father. "Stay here. You will be of no use out there; besides, you might get lost!"

Then Thumbling began to cry, and for the sake of peace his father put him in his pocket, and took him with him. When he was in the field, he took him out again, and set him in a furrow. While he was there, a great giant came over the hill. "Do you see that great bogy?" said his father, for he wanted to frighten the little fellow to make him good; "he is coming to fetch you."

The giant, however, had scarcely taken two steps with his long legs before he reached them. He took up little Thumbling carefully with two fingers, had a good look at him, and carried him off without saying one word. His father stood by dumb with terror, and he could only think that his child was lost, and that as long as he lived he should never set eyes on him again.

The giant carried him home and fed him on giant's food, and Thumbling grew and became tall and strong after the manner of giants. When two years had passed, the old giant took him into the forest to see what he was good for, and said, "Pull up a stock for yourself." The boy was already so strong that he tore up a young tree out of the earth by the roots. But the giant thought, "We must do better than that," took him back again, and fed him on giant's food for two years longer. At the next trial his strength had increased so much that he could tear an old tree out of the ground. That was still not enough for the giant; and he fed him for yet another two years, and then when he went with him into the forest and said, "Now, just tear up a proper stick for me," the boy tore up the strongest oak-tree he could find from the earth, and that was a mere trifle to him. "Now that will do," said the giant, "you are perfect," and he took him back to the field from whence he had brought him. His father was there following the plough.

The young giant went up to him and said, "Does my father see what a fine man his son has grown into?"

The farmer was alarmed, and said, "No, you are not my son. I don't want you. Go away!"

"Truly I am your son. Let me do your work. I can plough as well as you can, nay, better."

"No, no, you are not my son, and you cannot plough. Go away!"

However, as he was afraid of this great man, he let go of the plough, and stepped back. Then the youth took the plough, and just leaned on it with one hand, but his grasp was so strong that the plough went deep into the earth.

The farmer could not bear to see that, and called to him, "If you are determined to plough, you must not lean so hard. It's no good doing it that way." The youth, however, unharnessed the horses, and drew the plough himself, saying, "Just go home, Father, and bid my mother make ready a large dish of food, and in the meantime I will go over the field." Then the farmer went home, and ordered his wife to prepare his dinner.

The youth ploughed the field which was of two acres all by himself, and then he harnessed himself to the harrow, and harrowed the whole of the land, using two harrows at once. When he had done it, he went into the forest, and pulled up two oak-trees, took them upon his shoulders, and hung one harrow behind and one before, and then one of the horses behind and the other before and carried them all like a bundle of straw to his parents' house.

When he entered the yard, his mother did not recognize him, and asked, "Who is that horrible tall man?"

The father said, "That is our son."

"No, that cannot be our son," she said. "We never had such a tall one; ours was a little wee thing."

She called to him, "Go away, we do not want you!"

The youth said nothing, but led his horses to the stable and gave them oats and hay and all they needed. When he had done this, he went into the parlor, sat down on the bench and said, "Mother, now I should like something to eat. Will it soon be ready?"

Then she said, "Yes," and brought in two immense dishes full of food, which would have been enough to last herself and her husband for a week. The youth ate the whole of it himself, and asked if she had nothing more to set before him.

"No," she replied, "that is all we have."

"But that was only a taste, I must have more."

She did not dare to oppose him, and went and put a huge caldron full of food on the fire, and took it in when it was done.

"At length come a few crumbs," said he, and ate all there was, but it was still not sufficient to appease his hunger.

Then said he, "Father, I see well that with you I shall never have food enough. If you will get me an iron staff, a good strong one that I cannot break across my knees, I will go off out into the world."

The farmer was not sorry and put his two horses in his cart, and fetched from the smith a staff so large and thick that the two horses could only just bring it away. The youth laid it across his knees, and snap! he broke it in two like a bean-stick, and threw it away. The father then harnessed four horses, and brought a bar that was so long and thick, that the four horses could only just drag it. The son snapped this also in twain against his knees, threw it away, and said, "Father, this can be of no use to me; you must harness more horses, and bring a stronger staff."

So the father harnessed eight horses, and brought one, which was so long and thick that the eight horses could only just carry it. When the son took it in his hand, he broke a bit off the top of that also, and said, "Father, I see that you will not be able to procure me any such staff as I want, so I will stay with you no longer."

So he went away, and gave out that he was a smith's apprentice. He arrived at a village where lived a smith who was a greedy fellow, and who never did a kindness to any one, but wanted everything for himself. The youth went into the smithy to him, and asked if he needed a man. "Yes," said the smith, and looked at him, and thought, "That is a strong fellow who will hit hard and earn his bread well." So he asked, "How much wages do you want?"

"I don't want any at all," he replied, "only every fortnight, when the other men are paid, I will give you two blows, and you must bear them." This just pleased the miserly smith, for he thought he would save much money this way.

Next morning, the new man was to begin to work, but when the master brought the glowing bar, and the youth struck his first blow, the iron flew asunder, and the anvil sank so deep into the earth, that there was no bringing it out again. That made the miser angry, and he said, "Oh, but I can't make any use of you, you strike far too hard. What will you take for that one blow?"

Then said he, "I will only give you quite a little blow, that's all." And he raised his foot, and gave him such a kick that he flew away over four loads of hay. Then he sought out the thickest iron bar in the smithy for himself, took it as a stick in his hand, and went on his way.

When he had walked for some time, he came to a small farm, and asked the bailiff if he did not require a head servant.

"Yes," said the bailiff, "I can make use of one. You look a strong fellow who can do something. How much a year do you want as wages?"

He again replied that he wanted no wages at all, but that every year he would give him three blows, which he must bear. Then the bailiff was satisfied, for he, too, was a covetous fellow.

Next morning all the servants had to go to the wood, and the others were already up, but the head servant was still in bed. So one of them called to him, "Get up, it is time. We are going to the wood, and you must go with us."

"Oh," said he roughly, "you may just go, then. I shall be back again before any of you." And then he stayed in bed two hours longer.

At length he got up from his feather bed, but first he got himself two bushels of peas from the loft, made himself some broth and ate it at his leisure, and when that was done, went and harnessed the horses, and drove into the wood. Not far from the wood was a ravine through which the road passed, so he first drove the horses through and then stopped, and went back and took trees and brushwood and made a great barricade so that no horse could get through.

When he was entering the wood, the others were just driving out of it with their loaded carts to go home; then said he, "Drive on, I will still get home before you do."

He did not drive far into the wood, but at once tore two of the very largest trees of all out of the earth, threw them on his cart, and turned back. When he came to the barricade, the others were still standing there not able to get through.

"Don't you see," said he, "that if you had stayed with me, you would have got home just as quickly, and would have had another hour's sleep?" He now wanted to drive on, but his horses could not get the cart through, so he unharnessed them and laid them on the top of the cart, took the shafts in his own hands, and pulled it over just as easily as if it had been laden with feathers. When he was over, he said to the others, "There, you see, I have got over quicker than you," and drove on, and the others had to stay where they were.

In the yard, however, he took a tree in his hand, showed it to the bailiff, and said, "Isn't that a fine bundle of wood?"

Then said the bailiff to his wife, "This servant is a good one. Even if he does sleep it out, he is still home before the others."

So he served the bailiff a year, and when that was over, and the other servants were getting their wages, he said it was time for him to have his too. The bailiff, however, was afraid of the blows that he was to receive, and earnestly entreated him to excuse him from having them. Rather than that, said he, he himself would be head servant, and the youth should be bailiff.

"No," said he, "I won't be a bailiff. I am a foreman and that I'll stay, but I will take the payment which we agreed on."

The bailiff was willing to give him whatever he demanded, but it was of no use, the head servant said no to everything. Then the bailiff did not know what to do, and begged for a fortnight's delay, for he wanted to find some way of escape. The head servant consented to this and the bailiff summoned all his clerks together, and asked them to think the matter over, and give him advice. The clerks pondered for a long time, but at last they said that no one was sure of his life with the head servant, for he could kill a man as easily as a gnat, and that the bailiff ought to make him get into the well and clean it, and when he was down below, they would roll up one of the millstones that was lying there, and throw it on his head; and then he'd never see daylight again. The advice pleased the bailiff, and the head servant was quite willing to go down the well. So when he was standing down below at the bottom, they rolled the largest millstone down on to him and were quite sure they must have broken his skull, but he cried out, "Chase away those hens from the well, they are scratching in the sand up there, and throwing the dust into my eyes, so that I can't see." So the bailiff shouted out, "Shoo! shoo!" and pretended to frighten the hens away. When the head servant had finished his work, he climbed up and said, "Just look what a beautiful collar I have on," and behold it was the millstone which he was wearing round his neck.

The head servant now wanted to take his reward, but the bailiff again begged for a fortnight's delay. The clerks met together and advised him to send the head servant to the haunted mill to grind corn by night, for from thence as yet no man had ever returned alive. The proposal pleased the bailiff. He called the head servant that very evening, and ordered him to take eight bushels of corn to the mill, and grind it that night, for it was wanted at once. So the head servant went to the loft, and put two bushels in his right pocket, and two in his left, and took four in a sack that hung half on his back and half on his breast, and thus laden he went to the haunted mill. The miller told him that he could grind there very well by day, but not by night, for the mill was haunted, and that up to the present time whoever had gone into it at night had been found lying dead there in the morning.

He said, "I'll manage it, just you go away to bed." Then he went into the mill, and poured out the corn. About eleven o'clock he went into the miller's room, and sat down on the bench. When he had sat there a while, a door suddenly opened and a large table came in, and on the table, wine and roast meat placed themselves, and more good things besides, but everything came of itself, for there was no one there to carry it. After this the chairs pushed themselves up, but no people came, until all at once he beheld fingers, which handled knives and forks and laid food on the plates, but with this exception he saw nothing. As he was hungry and saw the food, he, too, placed himself at the table, ate with those who were eating and enjoyed it.

When he had had enough, and the others also had quite emptied their dishes, he distinctly heard all the candles being suddenly snuffed out, and as it was now pitch dark, he felt something like a box on the ear. Then he said, "If anything of that kind comes again, I shall strike out in return." And when he received a second box on the ear, he, too, struck out. And so it went on all night long. He took nothing without returning it, but repaid everything with interest and did not lay about him in vain. At daybreak everything became quiet again.

When the miller had got up, he came to look after him, wondering if he were still alive.

Then the youth said, "I have eaten my fill and have received some boxes on the ear, but I have given some in return." The miller rejoiced, and said that the mill was now released from the spell, and wanted to give him much money as a reward. But he said, "Money, I will not have, I have enough of it."

So he took his flour on his back and went home, telling the bailiff that he had done what he had been told to do and would now have the reward agreed on. When the bailiff heard that, he was quite beside himself with fear. He walked backwards and forwards in the room, and drops of perspiration ran down his forehead. Then he opened the window to get some fresh air, but before he was aware, the head servant had given him such a kick that he flew through the window out into the air, and so far away that no one ever saw him again.

Then said the head servant to the bailiff's wife, "If he does not come back, you must take the other blow."

She cried, "No, no, I cannot bear it," and opened the other window, because drops of perspiration were running down her forehead too. And he gave her such a kick that out she flew, and as she was lighter she went much higher than her husband. When her husband saw her, he shouted, "Hi! come to me here," but she replied, "You come to me, I cannot come to you." And there they hovered about in the air, and could not get near each other, and whether they are still hovering about or not, I do not know, but the young giant took up his iron bar and went on his way.

THE THREE
SONS OF FORTUNE

A FATHER ONCE CALLED his three sons before him, and he
gave to the first a cock, to the second a scythe, and to the
third a cat.

"I am already aged," said he, "and my death is nigh. Before it
comes I have wished to take thought for your future. Money I have
none, and these that I now give you may seem of little worth, but
all depends on your making wise use of them. Only seek out a
country where such things are still unknown, and your fortune is
made."

After the father's death the eldest set out with his cock, but
wherever he came the cock was already known; in the towns he saw
him from a long way off, sitting upon the steeples and turning
round with the wind, and in every village he heard more than one
crowing. No one would show any wonder at so well known a creature, so that it did not look as if he would make his fortune by it.

At last, however, it happened that he came to an island where the
people knew nothing about cocks, and did not even understand
how to reckon the time. They certainly knew when it was morning
or evening, but at night, if they lay awake, not one of them knew
how to find out the time.

"Look!" said he, "at this proud creature of mine! He has a crown
of rubies on his head, and wears spurs like a knight! He calls you
three times during the night, at fixed hours, and when he calls for
the last time, up comes the sun. But if he crows by broad daylight,
then take notice, for there will certainly be a change of weather."

195

The people were delighted. For a whole night they did not sleep, listening with wonder as the cock at two, at four, and at six o'clock, loudly and clearly proclaimed the time. They asked if this splendid bird was for sale, and how much he wanted for it.

"About as much gold as an ass can carry," answered he.

"A ridiculously small price for such a precious creature!" they all cried at once, and willingly gave him what he had asked.

When he came home with his wealth his brothers were astonished, and the second said, "Well, I will go forth and see whether I cannot get rid of my scythe as profitably." But it did not look as if he would, for laborers met him wherever he went, and they had scythes upon their shoulders as well as he.

At last, however, he chanced upon an island where the people knew nothing of scythes. When the corn was ripe there, they took

196

a cannon out to the fields and shot it down. Now this was rather an uncertain way of going to work. Often the shot went right over the corn, or sometimes hit the ears instead of the stalks, and shot them away, whereby much was lost. Besides, it made a terrible noise. So he set to work with his scythe and mowed the corn so quietly and quickly that the people gaped with astonishment. They agreed to give him what he wanted for the scythe, and he received a horse laden with as much gold as it could carry.

And now the third brother wanted to try his luck with his cat. He fared just like the others; so long as he stayed on the mainland she was worth nothing. Everywhere there were cats, and so many of them that the kittens were generally drowned as soon as they were born.

At last he sailed over to an island, and by luck it happened that no cats had ever yet been seen there, and the mice had got the upper hand so much that they danced over the tables and benches even whether the master were at home or not. The people complained bitterly of the plague. The King himself in his palace did not know how to secure himself against them. In every corner squeaked the mice, nibbling everything they could get at. But now the cat began her chase, and she soon cleared a couple of rooms of them, and the people all begged the King to buy the wonderful beast for the country. The King readily gave what was asked, which was a mule laden with gold, and the third brother came home with the greatest treasure of all.

The cat made herself merry with the mice in the royal palace, and killed so many that they could not be counted. At last she grew warm with the work and thirsty, so she stopped, and held up her head crying, "Miau, Miau!" When they heard this strange cry, the King and all his people were frightened, and in their terror all ran out of the palace at once. The King took counsel what had best be done. At last it was determined to send a herald to the cat, and demand that she should leave the palace, or if not, she must expect that force would be used against her. For the councilors said,

"Rather would we put up with the plague of mice, to which we are accustomed, than give up our lives to such a monster as this." A noble youth, therefore, was sent to ask the cat whether she would peaceably quit the castle? But the cat, whose thirst had become still greater, could only answer, "Miau! Miau!" The youth understood her to say, "Most certainly not! Most certainly not!" and took this answer to the King. "Then," said the councilors, "she shall yield to force." Cannons were brought out, and the palace was soon in flames. When the fire reached the room where the cat was sitting, she sprang safely out of the window, but the besiegers did not leave off until the whole palace was shot down to the ground.

THE POOR MILLER'S BOY
AND THE CAT

I N A CERTAIN MILL THERE LIVED an old miller who had neither wife nor child, and three apprentices served under him. As they had been with him several years, one day he said to them, "I am old, and want to sit in the chimney-corner, go out, and whichever of you brings the best horse home to me, to him will I give the mill, and in return for it he shall take care of me till my death."

The third boy, however, was the drudge, who was looked down upon by the others, and they begrudged the mill to him, and meant that he should not have it anyhow. They all three went out together, and when they came to the village, the two said to stupid Hans, "You may just as well stay here; as long as you live you will never get a horse."

Nevertheless Hans went with them, and at night they came to a cave in which they all lay down to sleep. The two sharp ones waited until Hans was fast asleep, and then they got up and made off, leaving him where he was. And they thought they had done a very clever thing, though really it turned out very ill for them in the end.

When the sun rose, and Hans woke up, he was lying in a deep cavern. He looked round him on every side and exclaimed, "O heavens! Where am I?" Then he got up and clambered out of the cave into the forest, and thought, "Here I am quite alone and deserted. How shall I obtain a horse now?"

As he went walking along buried in thought, he met a little tabby cat who said to him kindly, "Hans, where are you going?"

"Alas! You cannot help me."

"I well know what you are seeking," said the cat. "You wish to have a beautiful horse. Come with me, and be my faithful servant for seven years long, and then I will give you one more beautiful than any you have ever seen in your whole life."

"Well, this is a wonderful cat!" thought Hans, "but I've a good mind to see if she is telling the truth."

So she took him with her into her enchanted castle, where there were nothing but cats, who were her servants. They leaped nimbly upstairs and downstairs, and were all very merry and happy. In the evening when they sat down to dinner, three of them had to make music. One played the bassoon, the other the fiddle, and the third put the trumpet to his lips, and blew out his cheeks as much as ever he could. When they had dined, the table was cleared away, and the cat said, "Now, Hans, come and dance with me."

"No," said he, "I won't dance with a pussy cat. I have never done that yet."

"Then take him off to bed," said she to the cats.

So one of them lighted him to his bedroom, one pulled his shoes off, one his stockings, and at last one of them blew out the candle. Next morning they returned and helped him out of bed, one put his stockings on for him, one tied his garters, one brought his shoes, one washed him, and one dried his face with her tail.

"That's a very soft towel!" said Hans. He had to work for the cat, however, and chop wood every day, and for that he had an axe of silver, and the wedge and saw were of silver too and the mallet of copper. So he chopped up the wood, and lived there in the house and had good meat and drink, but never saw any one but the tabby cat and her servants.

Once she said to him, "Go and mow my meadow, and make the hay," and she gave him a scythe of silver, and a whetstone of gold, but bade him deliver them up again carefully. So Hans went and did what he was bidden, and when he had finished, he carried the scythe and whetstone and the hay to the house, and asked if the

time had not come for her to give him his reward.

"No," said the cat; "you must first do something more for me of the same kind. There are beams of silver, a carpenter's axe, a square, and everything that is needful, all of silver; with these build me a little house."

Then Hans built the little house, and said that he had now done everything, and still he had no horse. Nevertheless, the seven years had gone by with him as if they were six months. The cat asked him if he would like to see her horses?

"Yes," said Hans.

Then she opened the door of the little house, and there stood twelve horses—such horses, so sleek and well groomed, that his heart rejoiced at the sight of them.

And then she gave him something to eat and drink, and said, "Go home. I will not give you your horse to take away with you, but in three days I will follow you and bring it."

So Hans set out, and she showed him the way to the mill. She had, however, never once given him a new coat, and he had been obliged to keep on the dirty old smock-frock that he had brought with him, and that during the seven years had become ever so much too small for him.

When he reached home, the two other apprentices were there again as well, and each of them certainly had brought a horse with him, but one of them was a blind one, and the other lame. They

asked Hans where his horse was?

"It will follow me in three days," said he.

Then they laughed and said, "Indeed, stupid Hans, and where will you get a horse? It will be a fine one!"

Hans went into the parlor, but the miller said he should not sit down to table, for he was so ragged and torn that they would all be ashamed of him if any one came in. So they gave him a mouthful of food outside, and at night, when they went to rest, the two others would not let him have a bed, and at last he was forced to creep into the goose-house, and lie down on a little hard straw.

In the morning when he awoke, the three days had passed, and a coach drove up with six horses and they shone so bright that it was delightful to see them! And a servant led a seventh as well, and that one was for the poor miller's boy. Then a magnificent Princess alighted from the coach and went into the mill, and who should this Princess be but the little tabby cat who poor Hans had served for seven years!

She asked the miller where the miller's boy and drudge was? And the miller told her, "We cannot have him here in the mill, he's so ragged. He is lying in the goose-house."

Then the King's daughter said that they were to fetch him immediately. So they brought him out, and he had to hold his little smock-frock together as best he could to cover himself. The servants unpacked splendid garments and washed him and dressed him, and when that was done, no King could have looked more handsome. Then the maiden desired to see the horses that the other apprentices had brought home with them, and one of them was blind and the other lame. So she ordered the servant to bring the seventh horse, and when the miller saw that, he said such a horse as that had never yet entered his yard.

"And that is for the miller's third boy," said she.

"Then it's he who must have the mill," said the miller, but the King's daughter said that the horse there was for him, and that he was to keep his mill too, and she took her faithful Hans and set him in the coach, and drove away with him. They drove straight to the little house which he had built with the silver tools, and behold it was now a great castle, and everything inside it was of silver and gold. And then she married him, and he was rich, so rich that he had enough for all the rest of his life.

After this, let no one ever say that any one who is silly can never become a person of importance.

HANSEL AND GRETHEL

CLOSE TO A LARGE FOREST there lived a woodcutter with his wife and his two children. The boy was called Hansel, and the girl Grethel. They were always very poor, and had very little to live on; and at one time, when there was famine in the land, he could no longer procure daily bread.

One night he lay in bed worrying over his troubles, and he sighed and said to his wife, "What is to become of us? How are we to feed our poor children when we have nothing for ourselves?"

"I'll tell you what, husband," answered the woman, "tomorrow morning we will take the children out quite early into the thickest part of the forest. We will light a fire, and give each of them a piece of bread; then we will go to our work and leave them alone. They won't be able to find their way back, and so we shall be rid of them."

"Nay, wife," said the man; "we won't do that. I could never find it in my heart to leave my children alone in the forest; the wild animals would soon tear them to pieces."

"What a fool you are!" she said. "Then we must all four die of hunger. You may as well plane the boards for our coffins at once."

She gave him no peace till he consented. "But I grieve over the poor children all the same," said the man.

The two children could not go to sleep for hunger either, and they heard what their stepmother said to their father.

Grethel wept bitterly, and said, "All is over with us now!"

"Be quiet, Grethel!" said Hansel. "Don't cry; I will find some way out of it."

When the old people had gone to sleep, he got up, put on his little coat, opened the door, and slipped out. The moon was shining brightly, and the white pebbles round the house shone like newly-minted coins. Hansel stooped down and put as many into his pockets as they would hold.

Then he went back to Grethel and said, "Take comfort, little sister, and go to sleep. God won't forsake us." And then he went to bed again.

When the day broke, before the sun had risen, the woman came and said, "Get up, you lazybones; we are going into the forest to fetch wood."

Then she gave them each a piece of bread and said, "Here is something for your dinner, but mind you don't eat it before, for you'll get no more."

Grethel put the bread under her apron, for Hansel had the stones in his pockets. Then they all started for the forest.

When they had gone a little way, Hansel stopped and looked back at the cottage, and he did the same thing again and again.

His father said, "Hansel, what are you stopping to look back at? Take care, and put your best foot foremost."

"O Father!" said Hansel, "I am looking at my white cat, it is sitting on the roof, wanting to say good-bye to me."

"Little fool! That's no cat, it's the morning sun shining on the chimney."

But Hansel had not been looking at the cat; he had been dropping a pebble on to the ground each time he stopped. When they reached the middle of the forest, their father said:

"Now, children, pick up some wood, I want to make a fire to warm you."

Hansel and Grethel gathered the twigs together and soon made a huge pile. Then the pile was lighted, and when it blazed up, the woman said, "Now lie down by the fire and rest yourselves while we go and cut wood; when we have finished we will come back to fetch you."

Hansel and Grethel sat by the fire, and when dinnertime came they each ate their little bit of bread, and they thought their father was quite near because they could hear the sound of an axe. It was no axe, however, but a branch that the man had tied to a dead tree, and which blew backwards and forwards against it. They sat there such a long time that they got tired, their eyes began to close, and they were soon fast asleep.

When they woke it was dark night. Grethel began to cry: "How shall we ever get out of the wood!"

But Hansel comforted her, and said, "Wait a little till the moon rises, then we will soon find our way."

When the full moon rose, Hansel took his little sister's hand, and they walked on, guided by the pebbles, which glittered like newly-coined money. The walked the whole night, and at daybreak they found themselves back at their father's cottage.

They knocked at the door, and when the woman opened it and saw Hansel and Grethel, she said, "You bad children, why did you sleep so long in the wood? We thought you did not mean to come back any more."

But their father was delighted, for it had gone to his heart to leave them behind alone.

Not long after they were again in great destitution, and the children heard the woman at night in bed say to their father: "We have eaten up everything again but half a loaf, and then we are at the end of everything. The children must go away; we will take them further into the forest so that they won't be able to find their way back. There is nothing else to be done."

The man took it much to heart, and said, "We had better share our last crust with the children."

But the woman would not listen to a word he said; she only scolded and reproached him. Any one who once says A must also say B, and as he had given in the first time, he had to do so the second also. The children were again wide awake and heard what was said.

When the old people went to sleep Hansel again got up, meaning to go out and get some more pebbles, but the woman had locked the door and he couldn't get out. But he consoled his little sister, and said:

"Don't cry, Grethel; go to sleep. God will help us."

In the early morning the woman made the children get up, and gave them each a piece of bread, but it was smaller than the last. On the way to the forest Hansel crumbled it up in his pocket, and stopped every now and then to throw a crumb on to the ground.

"Hansel, what are you stopping to look about you for?" asked his father.

"I am looking at my dove which is sitting on the roof and wants to say good-bye to me," answered Hansel.

"Little fool!" said the woman, "that is no dove, it is the morning sun shining on the chimney."

Nevertheless, Hansel strewed the crumbs from time to time on the ground. The woman led the children far into the forest where they had never been in their lives before. Again they made a big fire, and the woman said:

"Stay where you are, children, and when you are tired you may go to sleep for a while. We are going further on to cut wood, and in the evening when we have finished we will come back and fetch you."

At dinnertime Grethel shared her bread with Hansel, for he had crumbled his up on the road. Then they went to sleep, and the evening passed, but no one came to fetch the poor children.

It was quite dark when they woke up, and Hansel cheered his little sister and said, "Wait a bit, Grethel, till the moon rises, then we can see the breadcrumbs that I scattered to show us the way home."

When the moon rose they started, but they found no breadcrumbs, for all the thousands of birds in the forest had pecked them up and eaten them.

Hansel said to Grethel, "We shall soon find the way."

But they could not find it. They walked the whole night, and all the next day from morning till night, but they could not get out of the wood.

They were very hungry, for they had nothing to eat but a few berries that they found. They were so tired that their legs would not carry them any further, and they lay down under a tree and went to sleep.

When they woke in the morning, it was the third day since they had left their father's cottage. They started to walk again, but they only got deeper and deeper into the wood, and if no help came they must perish.

At midday they saw a beautiful snow-white bird sitting on a tree. It sang so beautifully that they stood still to listen to it. When it stopped, it fluttered its wings and flew round them. They followed it till they came to a little cottage, on the roof of which it settled itself.

When they got quite near, they saw that the little house was made of bread, and it was roofed with cake; the windows were transparent sugar.

"This will be something for us," said Hansel. "We will have a good meal. I will have a piece of the roof, Grethel, and you can have a bit of the window; it will be nice and sweet."

Hansel stretched up and broke off a piece of the roof to try what it was like. Grethel went to the window and nibbled at that. A gentle voice called out from within:

"Nibbling, nibbling like a mouse,
Who's nibbling at my little house?"

The children answered:

"The wind, the wind doth blow
From heaven to earth below,"

and went on eating without disturbing themselves. Hansel, who found the roof very good, broke off a large piece for himself; and Grethel pushed a whole round pane out of the window, and sat down on the ground to enjoy it.

All at once the door opened and an old, old woman, supporting herself on a crutch, came hobbling out. Hansel and Grethel were so frightened that they dropped what they held in their hands.

But the old woman only shook her head, and said: "Ah, dear children, who brought you here? Come in and stay with me; you will come to no harm."

She took them by the hand and led them into the little house. A nice dinner was set before them, pancakes and sugar, milk, apples, and nuts. After this she showed them two little white beds into which they crept, and felt as if they were in heaven.

Although the old woman appeared to be so friendly, she was really a wicked old witch who was on the watch for children, and she had built the bread house on purpose to lure them to her. Whenever she could get a child into her clutches she cooked it and ate it, and considered it a grand feast. Witches have red eyes, and can't see very far, but they have keen scent like animals, and can perceive the approach of human beings.

When Hansel and Grethel came near her, she laughed wickedly to herself, and said scornfully, "Now I have them, they shan't escape me."

She got up early in the morning, before the children were awake, and when she saw them sleeping, with their beautiful rosy cheeks, she murmured to herself, "They will be dainty morsels."

She seized Hansel with her bony hand and carried him off to a little stable, where she shut him up with a barred door; he might shriek as loud as he liked, she took no notice of him. Then she went to Grethel and shook her till she woke, and cried:

"Get up, little lazybones, fetch some water and cook something nice for your brother; he is in the stable, and has to be fattened. When he is nice and fat, I will eat him."

Grethel began to cry bitterly, but it was no use, she had to obey the witch's orders. The best food was now cooked for poor Hansel, but Grethel only had the shells of crayfish.

The old woman hobbled to the stable every morning and cried, "Hansel, put your finger out for me to feel how fat you are."

Hansel put out a knucklebone, and the old woman, whose eyes were dim, could not see, and thought it was his finger, and she was much astonished that he did not get fat.

When four weeks had passed, and Hansel still kept thin, she became very impatient and would wait no longer.

"Now then, Grethel," she cried, "bustle along and fetch the water. Fat or thin, tomorrow I will kill Hansel and eat him."

Oh, how his poor little sister grieved. As she carried the water, the tears streamed down her cheeks.

"Dear God, help us!" she cried. "If only the wild animals in the forest had devoured us, we should, at least, have died together."

"You may spare your lamentations; they will do you no good," said the old woman.

Early in the morning Grethel had to go out to fill the kettle with water, and then she had to kindle a fire and hang the kettle over it.

"We will bake first," said the old witch. "I have heated the oven and kneaded the dough."

She pushed poor Grethel towards the oven, and said, "Creep in and see if it is properly heated, and then we will put the bread in."

211

She meant, when Grethel had got in, to shut the door and roast her.

But Grethel saw her intention, and said, "I don't know how to get in. How am I to manage it?"

"Stupid goose!" cried the witch. "The opening is big enough; you can see that I could get into it myself."

She hobbled up, and stuck her head into the oven. But Grethel gave her a push that sent the witch right in, and then she banged the door and bolted it.

"Oh! oh!" she began to howl horribly. But Grethel ran away and left the wicked witch to perish miserably.

Grethel ran as fast as she could to the stable. She opened the door and cried, "Hansel, we are saved. The old witch is dead."

Hansel sprang out, like a bird out of a cage when the door is set open. How delighted they were. They fell upon each other's necks, and kissed each other, and danced about for joy.

As they had nothing more to fear, they went into the witch's house, and they found chests in every corner full of pearls and precious stones.

"These are better than pebbles," said Hansel, as he filled his pockets.

Grethel said, "I must take something home with me too." And she filled her apron.

"But now we must go," said Hansel, "so that we may get out of this enchanted wood."

Before they had gone very far, they came to a great piece of water.

"We can't get across it," said Hansel; "I see not stepping-stones and no bridge."

"And there are no boats either," answered Grethel. "But there is a duck swimming. It will help us over if we ask it."

So she cried—

"Little duck, that cries quack, quack,
Here Grethel and here Hansel stand.
Quickly, take us on your back,
No path or bridge is there at hand!"

The duck came swimming towards them, and Hansel got on its back, and told his sister to sit on his knee.

"No," answered Grethel, "it will be too heavy for the duck; it must take us over one after the other."

The good creature did this, and when they had got safely over and walked for a while, the wood seemed to grow more and more familiar to them, and at last they saw their father's cottage in the distance. They began to run, and rushed inside, where they threw their arms round their father's neck. The man had not had a single happy moment since he had deserted his children in the wood, and in the meantime his wife was dead.

Grethel shook her apron and scattered the pearls and precious stones all over the floor, and Hansel added handful after handful out of his pockets.

So all their troubles came to an end, and they lived together as happily as possible.

HANS IN LUCK

HANS HAD SERVED HIS MASTER for seven years, when he one day said to him, "Master, my time is up. I want to go home to my mother; please give me my wages."

His master answered, "You have served me well and faithfully, and as the service has been, so shall the wages be"; and he gave him a lump of gold as big as his head.

Hans took out his pocket-handkerchief and tied up the gold in it, and then slung the bundle over his shoulder, and started on his homeward journey.

As he walked along, just dragging one foot after the other, a man on horseback appeared, riding fresh and gay along on his spirited horse.

"Ah!" said Hans, quite loud as he passed, "what a fine thing riding must be. You are as comfortable as if you were in an easy-chair; you don't stumble over any stones; you save your shoes; and you get over the road you needn't bother how."

The horseman, who heard him, stopped and said, "Hullo, Hans, why are you on foot?"

"I can't help myself," said Hans, "as I have this bundle to carry home. It is true that it is a lump of gold, but I can hardly hold my head up for it, and it weighs down my shoulder frightfully."

"I'll tell you what," said the horseman, "we will change. I will give you my horse, and you shall give me your bundle."

"With all my heart," said Hans; "but you will be rarely burdened with it."

The horseman dismounted, took the gold, and helped Hans up, put the bridle into his hands, and said: "When you want to go very fast, you must click your tongue and cry 'Gee-up, gee-up.'"

Hans was delighted when he found himself so easily riding along on horseback. After a time it occurred to him that he might be going faster, and he began to click with his tongue, and to cry "Gee-up, gee-up." The horse broke into a gallop, and before Hans knew where he was, he was thrown off into a ditch which separated the fields from the high road. The horse would have run away if a peasant coming along the road leading a cow had not caught it. Hans felt himself all over, and picked himself up; but he was very angry, and said to the peasant: "Riding is poor fun at times, when you have a nag like mine, which stumbles and throws you, and puts you in danger of breaking your neck. I will never mount it again. I think much more of that cow of yours. You can walk comfortably behind her, and you have her milk into the bargain every day, as well as butter and cheese. What would I not give for a cow like that!"

"Well," said the peasant, "if you have such a fancy for it as all that, I will exchange the cow for the horse."

Hans accepted the offer with delight, and the peasant mounted the horse and rode rapidly off.

Hans drove his cow peacefully on, and thought what a lucky bargain he had made. "If only I have a bit of bread, and I don't expect ever to be without that, I shall always have butter and cheese to eat with it. If I am thirsty, I only have to milk my cow and I have milk to drink. My heart! What more can you desire?"

When he came to an inn he made a halt, and in great joy he ate up all the food he had with him, all his dinner and his supper too, and he gave the last coins he had for half a glass of beer. Then he went on further in the direction of his mother's village, driving his cow before him. The heat was overpowering, and, as midday drew near, Hans found himself on a heath that took him an hour to cross.

He was so hot and thirsty that his tongue was parched and clung to the roof of his mouth.

"This can easily be set to rights," thought Hans. "I will milk my cow and sup up the milk." He tied her to a tree, and as he had no pail, he used his leather cap instead; but, try as hard as he liked, not a single drop of milk appeared. As he was very clumsy in his attempts, the impatient animal gave him a severe kick on his forehead with one of her hind legs. He was stunned by the blow, and fell to the ground, where he lay for some time, not knowing where he was.

Happily just then a butcher came along the road, trundling a young pig in a wheelbarrow.

"What is going on here?" he cried, as he helped poor Hans up.

Hans told him all that had happened.

The butcher handed him his flask and said, "Here, take a drink, it will do you good. The cow can't give any milk I suppose; she must be too old, and good for nothing but to be a beast of burden, or to go to the butcher."

"Oh dear!" said Hans, smoothing his hair. "Now who would ever have thought it! Killing the animal is all very well, but what kind of meat will it be? For my part, I don't like cow's flesh; it's not juicy enough. Now, if one had a nice young pig like that, it would taste ever so much better; and then, all the sausages!"

"Listen, Hans!" then said the butcher, "for your sake I will exchange, and let you have the pig instead of the cow."

"God reward your friendship!" said Hans, handing over the cow, as the butcher untied the pig, and put the halter with which it was tied into his hand.

Hans went on his way, thinking how well everything was turning out for him. Even if a mishap befell him, something else immediately happened to make up for it. Soon after this, he met a lad carrying a beautiful white goose under his arm. They passed the time of day, and Hans began to tell him how lucky he was, and what successful bargains he had made. The lad told him that he was taking the goose for a christening feast. "Just feel it," he went on, holding it up by the wings. "Feel how heavy it is; it's true they have been stuffing it for eight weeks. Whoever eats that roast goose will have to wipe the fat off both sides of his mouth."

"Yes, indeed!" answered Hans, weighing it in his hand; "but my pig is no light weight either."

Then the lad looked cautiously about from side to side, and shook his head. "Now, look here," he began, "I don't think it's all quite straight about your pig. One has just been stolen out of

Schultze's sty, in the village I have come from. I fear, I fear it is the
one you are leading. They have sent people out to look for it, and
it would be a bad business for you if you were found with it; the
least they would do would be to put you in the black hole."

Poor Hans was very much frightened at this. "Oh, dear! oh,
dear!" he said. "Do help me out of this trouble. You are more at
home here; take my pig, and let me have your goose."

"Well, I shall run some risk if I do, but I won't be the means of
getting you into a scrape."

So he took the rope in his hand, and quickly drove the pig up a
side road; and honest Hans, relieved of his trouble, plodded on with
the goose under his arm.

"When I really come to think it over," he said to himself, "I have
still had the best of the bargain. First, there is the delicious roast
goose, and then all the fat that will drip out of it in roasting will
keep us in goose-fat to eat on our bread for three months at least;
and, last of all, there are the beautiful white feathers which I will
stuff my pillow with, and then I shall need no rocking to send me
to sleep. How delighted my mother will be."

As he passed through the last village he came to a knife-grinder
with his cart, singing to his wheel as it buzzed merrily round—

> "Scissors and knives I grind so fast,
> And hang up my cloak against the blast."

Hans stopped to look at him, and at last he spoke to him and
said, "You must be doing a good trade to be so merry over your
grinding."

"Yes," answered the grinder. "The work of one's hands is the
foundation of a golden fortune. A good grinder finds money whenever he puts his hand into his pocket. But where did you buy that
beautiful goose?"

"I did not buy it; I exchanged my pig for it."

"And the pig?"

"Oh, I got that instead of my cow."

"And the cow?"

"I got that for a horse."

"And the horse?"

"I gave a lump of gold as big as my head for it."

"And the gold?"

"Oh, that was my wages for seven years of service."

"You certainly have known how to manage your affairs," said the grinder. "Now, if you could manage to hear the money jingling in your pockets when you got up in the morning, you would indeed have made your fortune."

"How shall I set about that?" asked Hans.

"You must be a grinder like me—nothing is needed for it but a whetstone; everything else will come of itself. I have one here which certainly is a little damaged, but you need not give me anything for it but your goose. Are you willing?"

"How can you ask me such a question?" said Hans. "Why, I shall be the happiest person in the world. If I can have some money every time I put my hand in my pocket, what more should I have to trouble about?"

So he handed him the goose, and took the whetstone in exchange.

"Now," said the grinder, lifting up an ordinary large stone that lay near on the road, "here is another good stone into the bargain. You can hammer out all your old nails on it to straighten them. Take it, and carry it off."

Hans shouldered the stone, and went on his way with a light heart, and his eyes shining with joy. "I must have been born in a lucky hour," he cried; "everything happens just as I want it, and as it would happen to a Sunday's child."

In the meantime, as he had been on foot since daybreak, he began to feel very tired, and he was also very hungry, as he had eaten all his provisions at once in his joy at his bargain over the cow. At last he could hardly walk any further, and he was obliged to stop every minute to rest. Then the stones were frightfully heavy, and he could not get rid of the thought that it would be very nice if he were not obliged to carry them any further. He dragged himself like a snail to a well in the fields, meaning to rest and refresh himself with a draught of the cool water. So as not to injure the stones by sitting on them, he laid them carefully on the edge of the well. Then he sat down, and was about to stoop down to drink when he inadvertently gave them a little push, and both the stones fell straight into the water.

When Hans saw them disappear before his very eyes he jumped for joy, and then knelt down and thanked God, with tears in his eyes, for having shown him this further grace, and relieved him of the heavy stones (which were all that remained to trouble him) without giving him anything to reproach himself with. "There is certainly no one under the sun so happy as I."

And so, with a light heart, free from every care, he now bounded on home to his mother.

THE BREMEN
TOWN MUSICIANS

ONCE UPON A TIME a man had an ass which for many years carried sacks to the mill without tiring. At last, however, its strength was worn out; it was no longer of any use for work. Accordingly its master began to ponder as to how best to cut down its keep. But the ass, seeing there was mischief in the air, ran away and started on the road to Bremen. There he though he could become a town musician.

When he had been traveling a short time, he fell in with a hound, who was lying panting on the road as though he had run himself off his legs.

"Well, what are you panting so for, Growler?" said the ass.

"Ah," said the hound, "just because I am old, and every day I get weaker, and also because I can no longer keep up with the pack, my master wanted to kill me, so I took my departure. But now, how am I to earn my bread?"

"Do you know what?" said the ass. "I am going to Bremen, and shall there become a town musician; come with me and take your part in the music. I shall play the lute, and you shall beat the kettle-drum."

The hound agreed, and they went on.

A short time after they came upon a cat, sitting in the road, with a face as long as a wet week.

"Well, what has been crossing you, Whiskers?" asked the ass.

"Who can be cheerful when he is out at elbows?" said the cat. "I am getting on in years, and my teeth are blunted and I prefer to

223

sit by the stove and purr instead of hunting round after mice. Just because of this my mistress wanted to drown me. I made myself scarce, but now I don't know where to turn."

"Come with us to Bremen," said the ass. "You are a great hand at serenading, so you can become a town musician."

The cat consented, and joined them.

Next the fugitives passed by a yard where a barn-door fowl was sitting on the door, crowing with all its might.

"You crow so loud you pierce one through and through," said the ass. "What is the matter?"

"Why! didn't I prophesy fine weather for Lady Day, when Our Lady washes the Christ Child's little garment and wants to dry it? But, notwithstanding this, because Sunday visitors are coming tomorrow, the mistress has no pity, and she has ordered the cook to make me into soup, so I shall have my neck wrung tonight. Now I am crowing with all my might while I have the chance."

"Come along, Red-Comb," said the ass; "you had better come with us. We are going to Bremen, and you will find a much better fate there. You have a good voice, and when we make music together, there will be quality in it."

The cock allowed himself to be persuaded, and they all four went off together. They could not, however, reach the town in one day, and by evening they arrived at a wood, where they determined to spend the night. The ass and the hound lay down under a big tree; the cat and the cock settled themselves in the branches, the cock flying right up to the top, which was the safest place for him. Before going to sleep he looked round once more in every direction; suddenly it seemed to him that he saw a light burning in the distance. He called out to his comrades that there must be a house not far off, for he saw a light.

"Very well," said the ass, "let us set out and make our way to it, for the entertainment here is very bad."

The hound thought some bones or meat would suit him too, so

they set out in the direction of the light, and soon saw it shining more clearly, and getting bigger and bigger, till they reached a brightly-lighted robbers' den. The ass, being the tallest, approached the window and looked in.

"What do you see, old Jackass?" asked the cock.

"What do I see?" answered the ass; "why, a table spread with delicious food and drink, and robbers seated at it enjoying themselves."

"That would just suit us," said the cock.

"Yes; if we were only there," answered the ass.

Then the animals took counsel as to how to set about driving the

robbers out. At last they hit upon a plan.

The ass was to take up his position with his forefeet on the windowsill, the hound was to jump on his back, the cat to climb up on to the hound, and last of all the cock flew up and perched on the cat's head. When they were thus arranged, at a given signal they all began to perform their music; the ass brayed, the hound barked, the cat mewed, and the cock crowed. Then they dashed through the window, shivering the panes. The robbers jumped up at the terrible noise; they thought nothing less than that a demon was coming in upon them, and fled into the wood in the greatest alarm. Then the four animals sat down to table, and helped themselves according to taste, and ate as though they had been starving for weeks. When they had finished they extinguished the light, and looked for sleeping places, each one to suit his nature and taste.

The ass lay down on the manure heap, the hound behind the door, the cat on the hearth near the warm ashes, and the cock flew up to the rafters. As they were tired from the long journey, they soon went to sleep.

When midnight was past, and the robbers saw from a distance that the light was no longer burning, and that all seemed quiet, the chief said:

"We ought not to have been scared by a false alarm," and ordered one of the robbers to go and examine the house.

Finding all quiet, the messenger went into the kitchen to kindle a light, and taking the cat's glowing, fiery eyes for live coals, he held a match close to them so as to light it. But the cat would stand no nonsense; it flew at his face, spat and scratched. He was terribly frightened and ran away.

He tried to get out by the back door, but the hound, who was lying there, jumped up and bit his leg. As he ran across the manure heap in front of the house, the ass gave him a good sound kick with his hind legs, while the cock, who had awoken at the uproar quite fresh and gay, cried out from his perch: "Cock-a-doodle-doo."

Thereupon the robber ran back as fast as he could to his chief, and said: "There is a gruesome witch in the house, who breathed on me and scratched me with her long fingers. Behind the door there stands a man with a knife, who stabbed me; while in the yard lies a black monster, who hit me with a club; and upon the roof the judge is seated, and he called out, 'Bring the rogue here,' so I hurried away as fast as I could."

Thenceforward the robbers did not venture again to the house, which, however, pleased the four Bremen musicians so much that they never wished to leave it again.

And he who last told the story has hardly finished speaking yet.

THE OLD SULTAN

A PEASANT ONCE HAD A faithful dog called Sultan, who had grown old and lost all his teeth, and could no longer keep fast hold of his quarry. One day when the peasant was standing in front of his house with his wife, he said, "Tomorrow I intend to shoot old Sultan; he is no longer any use."

His wife, who pitied the faithful animal, answered, "Since he has served us so long and honestly, we might at least keep him and feed him to the end of his days."

"What nonsense," said her husband; "you are a fool. He has not a tooth left in his head, and thieves are not a bit afraid of him now that they can get away from him. Even if he has served us well, he has been well fed in return."

The poor dog, who lay near, stretched out in the sun, heard all they said, and was sad at the thought that the next day was to be his last. Now, he had a good friend who was a wolf, and in the evening he slunk off into the wood, and complained to him of the fate which awaited him.

"Listen, comrade," said the wolf, "be of good cheer; I will help you in your need, for I have thought of a plan. Tomorrow your master and mistress are going hay-making, and they will take their little child with them because there will be nobody left at home. During their work they usually lay it under the hedge in the shade; you lie down as though to guard it. I will then come out of the wood and steal the child. You must rush quickly after me, as though you wanted to rescue the child. I will let it fall, and you will take it back to its parents again; they will think that you have saved it, and will be far too thankful to do you any harm. On the contrary, you will come into high favor, and they will never let you want again."

The plot pleased the dog, and it was carried out just as it was planned. The father cried out when he saw the wolf run across the field with his child in its mouth, but when old Sultan brought it back he was overjoyed, stroked him, and said: "Not a hair of your coat shall be hurt, and you shall have plenty to eat as long as you live." Then he said to his wife, "Go home immediately and prepare some broth for old Sultan that he won't need to bite, and bring the pillow out of my bed. I will give it to him to lie upon."

Henceforward old Sultan was as well off as he could wish. Soon afterwards the wolf paid him a visit, and rejoiced that all had turned out so well. "But, comrade," he said, "you must shut your eyes. Suppose some fine day I carry off one of your master's fat sheep? Nowadays it is hard to get one's living."

"Don't count on that," answered the dog. "I must remain true to my master—I shall never permit it."

The wolf, thinking that he had not spoken in earnest, came and crept in at night, and tried to carry off a sheep. But the peasant, to whom the faithful Sultan had betrayed the wolf's intention, spied him and belabored him soundly with a threshing-flail. The wolf was forced to retreat, but he called out to the dog, "Wait a bit, you wicked creature—you shall suffer for this."

The next morning he sent the boar to invite the dog into the wood, there to settle matters by a duel. Old Sultan could find no second except the cat, who had only three legs. When they came out the poor cat hobbled along, lifting up its tail with pain.

The wolf and his second were already in position; but when they saw their opponent coming they thought that he was bringing a sword, for they took the outstretched tail of the cat for one. And because the poor animal hobbled on three legs, they thought nothing less than that it was picking up stones to throw at them every time it stooped. Then both became frightened; the boar crept away into a thicket, and the wolf jumped up into a tree. The dog and the cat were astonished, when they arrived, at seeing no one about. The boar, however, had not been able to conceal himself completely; his ears still stuck out. While the cat was looking round cautiously, the boar twitched its ears; the cat, who thought that it was a mouse moving, sprang upon it, and began biting with a will. The boar jumped up and ran away, calling out: "The guilty party is up in that tree." The cat and the dog looked up and perceived the wolf, who, ashamed of having shown himself such a coward, made peace with the dog.

THE STRAW,
THE COAL, AND THE BEAN

ONCE THERE WAS A POOR old woman who lived in a village. She had collected a bundle of beans, and was going to cook them. So she prepared a fire on her hearth, and to make it burn up quickly she lighted it with a handful of straw. When she threw the beans into the pot, one escaped her unnoticed and slipped on to the floor, where it lay by a straw. Soon after, a glowing coal jumped out of the fire and joined the others. Then the straw began, and said, "Little friends, how came ye hither?"

The coal answered, "I have happily escaped the fire, and if I had not done so by force of will, my death would certainly have been a most cruel one. I should have been burnt to a cinder."

The bean said, "I also have escaped so far with a whole skin, but if the old woman had put me into the pot, I should have been pitilessly boiled down to broth like my comrades."

"Would a better fate have befallen me, then?" asked the straw. "The old woman packed all my brothers into the fire and smoke, sixty of them all done for at once. Fortunately, I slipped through her fingers."

"What are we to do now, though?" asked the coal.

"My opinion is," said the bean, "that, as we have escaped death, we must all keep together like good comrades, and so that we may run no further risks, we had better quit the country."

This proposal pleased both the others, and they set out together. Before long they came to a little stream, and, as there was neither path nor bridge, they did not know how to get over. The straw at last

had an idea, and said, "I will throw myself over and then you can walk across upon me like a bridge." So the straw stretched himself across from one side to the other, and the coal, which was of a fiery nature, tripped gaily over the newly-built bridge. But when it got to the middle and heard the water rushing below, it was frightened, and remained speechless, not daring to go any further. The straw, beginning to burn, broke in two and fell into the stream; the coal, falling with it, fizzled out in the water. The bean, who had cautiously remained on the bank, could not help laughing over the whole business, and, having begun, could not stop, but laughed till she split her sides. Now, all would have been up with her had not, fortunately, a wandering tailor been taking a rest by the stream. As he had a sympathetic heart, he brought out a needle and thread and stitched her up again. But, as he used black thread, all beans have a black seam to this day.

CLEVER ELSA

THERE WAS ONCE A MAN who had a daughter called Clever Elsa. When she was grown up, her father said, "We must get her married."

"Yes," said her mother. "If only somebody came who would have her."

At last a suitor named Hans came from a distance. He made an offer for her on condition that she really was as clever as she was said to be.

"Oh!" said her father, "she is a long-headed lass."

And her mother said, "She can see the wind blowing in the street, and hear the flies coughing."

"Well," said Hans, "if she is not really clever, I won't have her."

When they were at dinner, her mother said, "Elsa, go to the cellar and draw some beer."

Clever Elsa took the jug from the nail on the wall, and went to the cellar, clattering the lid as she went, to pass the time. When she reached the cellar she placed a chair near the cask so that she need not hurt her back by stooping. Then she put down the jug before her and turned the tap. And while the beer was running, so as not to be idle, she let her eyes rove all over the place, looking this way and that.

Suddenly she discovered a pickaxe just above her head, which a mason had by chance left hanging among the rafters.

Clever Elsa burst into tears, and said, "If I marry Hans, and we have a child, when it grows big, and we send it down to draw beer, the pickaxe will fall on its head and kill it." So there she sat crying and lamenting loudly at the impending mishap.

The others sat upstairs waiting for the beer, but Clever Elsa never came back.

Then the mistress said to her servant, "Go down to the cellar, and see why Elsa does not come back."

The maid went, and found Elsa sitting by the cask, weeping bitterly. "Why, Elsa, whatever are you crying for?" she asked.

"Alas!" she answered, "have I not cause to cry? If I marry Hans, and we have a child, when he grows big, and we send him down to draw beer, perhaps that pickaxe will fall on his head and kill him."

Then the maid said, "What a Clever Elsa we have"; and she, too, sat down by Elsa, and began to cry over the misfortune.

After a time, as the maid did not come back, and they were growing very thirsty, the master said to the serving-man, "Go down to the cellar and see what has become of Elsa and the maid."

The man went down, and there sat Elsa and the maid weeping together. So he said, "What are you crying for?"

"Alas!" said Elsa, "have I not enough to cry for? If I marry Hans, and we have a child, and we send it when it is big enough into the cellar to draw beer, the pickaxe will fall on its head and kill it."

The man said, "What a Clever Elsa we have"; and he, too, joined them and howled in company.

The people upstairs waited a long time for the serving-man, but as he did not come back, the husband said to his wife, "Go down to the cellar yourself, and see what has become of Elsa."

So the mistress went down and found all three making loud lamentations, and she asked the cause of their grief.

Then Elsa told her that her future child would be killed by the falling of the pickaxe when it was big enough to be sent to draw the beer. Her mother said with the others, "Did you ever see such a Clever Elsa as we have?"

Her husband upstairs waited some time, but as his wife did not return, and his thirst grew greater, he said, "I must go to the cellar myself to see what has become of Elsa."

But when he got to the cellar, and found all the others sitting together in tears, caused by the fear that a child which Elsa might

one day have, if she married Hans, might be killed by the falling of the pickaxe, when it went to draw beer, he too cried, "What a Clever Elsa we have!" Then, he, too, sat down and added his lamentations to theirs.

The bridegroom waited alone upstairs for a long time. Then, as nobody came back, he thought, "They must be waiting for me down there; I must go and see what they are doing."

So down he went, and when he found them all crying and lamenting in a heartbreaking manner, each one louder than the other, he asked, "What misfortune can possibly have happened?"

"Alas, dear Hans!" said Elsa, "if we marry and have a child, and we send it to draw beer when it is big enough, it may be killed if that pickaxe left hanging there were to fall on its head. Have we not cause to lament?"

"Well," said Hans, "more wits than this I do not need; and

as you are such a Clever Elsa I will have you for my wife."

He took her by the hand, led her upstairs, and they celebrated the marriage.

When they had been married for a while, Hans said, "Wife, I am going to work to earn some money. Could you go into the fields and cut the corn, so that we may have some bread?"

"Yes, my dear Hans; I will go at once."

When Hans had gone out, she made some good broth and took it into the field with her.

When she got there, she said to herself, "What shall I do, reap first, or eat first? I will eat first."

So she finished up the bowl of broth, which she found very satisfying. So she said again, "Which shall I do, sleep first, or reap first? I will sleep first." So she lay down among the corn and went to sleep.

Hans had been home a long time, and no Elsa came, so he said, "What a Clever Elsa I have. She is so industrious, she does not even come home to eat."

But as she still did not come, and it was getting dusk, Hans went out to see how much corn she had cut. He found that she had not cut any at all, and that she was lying there fast asleep. Hans hurried home to fetch a fowler's net with little bells on it, and this he hung around her without waking her. Then he ran home, shut the house door, and sat down to work.

At last, when it was quite dark, Clever Elsa woke up, and when she got up there was such a jangling, and the bells jingled at every step she took. She was terribly frightened, and wondered whether she really was Clever Elsa or not, and said, "Is it me, or is it not me?"

But she did not know what to answer, and stood for a time doubtful. At last she thought, "I will go home, and ask if it is me, or if it is not me. They will be sure to know."

She ran to the house, but found the door locked. So she knocked at the window, and cried, "Hans, is Elsa at home?"

"Yes," answered Hans, "she is!"

Then she started and cried, "Alas! then it is not me," and she went to another door. But when the people heard the jingling of the bells, they would not open the door, and nowhere would they take her in.

So she ran away out of the village, and was never seen again.

THE FISHERMAN
AND HIS WIFE

THERE WAS ONCE A FISHERMAN, who lived with his wife in a miserable little hovel close to the sea. He went to fish every day, and he fished and fished, and at last one day, as he was sitting looking deep down into the shining water, he felt something on his line. When he hauled it up there was a great flounder on the end of the line. The flounder said to him, "Listen, fisherman, I beg you not to kill me. I am no common flounder; I am an enchanted Prince! What good will it do you to kill me? I shan't be good to eat; put me back into the water, and leave me to swim about."

"Ho! ho!" said the fisherman, "you need not make so many words about it. I am quite ready to put back a flounder that can talk." And so saying, he put back the flounder into the shining water, and it sank down to the bottom, leaving a streak of blood behind it.

Then the fisherman got up and went back to his wife in the hovel. "Husband," she said, "have you caught nothing today?"

"No," said the man, "all I caught was one flounder, and he said he was an enchanted Prince, so I let him go swim again."

"Did you not wish for anything then?" asked the good-wife.

"No," said the man, "what was there to wish for?"

"Alas!" said his wife, "isn't it bad enough always to live in this wretched hovel! You might at least have wished for a nice clean cottage. Go back and call him, tell him I want a pretty cottage. He will surely give us that."

"Alas!" said the man, "what am I to go back there for?"

"Well," said the woman, "it was you who did catch him and let him go again; for certain he will do that for you. Be off now!"

The man was still not very willing to go, but he did not want to vex his wife, and at last he went back to the sea.

He found the sea no longer bright and shining, but dull and green. He stood by it and said—

> "Flounder, flounder in the sea,
> Prythee, hearken unto me:
> My wife, Ilsebil, must have her own will,
> And sends me to beg a boon of thee."

The flounder came swimming up, and said, "Well, what do you want?"

"Alas," said the man, "I had to call you, for my wife said I ought to have wished for something as I caught you. She doesn't want to live in our miserable hovel any longer, she wants a pretty cottage."

"Go home again then," said the flounder. "She has her wish fully."

The man went home and found his wife no longer in the old hut, but a pretty little cottage stood in its place, and his wife was sitting on a bench by the door.

She took him by the hand, and said, "Come and look in here—isn't this much better?"

They went inside and found a pretty sitting-room, and a bed-room with a bed in it, a kitchen and a larder furnished with everything of the best in tin and brass and every possible requisite. Outside there was a little yard with chickens and ducks, and a little garden full of vegetables and fruit.

"Look!" said the woman, "is not this nice?"

"Yes," said the man, "and so let it remain. We can live here very happily."

"We will see about that," said the woman. With that they ate something and went to bed.

Everything went well for a week or more, and then said the wife, "Listen, husband, this cottage is too cramped, and the garden is too small. The flounder could have given us a bigger house. I want to live in a big stone castle. Go to the flounder, and tell him to give us a castle."

"Alas, wife," said the man, "the cottage is good enough for us; what should we do with a castle?"

"Never mind," said his wife, "but go to the flounder, and he will manage it."

"Nay, wife," said the man, "the flounder gave us the cottage. I don't want to go back; as likely as not he'll be angry."

"Go, all the same," said the woman. "He can do it easily enough, and willingly into the bargain. Just go!"

The man's heart was heavy, and he was very unwilling to go. He said to himself, "It's not right." But at last he went.

He found the sea was no longer green; it was still calm, but dark violet and grey. He stood by it and said—

> "Flounder, flounder in the sea,
> Prythee, hearken unto me:
> My wife, Ilsebil, must have her own will,
> And sends me to beg a boon of thee."

"Now, what do you want?" said the flounder.

"Alas," said the man, half scared, "my wife wants a big stone castle."

"Go home again," said the flounder. "She is standing at the door of it."

Then the man went away thinking he would find no house, but when he got back he found a great stone palace, and his wife standing at the top of the steps, waiting to go in.

She took him by the hand and said, "Come in with me."

With that they went in and found a great hall paved with marble slabs, and numbers of servants in attendance, who opened the great doors for them. The walls were hung with beautiful tapestries, and the rooms were furnished with golden chairs and tables, while rich carpets covered the floors, and crystal chandeliers hung from the ceilings. The tables groaned under every kind of delicate food and the most costly wines. Outside the house there was a great courtyard, with stabling for horses, and cows, and many fine carriages. Beyond this there was a great garden filled with the loveliest flowers, and fine fruit-trees. There was also a park, half a mile long, and in it were stags and hinds, and hares, and everything of the kind one could wish for.

"Now," said the woman, "is not this worth having?"

"Oh yes," said the man, "and so let it remain. We will live in this beautiful palace and be content."

"We will think about that," said his wife, "and sleep upon it."

With that they went to bed.

Next morning the wife woke up first; day was just dawning, and from her bed she could see the beautiful country around her. Her husband was still asleep, but she pushed him with her elbow, and said, "Husband, get up and peep out of the window. See here, now, could we not be King over all this land? Go to the flounder. We will be King."

"Alas, wife," said the man, "what should we be King for? I don't want to be King."

"Ah," said his wife, "if you will not be King, I will. Go to the flounder. I will be King."

"Alas, wife," said the man, "whatever do you want to be King for? I don't like to tell him."

"Why not?" said the woman. "Go you must. I will be King."

So the man went, but he was quite sad because his wife would be King.

"It is not right," he said. "It is not right."

When he reached the sea, he found it dark, grey, and rough, and evil smelling. He stood there and said—

> "Flounder, flounder in the sea,
> Prythee, hearken unto me:
> My wife, Ilsebil, must have her own will,
> And sends me to beg a boon of thee."

"Now, what does she want?" said the flounder.

"Alas," said the man, "she wants to be King now."

"Go back. She is King already," said the flounder.

So the man went back, and when he reached the palace he found that it had grown much larger, and a great tower had been added with handsome decorations. There was a sentry at the door, and numbers of soldiers were playing drums and trumpets. As soon as he got inside the house, he found everything was marble and gold, and the hangings were of velvet, with great golden tassels. The doors of the saloon were thrown wide open, and he saw the whole court assembled. His wife was sitting on a lofty throne of gold and diamonds; she wore a golden crown, and carried in one hand a scepter of pure gold. On each side of her stood her ladies in a long row, every one a head shorter than the next.

He stood before her, and said, "Alas, wife, are you now King?"

"Yes," she said, "now I am King."

He stood looking at her for some time, and then he said, "Ah, wife, it is a fine thing for you to be King; now we will not wish to be anything more."

"Nay, husband," she answered, quite uneasily. "I find the time hang very heavy on my hands. I can't bear it any longer. Go back to the flounder. King I am, but I must also be Emperor."

"Alas, wife," said the man. "Why do you now want to be Emperor?"

"Husband," she answered, "go to the flounder. Emperor I will be."

"Alas, wife," said the man. "Emperor he can't make you, and I won't ask him. There is only one Emperor in the country; and Emperor the flounder cannot make you, that he can't."

"What?" said the woman. "I am King, and you are but my husband. To him you must go, and that right quickly. If he can make a King, he can also make an Emperor. Emperor I will be, so go quickly."

He had to go, but he was quite frightened. And as he went, he thought, "This won't end well. Emperor is too shameless. The flounder will make an end of the whole thing."

With that he came to the sea, but now he found it quite black, and heaving up from below in great waves. It tossed to and fro, and a sharp wind blew over it, and the man trembled. So he stood there, and said—

"Flounder, flounder in the sea,
Prythee, hearken unto me:
My wife, Ilsebil, must have her own will,
And sends me to beg a boon of thee."

"What does she want now?" said the flounder.

"Alas, flounder," he said, "my wife wants to be Emperor."

"Go back," said the flounder. "She is Emperor."

So the man went back, and when he got to the door, he found that the whole palace was made of polished marble, with alabaster figures and golden decorations. Soldiers marched up and down before the doors, blowing their trumpets and beating their drums. Inside the palace, counts, barons, and dukes walked about as attendants, and they opened to him the doors, which were of pure gold.

He went in, and saw his wife sitting on a huge throne made of solid gold. It was at least two miles high. She had on her head a great golden crown set with diamonds three yards high. In one hand she held the scepter, and in the other the orb of empire. On each side of her stood the gentlemen-at-arms in two rows, each one a little smaller than the other, from giants two miles high down to the tiniest dwarf no bigger than my little finger. She was surrounded by Princes and dukes.

Her husband stood still, and said, "Wife, are you now Emperor?"

"Yes," said she, "now I am Emperor."

Then he looked at her for some time, and said, "Alas, wife, how much better off are you for being Emperor?"

"Husband," she said, "what are you standing there for? Now I am Emperor, I mean to be Pope! Go back to the flounder."

"Alas, wife," said the man, "what will you not want? Pope you cannot be. There is only one Pope in Christendom. That's more than the flounder can do."

"Husband," she said, "Pope I will be; so go at once. I must be Pope this very day."

"No, wife," he said. "I dare not tell him. It's no good; it's too monstrous altogether. The flounder cannot make you Pope."

"Husband," said the woman, "don't talk nonsense. If he can make an Emperor, he can make a Pope. Go immediately. I am Emperor, and you are but my husband, and you must obey."

So he was frightened and went, but he was quite dazed. He shivered and shook, and his knees trembled.

A great wind arose over the land, the clouds flew across the sky, and it grew as dark as night. The leaves fell from the trees, and the water foamed and dashed upon the shore. In the distance the ships were being tossed to and fro on the waves, and he heard them firing signals of distress. There was still a little patch of blue in the sky among the dark clouds, but towards the south they were red and heavy, as in a bad storm. In despair, he stood and said—

> "Flounder, flounder in the sea,
> Prythee, hearken unto me:
> My wife, Ilsebil, must have her own will,
> And sends me to beg a boon of thee."

"Now, what does she want?" said the flounder.

"Alas," said the man, "she wants to be Pope!"

"Go back. Pope she is," said the flounder.

So back he went, and he found a great church surrounded with palaces. He pressed through the crowd, and inside he found thousands and thousands of lights, and his wife, entirely clad in gold, was sitting on a still higher throne, with three golden crowns upon her head, and she was surrounded with priestly state. On each side of her were two rows of candles, the biggest as thick as a tower, down to the tiniest little taper. Kings and Emperors were on their knees before her, kissing her shoe.

"Wife," said the man, looking at her, "are you now Pope?"

"Yes," said she. "Now I am Pope."

So there he stood gazing at her, and it was like looking at a shining sun.

"Alas, wife," he said, "are you better off for being Pope?" At first she sat as stiff as a post, without stirring. Then he said, "Now, wife, be content with being Pope; higher you cannot go."

"I will think about that," said the woman, and with that they both went to bed. Still she was not content, and could not sleep for her inordinate desires. The man slept well and soundly, for he had walked about a great deal in the day; but his wife could think of nothing but what further grandeur she could demand. When the dawn reddened the sky she raised herself up in bed and looked out of the window, and when she saw the sun rise, she said:

"Ha! Can I not cause the sun and the moon to rise? Husband!"

she cried, digging her elbow into his side, "wake up and go to the flounder. I will be Lord of the Universe."

Her husband, who was still more than half asleep, was so shocked that he fell out of bed. He thought he must have heard wrong. He rubbed his eyes, and said, "Alas, wife, what did you say?"

"Husband," she said, "if I cannot be Lord of the Universe, and cause the sun and moon to set and rise, I shall not be able to bear it. I shall never have another happy moment."

She looked at him so wildly that it caused a shudder to run through him.

"Alas, wife," he said, falling on his knees before her, "the flounder can't do that. Emperor and Pope he can make, but that is indeed beyond him. I pray you, control yourself and remain Pope."

Then she flew into a terrible rage. Her hair stood on end; she kicked him and screamed—

"I won't bear it any longer. Will you go!"

Then he pulled on his trousers and tore away like a madman. Such a storm was raging that he could hardly keep his feet. Houses and trees quivered and swayed, and mountains trembled, and the rocks rolled into the sea. The sky was pitchy black; it thundered and lightened, and the sea ran in black waves mountains high, crested with white foam. He shrieked out, but could hardly make himself heard—

> "Flounder, flounder in the sea,
> Prythee, hearken unto me:
> My wife, Ilsebil, must have her own will,
> And sends me to beg a boon of thee."

"Now, what does she want?" asked the flounder.
"Alas," he said, "she wants to be Lord of the Universe."
"Now she must go back to her old hovel; and there she is."
So there they are to this very day.

THE WREN AND THE BEAR

ONCE UPON A TIME, in the summer, a bear and a wolf were taking a walk in a wood when the bear heard a bird singing most beautifully, and he said, "Brother wolf, what kind of bird is that singing so beautifully?"

"That is the King of the birds, and we must bow down to it."

But really it was a wren.

"If that is so," said the bear, "I should like to see his royal palace. Come, you must take me to it."

"That's not so easy," said the wolf. "You must wait till the Queen comes."

Soon after, the Queen made her appearance, bringing food in her beak, and the King came with her to feed their little ones. The bear would have liked to go in at once, but the wolf held him by the sleeve, and said, "No, now you must wait till the King and Queen fly away again."

So they marked the opening of the nest, and trudged on. But the bear had no rest till he could see the royal palace, and before long he went back.

The King and the Queen had gone out again. He peeped in, and saw five or six young ones lying in the nest.

"Is that the royal palace?" cried the bear. "What a miserable place! And do you mean to say that you are royal children? You must be changelings!"

When the young wrens heard this, they were furious, and shrieked, "No, indeed we're not. Our parents are honest people.

We must have this out with you."

The bear and the wolf were very much frightened. They turned round and ran home to their dens.

But the young wrens continued to shriek and scream aloud, and when their parents came back with more food, they said, "We won't touch so much as the leg of a fly, even if we starve, till you tell us whether we are really your lawful children or not. The bear has been here calling us names."

Then said the old King, "Only be quiet, and this shall be seen to."

Thereupon he and his wife the Queen flew off to the bear in his den, and called in to him, "Old Bruin, why have you been calling our children names? It will turn out badly for you, and it will lead to a bloody war between us."

So war was declared, and all the four-footed animals were called together—the ox, the ass, the cow, the stag, the roedeer, and every other creature on the earth.

But the wren called together every creature that flew in the air, not only birds both large and small, but also the gnats, the hornets, the bees, and the flies.

When the time came for the war to begin, the wren sent out scouts to discover where the commanding generals of the enemy were to be found. The gnats were the most cunning of all. They swarmed in the wood where the enemy assembled, and at last they hid themselves under a leaf of the tree where the orders were being given.

The bear called the fox up to him and said, "You are the slyest of all the animals, Reynard. You shall be our general, and lead us."

"Very good," said the fox. "But what shall we have for a signal?" But nobody could think of anything. Then said the fox, "I have a fine, long, bushy tail, which almost looks like a red feather brush. When I hold my tail erect, things are going well, and you must march forward at once. But if it droops, you must all run away as hard as ever you can."

When the gnats heard this they flew straight home and told the wrens every detail.

When the day broke, all the four-footed animals came rushing to the spot where the battle was to take place. They came with such a tramping that the earth shook.

The wren and his army also came swarming through the air; they fluttered and buzzed enough to terrify one. And then they made for one another.

The wren sent the hornet down with orders to seat herself under the tail of the fox and to sting him with all her might.

When the fox felt the first sting he quivered, and raised one leg in the air. But he bore it bravely, and kept his tail erect. At the second sting he was forced to let it droop for a moment, but the third time he could bear it no longer; he screamed, and down went his tail between his legs. When the animals saw this they thought all was lost, and off they ran helter-skelter, as fast as they could go, each to his own den.

So the birds won the battle.

When it was over the King and the Queen flew home to their children, and cried, "Children, be happy! Eat and drink to your hearts' content; we have won the battle."

But the young wrens said, "We won't eat till the bear comes here to make an apology, and says that we are really and truly your lawful children."

The wren flew to the bear's den, and cried, "Old Bruin, you will have to come and apologize to my children for calling them names, or else you will have all your ribs broken."

So in great terror the bear crept to the nest and apologized, and at last the young wrens were satisfied, and they ate and drank and made merry till far into the night.

THE FROG PRINCE

IN THE OLDEN TIME, WHEN wishing was some good, there lived
a King whose daughters were all beautiful, but the youngest was
so lovely that even the sun, that looked on many things, could
not but marvel when he shone upon her face.

Near the King's palace there was a large dark forest, and in the
forest, under an old lime-tree, was a well. When the day was very hot
the Princess used to go into the forest and sit upon the edge of this
cool well. When she was tired of doing nothing she would play with
a golden ball, throwing it up in the air and catching it again, and this
was her favorite game. Now on one occasion it so happened that the
ball did not fall back into her hand stretched up to catch it, but
dropped to the ground and rolled straight into the well. The Princess
followed it with her eyes, but it disappeared, for the well was so very
deep that it was quite impossible to see the bottom. Then she began
to cry bitterly, and nothing would comfort her.

As she was lamenting in this manner, some one called out to her,
"What is the matter, Princess? Your lamentations would move the
heart of a stone."

She looked round towards the spot whence the voice came, and
saw a frog stretching its broad, ugly face out of the water.

"Oh, it's you, is it, old splasher? I am crying for my golden ball
which has fallen into the water."

"Be quiet then, and stop crying," answered the frog. "I know what
to do; but what will you give me if I get you back your plaything?"

"Whatever you like, you dear old frog," she said. "My clothes, my pearls and diamonds, or even the golden crown upon my head."

The frog answered, "I care neither for your clothes, your pearls and diamonds, nor even your golden crown. But if you will be fond of me, and let me be your playmate, sit by you at table, eat out of your plate, drink out of your cup, and sleep in your little bed—if you will promise to do all this, I will go down and fetch your ball."

"I will promise anything you like to ask, if only you will get me back my ball."

She thought, "What is the silly old frog chattering about? He lives in the well, croaking with his mates, and he can't be the companion of a human being."

As soon as the frog received her promise, he ducked his head under the water and disappeared. After a little while, back he came with the ball in his mouth, and threw it on to the grass beside her.

The princess was full of joy when she saw her pretty toy again, picked it up, and ran off with it.

"Wait, wait," cried the frog. "Take me with you. I can't run as fast as you can."

But what was the good of his crying "Croak, croak," as loud as he could? She did not listen to him, but hurried home, and forgot all about the poor frog, and he had to go back to his well.

The next day, as she was sitting at dinner with the King and all the courtiers, eating out of her golden plate, something came flopping up the stairs, flip, flap, flip, flap. When it reached the top it knocked at the door, and cried, "Youngest daughter of the King, you must let me in." She ran to see who it was. When she opened the door and saw the frog she shut it again very quickly, and went back to the table, for she was very much frightened.

The King saw that her heart was beating very fast, and he said, "My child, what is the matter? Is there a giant at the door wanting to take you away?"

"Oh no!" she said. "It's not a giant, but a hideous frog."

"What does the frog want with you?"

"Oh, Father dear, last night, when I was playing by the well in the forest, my golden ball fell into the water. And I cried, and the frog got it out for me. And then, because he insisted on it, I promised that he should be my playmate. But I never thought that he would come out of the water, but there he is, and he wants to come in to me."

He knocked at the door for the second time, and sang—

"Youngest daughter of the King,
Take me up, I sing;
Know'st thou not what yesterday
Thou to me didst say
By the well in forest dell.
Youngest daughter of the King,
Take me up, I sing."

Then said the King, "What you have promised you must perform. Go and open the door for him."

So she opened the door, and the frog shuffled in, keeping close to her feet, till he reached her chair. Then he cried, "Lift me up beside you." She hesitated, till the King ordered her to do it. When the frog was put on the chair, he demanded to be placed upon the table, and then he said, "Push your golden plate nearer that we may eat together." She did as he asked her, but very unwillingly, as could easily be seen. The frog made a good dinner, but the Princess could not swallow a morsel. At last he said, "I have eaten enough, and I am tired, carry me into your bedroom and arrange your silken bed, that we may go to sleep."

The Princess began to cry, for she was afraid of the clammy frog, which she did not dare to touch, and which was now to sleep in her pretty little silken bed. But the King grew very angry, and said, "You must not despise any one who has helped you in your need."

So she seized him with two fingers, and carried him upstairs, where she put him in a corner of her room. When she got into bed, he crept up to her, and said, "I am tired, and I want to go to sleep as well as you. Lift me up, or I will tell your father."

She was very angry, picked him up, and threw him with all her might against the wall, saying, "You may rest there as well as you can, you hideous frog." But when he fell to the ground, he was no longer a hideous frog, but a handsome Prince with beautiful friendly eyes.

And at her father's wish he became her beloved companion and husband. He told her that he had been bewitched by a wicked fairy, and nobody could have released him from the spells but she herself.

Next morning, when the sun rose, a coach drove up drawn by eight milk-white horses, with white ostrich plumes on their heads, and golden harness. Behind stood faithful Henry, the Prince's body-servant. The faithful fellow had been so distressed when his master was changed into a frog, that he had caused three iron bands to be placed round his heart, lest it should break from grief and pain.

The coach had come to carry the young pair back into the Prince's own kingdom. The faithful Henry helped both of them into the coach and mounted again behind, delighted at his master's deliverance.

They had only gone a little way when the Prince heard a cracking behind him, as if something were breaking. He turned round, and cried—

> "'Henry, the coach is giving way!'
> 'No, sir, the coach is safe, I say,
> A band from my heart has fall'n in twain,
> For long I suffered woe and pain,
> While you a frog within a well
> Enchanted were by witch's spell!'"

Once more he heard the same snapping and cracking, and then again. The Prince thought it must be some part of the carriage giving way, but it was only the bands round faithful Henry's heart that were snapping, because of his great joy at his master's deliverance and happiness.

THE ADVENTURES OF
CHANTICLEER AND PARTLET

I. HOW THEY WENT
TO THE HILLS TO EAT NUTS

CHANTICLEER SAID TO PARTLET one day, "The nuts must be ripe. Now we will go up the hill together and have a good feast before the squirrel carries them all off."

"All right," said Partlet, "Come along. We'll have a fine time." So they went away up the hill, and, as it was a bright day, they stayed till evening.

Now whether they really had grown fat, or whether it was merely pride, I do not know, but, whatever the reason, they would not walk home, and Chanticleer had to make a little carriage of nutshells. When it was ready, Partlet took her seat in it, and said to Chanticleer, "Now you get between the shafts."

"That's all very fine," said Chanticleer, "but I would sooner go home on foot than put myself in harness. I will sit on the box and drive, but draw it myself I never will."

As they were squabbling over this, a duck quacked out, "You thievish folk! Who told you to come to my nut-hill? Just you wait, you will suffer for it."

Then she rushed at Chanticleer with open bill, but he was not to be taken by surprise, and fell upon her with his spurs till she cried out for mercy. At last she allowed herself to be harnessed to the carriage. Chanticleer seated himself on the box as coachman, and cried out unceasingly, "Now, duck, run as fast as you can."

When they had driven a little way they met two foot passengers, a pin and a needle. They called out, "Stop! Stop!" They said it would soon be pitch dark, and they couldn't walk a step further, the road was so dirty, might they not have a lift? They had been to the Tailor's Inn by the gate, and had lingered over their beer.

As they were both very thin, and did not take up much room, Chanticleer allowed them to get in, but he made them promise not to tread either on his toes, or on Partlet's. Late in the evening they came to an inn, and as they did not want to drive any further in the dark, and the duck was getting rather uncertain on her feet, tumbling from side to side, they drove in.

The landlord at first made many objections to having them, and said the house was already full. Perhaps he thought they were not very grand folk. But at last, by dint of persuasive words, and promising him the egg that Mrs. Partlet had laid on the way, and also that he should keep the duck, who laid an egg every day, he consented to let them stay the night.

Then they had a meal served to them, and feasted, and passed the time in rioting.

In the early dawn, before it grew light, and every one was asleep, Parlet woke up Chanticleer, fetched the egg, pecked a hole in it, and between them they ate it all up, and threw the shells on to the hearth. Then they went to the needle, which was still asleep, seized it by the head and stuck it in the cushion of the landlord's armchair; the pin they stuck in his towel, and then, without more ado, away they flew over the heath. The duck, which preferred to sleep in the open air, and had stayed in the yard, heard them whizzing by, and bestirred herself. She found a stream, and swam away down it; it was a much quicker way to get on than being harnessed to a carriage.

A couple of hours later, the landlord, who was the first to leave his pillow, got up and washed. When he took up the towel to dry himself, he scratched his face and made a long red line from ear to ear. Then he went to the kitchen to light his pipe, but when he stooped over the hearth the eggshells flew into his eye.

"Everything goes to my head this morning," he said angrily, as he dropped on to the cushion of his grandfather's armchair. But he quickly bounded up again, and shouted, "Gracious me!" for the needle had run into him, and this time not in the head. He grew furious, and his suspicions immediately fell on the guests who had come in so late the night before. When he went to look for them, they were nowhere to be seen. Then he swore never to take such ragamuffins into his house again, for they ate a great deal, paid nothing, and played tricks, by way of thanks, into the bargain.

II. THE VISIT TO MR. KORBES

Another day, when Partlet and Chanticleer were about to take a journey, Chanticleer built a fine carriage with four red wheels, and harnessed four little mice to it. Mrs. Partlet seated herself in it with Chanticleer, and they drove off together.

Before long they met a cat. "Whither away?" said she. Chanticleer answered—

> "All on our way
> A visit to pay
> To Mr. Korbes at his house today."

"Take me with you," said the cat.

Chanticleer answered, "With pleasure. Sit down behind, so that you don't fall out forwards."

> "My wheels are so red, pray have a care
> From any splash of mud to spare.
> Little wheels hurry!
> Little mice scurry!
> All on our way

> A visit to pay
> To Mr. Korbes at his house today."

Then came a millstone, an egg, a duck, a pin, and, last of all, a needle. They all took their places in the carriage and went with the rest.

But when they arrived at Mr. Korbes' house, he wasn't in. The mice drew the carriage into the coach-house, Partlet and Chanticleer flew on to a perch, the cat sat down by the fire, the duck lay down by the well-pole. The egg rolled itself up in the towel, the pin stuck itself into the cushion, the needle sprang into the pillow on the bed, and the millstone laid itself over the door.

When Mr. Korbes came home, and went to the hearth to make a fire, the cat threw ashes into his face. He ran into the kitchen to wash, and the duck squirted water into his face. Seizing the towel to dry himself, the egg rolled out, broke, and stuck up one of his eyes. He wanted to rest, and sat down in his armchair, when the pin pricked him. He grew very angry, threw himself on the bed and laid his head on the pillow, when the needle ran into him and made him cry out. In a fury he wanted to rush into the open air, but when he got to the door, the millstone fell on his head and killed him. What a bad man Mr. Korbes must have been!

III. THE DEATH OF PARTLET

Partlet and Chanticleer went to the nut-hill on another occasion, and they arranged that whichever of them found a nut should share it with the other.

Partlet found a huge nut, but said nothing about it, and meant to eat it all herself, but the kernel was so big that she could not swallow it. It stuck in her throat, and she was afraid she would be choked. She shrieked, "Chanticleer, Chanticleer, run and fetch some water as fast as you can, or I shall choke!"

So Chanticleer ran as fast as he could to the well, and said, "Well, well, you must give me some water! Partlet is out on the nut-hill; she has swallowed a big nut, and is choking."

The well answered, "First you must run to my bride, and tell her to give you some red silk."

Chanticleer ran to the bride, and said, "Bride, bride, give me some red silk. I will give the silk to the well, and the well will give me some water to take to Partlet, for she has swallowed a big nut, and is choking."

The bride answered, "Run first and fetch me a wreath which I left hanging on a willow."

So Chanticleer ran to the willow, pulled the wreath off the branch, and brought it to the bride. The bride gave him the red silk, which he took to the well, and the well gave him the water for it. Then Chanticleer took the water to Partlet, but as it happened she had choked in the meantime, and lay there dead and stiff. Chanticleer's grief was so great that he cried aloud, and all the animals came and condoled with him.

Six mice built a little car to draw Partlet to the grave, and when the car was ready they harnessed themselves to it, and drew Partlet away.

On the way, Reynard the fox joined them. "Where are you going, Chanticleer?"

"I'm going to bury my wife, Partlet."

"May I go with you?"

> "Jump up behind, we're not yet full,
> A weight in front, my nags can't pull."

So the fox took a seat at the back, and he was followed by the wolf, the bear, the stag, the lion, and all the other animals of the forest. The procession went on, till they came to a stream.

"How shall we ever get over?" said Chanticleer.

A straw was lying by the stream, and it said, "I will stretch myself across, and then you can pass over upon me."

But when the six mice got on to the straw it collapsed, and the mice fell into the water with it, and they were all drowned.

RAPUNZEL

THERE WAS ONCE A MAN and his wife who had long wished in vain for a child, when at last they had reason to hope that heaven would grant their wish. There was a little window at the back of their house, which overlooked a beautiful garden, full of lovely flowers and shrubs. It was, however, surrounded by a high wall, and nobody dared to enter it, because it belonged to a powerful witch, who was feared by everybody.

One day the woman, standing at this window and looking into the garden, saw a bed planted with beautiful rampion. It looked so fresh and green that it made her long to eat some of it. This longing increased every day, and as she knew it could never be satisfied, she began to look pale and miserable, and to pine away. Then her husband was alarmed, and said, "What ails you, my dear wife?"

"Alas!" she answered, "if I cannot get any of the rampion from the garden behind our house to eat, I shall die."

Her husband, who loved her, thought, "Before you let your wife die, you must fetch her some of that rampion, cost what it may." So in the twilight he climbed over the wall into the witch's garden, hastily picked a handful of rampion, and took it back to his wife. She immediately dressed it, and ate it up very eagerly. It was so very, very nice, that the next day her longing for it increased threefold. She could have no peace unless her husband fetched her some more. So in the twilight he set out again, but when he got over the wall he was terrified to see the witch before him.

"How dare you come into my garden like a thief, and steal my rampion?" she said, with angry looks. "It shall be the worse for you!"

"Alas!" he answered, "be merciful to me. I am only here from necessity. My wife sees your rampion from the window, and she has such a longing for it, that she would die if she could not get some of it."

The anger of the witch abated, and she said to him, "If it is as you say, I will allow you to take away with you as much rampion as you like, but on one condition. You must give me the child that your wife is about to bring into the world. I will care for it like a mother, and all will be well with it." In his fear the man consented to everything, and when the baby was born, the witch appeared, gave it the name of Rapunzel (which meant "rampion"), and took it away with her.

Rapunzel was the most beautiful child under the sun. When she was twelve years old, the witch shut her up in a tower that stood in a wood. It had neither staircase nor doors, and only a little window quite high up in the wall. When the witch wanted to enter the tower, she stood at the foot of it, and cried—

"Rapunzel, Rapunzel, let down your hair."

Rapunzel had splendid long hair, as fine as spun gold. As soon as she heard the voice of the witch, she unfastened her plaits and twisted them round a hook by the window. They fell twenty ells downwards, and the witch climbed up by them.

It happened a couple of years later that the King's son rode through the forest, and came close to the tower. From thence he heard a song so lovely, that he stopped to listen. It was Rapunzel, who in her loneliness made her sweet voice resound to pass away the time. The King's son wanted to join her, and he sought for the door of the tower, but there was none to find.

He rode home, but the song had touched his heart so deeply that he went into the forest every day to listen to it. Once, when he was hidden behind a tree, he saw a witch come to the tower and call out—

"Rapunzel, Rapunzel, let down your hair."

Then Rapunzel lowered her plaits of hair and the witch climbed up to her.

"If that is the ladder by which one ascends," he thought, "I will try my luck myself." And the next day, when it began to grow dark, he went to the tower and cried—

"Rapunzel, Rapunzel, let down your hair."

The hair fell down at once, and the King's son climbed up by it.

At first Rapunzel was terrified, for she had never set eyes on a man before, but the King's son talked to her kindly, and told her that his heart had been so deeply touched by her song that he had no peace, and he was obliged to see her. Then Rapunzel lost her fear, and when he asked if she would have him for her husband, and she saw that he was young and handsome, she thought, "He will love me better than old Mother Gothel." So she said, "Yes," and laid her hand in his. She said, "I will gladly go with you, but I do not know how I am to get down from this tower. When you come, will you bring a skein of silk with you every time. I will twist it into a ladder, and when it is long enough I will descend by it, and you can take me away with you on your horse."

She arranged with him that he should come and see her every evening, for the old witch came in the daytime.

The witch discovered nothing, till suddenly Rapunzel said to her, "Tell me, Mother Gothel, how can it be that you are so much heavier to draw up than the young Prince who will be here before long?"

"Oh, you wicked child, what do you say? I thought I had separated you from all the world, and yet you have deceived me." In her rage she seized Rapunzel's beautiful hair, twisted it twice round her left hand, snatched up a pair of shears and cut off the plaits, which fell to the ground. She was so merciless that she took poor Rapunzel away into a wilderness, where she forced her to live in the greatest grief and misery.

In the evening of the day on which she had banished Rapunzel, the witch fastened the plaits that she had cut off to the hook by the window, and when the Prince came and called, "Rapunzel, Rapunzel, let down your hair," she lowered the hair. The Prince climbed up, but there he found not his beloved Rapunzel, but the witch, who looked at him with angry and wicked eyes.

"Ah!" she cried mockingly, "you have come to fetch your ladylove, but the pretty bird is no longer in her nest. She can sing no more, for the cat has seized her, and it will scratch your own eyes out too. Rapunzel is lost to you; you will never see her again."

The Prince was beside himself with grief, and in his despair he sprang out of the window. He was not killed, but his eyes were scratched out by the thorns among which he fell. He wandered about blind in the wood, and had nothing but roots and berries to eat. He did nothing but weep and lament over the loss of his beloved wife Rapunzel. In this way he wandered about for some years, till at last he reached the wilderness where Rapunzel had been living in great poverty with the twins who had been born to her, a boy and a girl.

He heard a voice that seemed very familiar to him, and he went towards it. Rapunzel knew him at once, and fell weeping upon his neck. Two of her tears fell upon his eyes, and they immediately grew quite clear, and he could see as well as ever. He took her to his kingdom, where he was received with joy, and they lived long and happily together.

THE VALIANT TAILOR

ATAILOR WAS SITTING ON his table at the window one summer morning. He was a good fellow, and stitched with all his might. A peasant woman came down the street, crying, "Good jam for sale! Good jam for sale!"

This had a pleasant sound in the tailor's ears; he put his pale face out of the window, and cried, "You'll find a sale for your wares up here, good woman."

The woman went up the three steps to the tailor, with the heavy basket on her head, and he made her unpack all her pots. He examined them all, lifted them up, smelt them, and at last said, "The jam seems good. Weigh me out four ounces, good woman, and should it come over the quarter pound, it will be all the same to me."

The woman, who had hoped for a better sale, gave him what he asked for, but went away cross, and grumbling to herself.

"That jam will be a blessing to me," cried the tailor. "It will give me strength and power." He brought his bread out of the cupboard, cut a whole slice, and spread the jam on it. "It won't be a bitter morsel," said he, "but I will finish this waistcoat before I stick my teeth into it."

He put the bread down by his side, and went on with his sewing, but in his joy the stitches got bigger and bigger. The smell of the jam rose to the wall, where the flies were clustered in swarms, and tempted them to come down, and they settled on the jam in masses.

"Ah! who invited you?" cried the tailor, chasing away his unbidden guests. But the flies, who did not understand his language, were not to be got rid of so easily, and came back in greater numbers than ever. At last the tailor came to the end of his patience, and seizing a bit of cloth, he cried, "Wait a bit, and I'll give it you!" So saying, he struck out at them mercilessly. When he looked, he found no fewer than seven dead and motionless. "So that's the kind of fellow you are," he said, admiring his own valor. "The whole town shall know of this."

In great haste he cut out a belt for himself, and stitched on it, in big letters, "Seven at one blow!" "The town!" he then said, "the whole world shall know of it!" And his heart wagged for very joy like the tail of a lamb. The tailor fastened the belt round his waist, and wanted to start out into the world at once; he found his workshop too small for his valor. Before starting, he searched the house to see if there was anything to take with him. He only found an old cheese, but this he put into his pocket. By the gate he saw a bird entangled in a thicket, and he put that into his pocket with the cheese. Then he boldly took to the road, and as he was light and active, he felt no fatigue. The road led up a mountain, and when he reached the highest point, he found a huge giant sitting there comfortably looking round him.

The tailor went pluckily up to him, and addressed him.

"Good day, comrade, you are sitting there surveying the wide world, I suppose. I am just on my way to try my luck. Do you feel inclined to go with me?"

The giant looked scornfully at the tailor, and said, "You jackanapes! You miserable ragamuffin!"

"That may be," said the tailor, unbuttoning his coat and showing the giant his belt. "You may just read what kind of fellow I am."

The giant read, "Seven at one blow," and thought that it was people the tailor had slain; so it gave him a certain amount of respect for the little fellow. Still, he thought he would try him; so he picked up a stone and squeezed it till the water dropped out of it.

"Do that," he said, "if you have the strength."

"No more than that!" said the tailor. "Why, it's a mere joke to me."

He put his hand into his pocket, and pulling out the bit of soft cheese, he squeezed it till the moisture ran out.

"I guess that will equal you," said he.

The giant did not know what to say, and could not have believed it of the little man.

Then the giant picked up a stone, and threw it up so high that one could scarcely follow it with the eye.

"Now, then, you sample of a mannikin, do that after me."

"Well thrown!" said the tailor, "but the stone fell to the ground again. Now I will throw one for you which will never come back again."

So saying, he put his hand into his pocket, took out the bird, and threw it into the air. The bird, rejoiced at its freedom, soared into the air, and was never seen again.

"What do you think of that, comrade?" asked the tailor.

"You can certainly throw, but now we will see if you are in a condition to carry anything," said the giant.

He led the tailor to a mighty oak that had been felled, and which lay upon the ground.

"If you are strong enough, help me out of the wood with this tree," he said.

"Willingly," answered the little man. "You take the trunk on your shoulder, and I will take the branches; they must certainly be the heaviest."

The giant accordingly took the trunk on his shoulder; but the tailor seated himself on one of the branches, and the giant, who could not look round, had to carry the whole tree, and the tailor into the bargain. The tailor was very merry on the end of the tree, and whistled, "Three tailors rode merrily out of the town," as if tree-carrying were a joke to him.

When the giant had carried the tree some distance, he could go no further, and exclaimed, "Look out, I am going to drop the tree."

The tailor sprang to the ground with great agility, and seized the tree with both arms, as if he had been carrying it all the time. He said to the giant, "Big fellow as you are, you can't carry a tree."

After a time they went on together, and when they came to a cherry-tree, the giant seized the top branches, where the cherries ripened first, bent them down, put them in the tailor's hand, and told him to eat. The tailor, however, was much too weak to hold the tree, and when the giant let go, the tree sprang back, carrying the tailor with it into the air. When he reached the ground again, without any injury, the giant said, "What's this? Haven't you the strength to hold a feeble sapling?"

"It's not strength that's wanting," answered the tailor. "Do you think that would be anything to one who killed seven at a blow? I sprang over the tree because some sportsmen were shooting among the bushes. Spring after me if you like."

The giant made the attempt, but he could not clear the tree, and stuck among the branches. So here, too, the tailor had the advantage of him.

The giant said, "If you are such a gallant fellow, come with me to our cave, and stay the night with us."

The tailor was quite willing, and went with him. When they reached the cave, they found several other giants sitting round a fire, and each one held a roasted sheep in his hand, which he was eating. The tailor looked about him, and thought, "It is much more roomy here than in my workshop."

The giant showed him a bed, and told him to lie down and have a good sleep. The bed was much too big for the tailor, so he did not lie down in it, but crept into a corner. At midnight, when the giant thought the tailor would be in a heavy sleep, he got up, took a big oak club, and with one blow crashed right through the bed, and thought he had put an end to the grasshopper. Early in the morning the giants went out into the woods, forgetting all about the tailor, when all at once he appeared before them, as lively as possible. They were terrified, and thinking he would strike them all dead, they ran off as fast as ever they could.

The tailor went on his way, always following his own pointed nose. When he had walked for a long time, he came to the courtyard of a royal palace. He was so tired that he lay down on the grass and went to sleep. While he lay and slept, the people came and inspected him on all sides, and they read on his belt, "Seven at one blow." "Alas!" they said, "why does this great warrior come here in time of peace; he must be a mighty man."

They went to the King and told him about it; and they were of opinion that, should war break out, he would be a useful and powerful man, who should on no account be allowed to depart. This advice pleased the King, and he sent one of his courtiers to the tailor to offer him a military appointment when he woke up. The messenger remained standing by the tailor, till he opened his eyes and stretched himself, and then he made the offer.

"For that very purpose have I come," said the tailor. "I am quite ready to enter the King's service."

So he was received with honor, and a special dwelling was assigned to him.

The soldiers, however, bore him a grudge, and wished him a thousand miles away. "What will be the end of it?" they said to each other. "When we quarrel with him, and he strikes out, seven of us will fall at once. One of us can't cope with him." So they took a resolve, and went all together to the King, and asked for their discharge. "We are not made," said they, "to hold our own with a man who strikes seven at one blow."

It grieved the King to lose all his faithful servants for the sake of one man; he wished he had never set eyes on the tailor, and was quite ready to let him go. He did not dare, however, to give him his dismissal, for he was afraid that he would kill him and all his people, and place himself on the throne. He pondered over it for a long time, and at last he thought of a plan. He sent for the tailor, and said

273

that as he was so great a warrior, he would make him an offer. In a forest in his kingdom lived two giants, who, by robbery, murder, burning, and laying waste, did much harm. No one dared approach them without being in danger of his life. If he could subdue and kill these two giants, he would give him his only daughter to be his wife, and half his kingdom as a dowry; also he would give him a hundred horsemen to accompany and help him.

"That would be something for a man like me," thought the tailor. "A beautiful Princess and half a kingdom are not offered to one every day." "Oh yes," was his answer, "I will soon subdue the giants, and that without the hundred horsemen. He who slays seven at a blow need not fear two." The tailor set out at once, accompanied by the hundred horsemen, but when he came to the edge of the forest, he said to his followers, "Wait here, I will soon make an end of the giants by myself."

Then he disappeared into the wood; he looked about to the right and to the left. Before long he espied both the giants lying under a tree fast asleep, and snoring. Their snores were so tremendous that they made the branches of the tree dance up and down. The tailor, who was no fool, filled his pockets with stones, and climbed up the tree. When he got halfway up, he slipped on to a branch just above the sleepers, and then hurled the stones, one after another, on to one of them.

It was some time before the giant noticed anything; then he woke up, pushed his companion, and said, "What are you hitting me for?"

"You're dreaming," said the other. "I didn't hit you." They went to sleep again, and the tailor threw a stone at the other one. "What's that?" he cried. "What are you throwing at me?"

"I'm not throwing anything," answered the first one, with a growl.

They quarreled over it for a time, but as they were sleepy, they made it up, and their eyes closed again.

The tailor began his game again, picked out his biggest stone, and threw it at the first giant as hard as he could.

"This is too bad," said the giant, flying up like a madman. He pushed his companion against the tree with such violence that it shook. The other paid him back in the same coin, and they worked themselves up into such a rage that they tore up trees by the roots, and hacked at each other till they both fell dead upon the ground.

Then the tailor jumped down from his perch. "It was very lucky," he said, "that they did not tear up the tree I was sitting on, or I should have had to spring on to another like a squirrel, but we are nimble fellows." He drew his sword, and gave each of the giants two or three cuts in the chest. Then he went out to the horsemen, and said, "The work is done. I have given both of them the finishing stroke, but it was a difficult job. In their distress they tore trees up by the root to defend themselves, but all that's no good when a man like me comes, who slays seven at a blow."

"Are you not wounded?" then asked the horsemen.

"There was no danger," answered the tailor. "Not a hair of my head was touched."

The horsemen would not believe him, and rode into the forest to see. There, right enough, lay the giants in pools of blood, and round about them, the uprooted trees.

The tailor now demanded his promised reward from the King, but he, in the meantime, had repented of this promise, and was again trying to think of a plan to shake him off.

"Before I give you my daughter and the half of my kingdom, you must perform one more doughty deed. There is a unicorn that runs about in the forests doing vast damage; you must capture it."

"I have even less fear of one unicorn than of two giants. Seven at one stroke is my style." He took a rope and an axe, and went into the wood, and told his followers to stay outside. He did not have long to wait. The unicorn soon appeared, and dashed towards the tailor, as if it meant to run him through with its horn on the spot. "Softly, softly," cried the tailor. "Not so fast." He stood still, and waited till the animal got quite near, and then he very nimbly dodged behind a tree. The unicorn rushed at the tree, and ran its horn so hard into the trunk that it had not strength to pull it out again, and so it was caught. "Now I have the prey," said the tailor, coming from behind the tree. He fastened the rope round the creature's neck, and, with his axe, released the horn from the tree. When this was done he led the animal away, and took it to the King.

Still the King would not give him the promised reward, but made a third demand of him. Before the marriage, the tailor must catch a boar that did much damage in the woods. The huntsmen were to help him.

"Willingly," said the tailor. "That will be mere child's play."

He did not take the huntsmen into the wood with him, at which they were well pleased, for they had already more than once had such a reception from the boar that they had no wish to encounter him again. When the boar saw the tailor, it flew at him with foaming mouth, and, gnashing its teeth, tried to throw him to the ground, but the nimble hero darted into a little chapel that stood near. He jumped out again immediately by the window. The boar rushed in after the tailor; but he by this time was hopping about outside, and quickly shut the door upon the boar. So the raging animal was caught, for it was far too heavy and clumsy to jump out of the window. The tailor called the huntsmen up to see the captive with their own eyes.

The hero then went to the King, who was now obliged to keep his word, whether he liked it or not, so he handed over his daughter and half his kingdom to him. Had he known that it was no warrior but only a tailor who stood before him, he would have taken it even more to heart. The marriage was held with much pomp, but little joy, and a King was made out of a tailor.

After a time the young Queen heard her husband talking in his sleep, and saying, "Apprentice, bring me the waistcoat, and patch the trousers, or I will break the yard measure over your head." So in this manner she discovered the young gentleman's origin. In the morning she complained to the King, and begged him to rid her of a husband who was nothing more than a tailor.

The King comforted her, and said, "Tonight, leave your bedroom door open. My servants shall stand outside, and when he is asleep they shall go in and bind him. They shall then carry him away, and put him on board a ship which will take him far away."

The lady was satisfied with this, but the tailor's armor-bearer, who was attached to his young lord, told him the whole plot.

"I will put a stop to their plan," said the tailor.

At night he went to bed as usual with his wife. When she thought he was asleep, she got up, opened the door, and went to bed again. The tailor, who had only pretended to be asleep, began to cry out in a clear voice, "Apprentice, bring me the waistcoat, and you patch the trousers, or I will break the yard measure over your head. I have slain seven at a blow, killed two giants, led captive a unicorn, and caught a boar; should I be afraid of those who are standing outside my chamber door?"

When they heard the tailor speaking like this, the servants were overcome by fear, and ran away as if wild animals were after them, and none of them would venture near him again.

So the tailor remained a King till the day of his death.

THE GOLDEN BIRD

ALONG TIME AGO THERE was a King who had a lovely
pleasure-garden round his palace, and in it stood a tree that
bore golden apples. When the apples were nearly ripe they
were counted, but the very next morning one was missing.

This was reported to the King, and he ordered a watch to be set
every night under the tree.

The King had three sons, and he sent the eldest into the garden
at nightfall. But by midnight he was overcome with sleep, and in
the morning another apple was missing.

On the following night the second son had to keep watch, but
he fared no better. When the clock struck twelve, he too was fast
asleep, and in the morning another apple was gone.

The turn to watch now came to the third son. He was quite
ready, but the King had not much confidence in him, and thought
that he would accomplish even less than his brothers. At last, however, he gave his permission. So the youth lay down under the tree
to watch, determined not to let sleep get the mastery over him.

As the clock struck twelve there was a rustling in the air, and by
the light of the moon he saw a bird, whose shining feathers were of
pure gold. The bird settled on the tree, and was just plucking an
apple when the young Prince shot an arrow at it. The bird flew
away, but the arrow hit its plumage, and one of the golden feathers
fell to the ground. The Prince picked it up, and in the morning
took it to the King and told him all that he had seen in the night.

The King assembled his council, and everybody declared that a feather like that was worth more than the whole kingdom. "If the feather is worth so much," said the King, "one will not satisfy me; I must and will have the whole bird."

The eldest, relying on his cleverness, set out in search of the bird, and thought that he would be sure to find it soon.

When he had gone some distance he saw a fox sitting by the edge of a wood; he raised his gun and aimed at it. The fox cried out, "Do not shoot me, and I will give you some good advice. You are going to look for the Golden Bird; you will come to a village at nightfall, where you will find two inns opposite each other. One of them will be brightly lighted, and there will be noise and revelry going on in it. Be sure you do not choose that one, but go into the other, even if you don't like the look of it so well."

"How can a stupid animal like that give me good advice?" thought the King's son, and he pulled the trigger, but missed the fox, who turned tail and made off into the wood.

Thereupon the Prince continued his journey, and at nightfall reached the village with the two inns. Singing and dancing were going on in the one, and the other had a poverty-stricken and decayed appearance.

"I should be a fool," he said, "if I were to go to that miserable place with this good one so near."

So he went into the noisy one, and lived there in rioting and revelry, forgetting the bird, his father, and all his good counsels.

When some time had passed and the eldest son did not come back, the second prepared to start in quest of the Golden Bird. He met the fox, as the eldest son had done, and it gave him the same good advice, of which he took just as little heed.

He came to the two inns, and saw his brother standing at the window of the one whence sounds of revelry proceeded. He could not withstand his brother's calling, so he went in and gave himself up to a life of pleasure.

Again some time passed, and the King's youngest son wanted to

go out to try his luck. But his father would not let him go.

"It is useless," he said. "He will be even less able to find the Golden Bird than his brothers, and when any ill luck overtakes him, he will not be able to help himself; he has no backbone."

But at last, because he gave him no peace, he let him go. The fox again sat at the edge of the wood, begged for its life, and give its good advice. The Prince was good-natured, and said, "Be calm, little fox, I will do you no harm."

"You won't repent it," answered the fox. "And so that you may get along faster, come and mount on my tail."

No sooner had he seated himself than the fox began to run, and away they flew over stock and stone, at such a pace that his hair whistled in the wind.

When they reached the village, the Prince dismounted, and following the good advice of the fox, he went straight to the mean inn without looking about him, and there he passed a peaceful night. In the morning when he went out into the fields, there sat the fox, who said, "I will now tell you what you must do next. Walk straight on till you come to a castle, in front of which a whole regiment of soldiers is encamped. Don't be afraid of them; they will all be asleep and snoring. Walk through the midst of them straight into the castle, and through all the rooms, and at last you will reach an apartment where the Golden Bird will be hanging in a common wooden cage. A golden cage stands near it for show, but beware! Whatever you do, you must not take the bird out of the wooden cage to put it into the other, or it will be the worse for you."

After these words the fox again stretched out his tail, and the Prince took his seat on it, and away they flew over stock and stone, till his hair whistled in the wind.

When he arrived at the castle, he found everything just as the fox had said.

The Prince went to the room where the Golden Bird hung in the wooden cage, with a golden cage standing by, and the three golden apples were scattered about the room. He thought it would be absurd to leave the beautiful bird in the common old cage, so he opened the door, caught it, and put it into the golden cage. But as he did it, the bird uttered a piercing shriek. The soldiers woke up, rushed in, and carried him away to prison. Next morning he was taken before a judge, and, as he confessed all, he was sentenced to death. The King, however, said that he would spare his life on one condition, and this was that he should bring him the Golden Horse that runs faster than the wind. In addition, he should have the Golden Bird as a reward.

So the Prince set off with many sighs; he was very sad, for where was he to find the Golden Horse?

Then suddenly he saw his old friend the fox sitting on the road. "Now you see," said the fox, "all this has happened because you did not listen to me. All the same, keep up your spirits; I will protect you and tell you how to find the Golden Horse. You must keep straight along the road, and you will come to a palace, in the stable of which stands the Golden Horse. The grooms will be lying round the stable, but they will be fast asleep and snoring, and you can safely lead the horse through them. Only, one thing you must beware of. Put the old saddle of wood and leather upon it, and not the golden one hanging near, or you will rue it."

Then the fox stretched out his tail, the Prince took his seat, and away they flew over stock and stone, till his hair whistled in the wind.

Everything happened just as the fox had said. The Prince came to the stable where the Golden Horse stood, but when he was about to put the old saddle on its back, he thought, "Such a beautiful animal will be disgraced if I don't put the good saddle upon him, as he deserves." Hardly had the golden saddle touched the horse than he began neighing loudly. The grooms awoke, seized the Prince, and threw him into a dungeon.

The next morning he was taken before a judge, and condemned to death; but the King promised to spare his life, and give him the Golden Horse as well, if he could bring him the beautiful Princess out of the golden palace. With a heavy heart the Prince set out, when to his delight he soon met the faithful fox.

"I ought to leave you to your fate," he said. "But I will have pity on you and once more help you out of your trouble. Your road leads straight to the golden palace—you will reach it in the evening; and at night, when everything is quiet, the beautiful Princess will go to the bathroom to take a bath. As she goes along, spring forward and give her a kiss, and she will follow you. Lead her away with you. Only on no account allow her to bid her parents good-bye, or it will go badly with you."

Again the fox stretched out his tail, the Prince seated himself upon it, and off they flew over stock and stone, till his hair whistled in the wind.

When he got to the palace, it was just as the fox had said. He waited till midnight, and when the whole palace was wrapped in sleep, and the maiden went to take a bath, he sprang forward and gave her a kiss. She said she was quite willing to go with him, but she implored him to let her say good-bye to her parents. At first he refused; but as she cried, and fell at his feet, at last he gave her leave. Hardly had the maiden stepped up to her father's bed, when he and every one else in the palace woke up. The Prince was seized, and thrown into prison.

Next morning the King said to him, "Your life is forfeited, and it can only be spared if you clear away the mountain in front of my window, which shuts out the view. It must be done in eight days, and if you accomplish the task you shall have my daughter as a reward."

So the Prince began his labors, and he dug and shoveled without ceasing. On the seventh day, when he saw how little he had done, he became very sad, and gave up all hope. However, in the evening the fox appeared and said, "You do not deserve any help from me, but lie down and go to sleep; I will do the work." In the morning when he woke and looked out of the window, the mountain had disappeared.

Overjoyed, the Prince hurried to the King and told him that his condition was fulfilled, and, whether he liked it or not, he must keep his word and give him his daughter.

So they both went away together, and before long the faithful fox joined them.

"You certainly have got the best thing of all," said he. "But to the maiden of the golden palace the Golden Horse belongs."

"How am I to get it?" asked the Prince.

"Oh! I will tell you that," answered the fox. "First take the beautiful maiden to the King who sent you to the golden palace. There will be great joy when you appear, and they will bring out the Golden Horse to you. Mount it at once, and shake hands with everybody, last of all with the beautiful maiden; and when you have taken her hand firmly, pull her up beside you with a swing and gallop away. No one will be able to catch you, for the horse goes faster than the wind."

All this was successfully done, and the Prince carried off the beautiful maiden on the Golden Horse.

The fox was not far off, and he said to the Prince, "Now I will help you to get the Golden Bird, too. When you approach the castle where the Golden Bird lives, let the maiden dismount, and I will take care of her. Then ride with the Golden Horse into the courtyard of the castle; there will be great rejoicing when they see you, and they will bring out the Golden Bird to you. As soon as you have the cage in your hand, gallop back to us and take up the maiden again."

When these plans had succeeded, and the Prince was ready to ride on with all his treasures, the fox said to him, "Now you must reward me for my help."

"What do you want?" asked the Prince.

"When you reach that wood, shoot me dead and cut off my head and my paws."

"That would indeed be gratitude!" said the Prince. "I can't possibly promise to do such a thing."

The fox said, "If you won't do it, I must leave you; but before I go I will give you one more piece of advice. Beware of two things— buy no gallows-birds, and don't sit on the edge of a well." Saying which, he ran off into the wood.

The Prince thought, "That is a strange animal; what whims he has. Who on earth would want to buy gallows-birds! And the desire to sit on the edge of a well has never yet seized me!"

He rode on with the beautiful maiden, and the road led him through the village where his two brothers had stayed behind. There was a great hubbub in the village, and when he asked what it was about, he was told that two persons were going to be hanged.

When he got nearer he saw that they were his brothers, who had wasted their possessions and done all sorts of evil deeds. He asked if they could not be set free.

"Yes, if you'll ransom them," answered the people. "But why will you throw your money away in buying off such wicked people?"

He did not stop to reflect, however, but paid the ransom for them, and when they were set free they all journeyed on together.

They came to the wood where they had first met the fox. It was deliciously cool there, while the sun was broiling outside, so the two brothers said, "Let us sit down here by the well to rest a little and eat and drink." The Prince agreed, and during the conversation he forgot what he was about, and, never dreaming of any foul play, seated himself on the edge of the well. But his two brothers threw him backwards into it, and went home to their father, taking with them the maiden, the horse, and the bird.

"Here we bring you not only the Golden Bird, but the Golden Horse, and the maiden from the golden palace, as our booty."

Thereupon there was great rejoicing; but the horse would not eat, the bird would not sing, and the maiden sat and wept all day.

The youngest brother had not perished, however. Happily the well was dry, and he fell upon soft moss without taking any harm. Only, he could not get out.

Even in this great strait the faithful fox did not forsake him, but came leaping down and scolded him for not taking his advice. "I can't leave you to your fate, though. I must help you to get back to the light of day." He told him to take tight hold of his tail, and then he dragged him up. "You are not out of every danger even now," said the fox. "Your brothers were not sure of your death, so they have set watchers all over the wood to kill you if they see you."

A poor old man was sitting by the roadside, and the Prince exchanged clothes with him, and by this means he succeeded in reaching the King's court.

Nobody recognized him, but the bird began to sing, the horse began to eat, and the beautiful maiden left off crying.

In astonishment the King asked, "What does all this mean?"

The maiden answered, "I do not know. But I was very sad, and now I am gay. It seems to me that my true bridegroom must have come."

She told the King all that had happened, although the two brothers had threatened her with death if she betrayed anything. The King ordered every person in the palace to be brought before him. Among them came the Prince disguised as an old man in all his rags, but the maiden knew him at once, and fell on his neck. The wicked brothers were seized and put to death, but the Prince was married to the beautiful maiden, and proclaimed heir to the King.

But what became of the poor fox? Long afterwards, when the Prince went out into the fields one day, he met the fox, who said, "You have everything that you can desire, but there is no end to my misery. It still lies in your power to release me." And again he implored the Prince to shoot him dead, and to cut off his head and his paws.

At last the Prince consented to do as he was asked, and no sooner was it done than the fox was changed into a man, no other than the brother of the beautiful Princess, at last set free from the evil spell which so long had lain upon him.

There was nothing now wanting to their happiness for the rest of their lives.

THE MOUSE,
THE BIRD, AND THE SAUSAGE

ONCE UPON A TIME, a mouse, a bird, and a sausage went into partnership. They kept house together long and amicably, and thus had increased their possessions. It was the bird's work to fly to the forest every day and bring back wood. The mouse had to carry water, make up the fire, and set the table, while the sausage did the cooking.

Whoever is too well off is always eager for something new.

One day the bird met a friend, to whom it sang the praises of its comfortable circumstances. But the other bird scolded it, and called it a poor creature who did all the hard work, while the other two had an easy time at home. For when the mouse had made up the fire, and carried the water, she betook herself to her little room to rest till she was called to lay the table. The sausage only had to stay by the hearth and take care that the food was nicely cooked. When it was nearly dinnertime, she passed herself once or twice through the broth and the vegetables, and they were then buttered, salted, and flavored, ready to eat. Then the bird came home, laid his burden aside, and they all sat down to table, and after their meal they slept their fill till morning. It was indeed a delightful life.

Another day the bird, owing to the instigations of his friend, declined to go and fetch any more wood, saying that he had been drudge long enough, and had only been their dupe. They must now make a change and try some other arrangement.

In spite of the fervent entreaties of the mouse and the sausage, the bird got his way. They decided to draw lots, and the lot fell on

the sausage, who was to carry the wood. The mouse became cook, and the bird was to fetch water.

What was the result?

The sausage went out into the forest, the bird made up the fire, while the mouse put on the pot and waited alone for the sausage to come home, bringing wood for the next day. But the sausage stayed away so long that the other two suspected something wrong, and the bird flew out to take the air in the hope of meeting her. Not far off he fell in with a dog which had met the poor sausage and fallen upon her as lawful prey, seized her, and quickly swallowed her.

The bird complained bitterly to the dog of his barefaced robbery, but it was no good, for the dog said he had found forged letters on the sausage, whereby her life was forfeit to him.

The bird took the wood and flew sadly home with it, and related what he had seen and heard. They were much upset, but they determined to do the best they could and stay together. So the bird laid the table, and the mouse prepared their meal. She tried to cook it, and, like the sausage, to dip herself in the vegetables so as to flavor them. But before she got well into the midst of them she came to a standstill, and in the attempt lost her hair, skin, and life itself.

When the bird came back and wanted to serve up the meal,

there was no cook to be seen. The bird in his agitation threw the wood about, called and searched everywhere, but could not find his cook. Then, owing to his carelessness, the wood caught fire and there was a blaze. The bird hastened to fetch water, but the bucket fell into the well and the bird with it; he could not recover himself, and so he was drowned.

RED RIDING HOOD

THERE WAS ONCE A SWEET little maiden, who was loved by all who knew her, but she was especially dear to her grandmother, who did not know how to make enough of the child. Once she gave her a little red velvet cloak. It was so becoming, and she liked it so much, that she would never wear anything else, and so she got the name of Red Riding Hood.

One day her mother said to her, "Come here, Red Riding Hood, take this cake and a bottle of wine to Grandmother. She is weak and ill, and they will do her good. Go quickly, before it gets hot, and don't loiter by the way, or run, or you will fall down and break the bottle, and there would be no wine for Grandmother. When you get there, don't forget to say 'Good morning' prettily, without staring about you."

"I will do just as you tell me," Red Riding Hood promised her mother.

Her grandmother lived away in the woods, a good half-hour from the village. When she got to the wood, she met a wolf. But Red Riding Hood did not know what a wicked animal he was, so she was not a bit afraid of him.

"Good morning, Red Riding Hood," he said.

"Good morning, wolf," she answered.

"Whither away so early, Red Riding Hood?"

"To Grandmother's."

"What have you got in your basket?"

"Cake and wine. We baked yesterday, so I'm taking a cake to

Granny. She wants something to make her well."

"Where does your grandmother live, Red Riding Hood?"

"A good quarter of an hour further into the wood. Her house stands under three big oak trees, near a hedge of nut trees which you must know," said Red Riding Hood.

The wolf thought, "This tender little creature will be a plump morsel. She will be nicer than the old woman. I must be cunning, and snap them both up."

He walked along with Red Riding Hood for a while, then he said, "Look at the pretty flowers, Red Riding Hood. Why don't you look about you? I don't believe you even hear the birds sing, you are just as solemn as if you were going to school. Everything else is so gay out here in the woods."

Red Riding Hood raised her eyes, and when she saw the sunlight dancing through the trees, and all the bright flowers, she thought, "I'm sure Granny would be pleased if I took her a bunch of fresh flowers. It is still quite early; I shall have plenty of time to pick them."

So she left the path, and wandered off among the trees to pick the flowers. Each time she picked one, she always saw another prettier one further on. So she went deeper and deeper into the forest.

In the meantime the wolf went straight off to the grandmother's cottage, and knocked at the door.

"Who is there?"

"Red Riding Hood, bringing you a cake and some wine. Open the door!"

"Press the latch!" cried the old woman. "I am too weak to get up."

The wolf pressed the latch, and the door sprang open. He went straight in and up to the bed without saying a word, and ate up the poor old woman. Then he put on her nightdress and nightcap, got into bed, and drew the curtains.

Red Riding Hood ran about picking flowers till she could carry no more, and then she remembered her grandmother again. She was astonished when she got to the house to find the door open, and when she entered the room everything seemed so strange.

She felt quite frightened, but she did not know why. "Generally I like coming to see Grandmother so much," she thought. She cried, "Good morning, Grandmother," but she received no answer.

Then she went up to the bed and drew the curtains back. There lay her grandmother, but she had drawn her cap down over her face, and she looked very odd.

"O Grandmother, what big ears you have got," she said.

"The better to hear with, my dear."

"Grandmother, what big eyes you have got."

"The better to see with, my dear."

"What big hands you have got, Grandmother."

"The better to catch hold of you with, my dear."

"But, Grandmother, what big teeth you have got."

"The better to eat you up with, my dear."

Hardly had the wolf said this, than he made a spring out of bed, and devoured poor little Red Riding Hood. When the wolf had satisfied himself, he went back to bed and he was soon snoring loudly.

A huntsman went past the house, and thought, "How loudly the old lady is snoring. I must see if there is anything the matter with her."

So he went into the house, and up to the bed, where he found the wolf fast asleep. "Do I find you here, you old sinner?" he said. "Long enough have I sought you."

He raised his gun to shoot, when it just occurred to him that perhaps the wolf had eaten up the old lady, and that she might still be saved. So he took a knife and began cutting open the sleeping wolf. At the first cut he saw the little red cloak, and after a few more slashes, the little girl sprang out, and cried, "Oh, how frightened I was, it was so dark inside the wolf!" Next the old grandmother came out, alive, but hardly able to breathe.

Red Riding Hood brought some big stones with which they

filled the wolf, so that when he woke and tried to spring away, they dragged him back, and he fell down dead.

They were all quite happy now. The huntsman skinned the wolf, and took the skin home. The grandmother ate the cake and drank the wine that Red Riding Hood had brought, and she soon felt quite strong. Red Riding Hood thought, "I will never again wander off into the forest as long as I live, if my mother forbids it."

THE ROBBER BRIDEGROOM

T HERE WAS ONCE A MILLER, who had a beautiful daughter.
When she grew up, he wanted to have her married and settled. He thought, "If a suitable bridegroom come and ask
for my daughter, I will give her to him."

Soon after a suitor came who appeared to be rich, and as the
miller knew nothing against him he promised his daughter to him.
The maiden, however, did not like him as a bride ought to like her
bridegroom, nor had she any faith in him. Whenever she looked at
him, or thought about him, a shudder came over her. One day he
said to her, "You are my betrothed, and yet you have never been to
see me."

The maiden answered, "I don't even know where your house is."

Then the bridegroom said, "My house is in the depths of the
forest."

She made excuses, and said she could not find the way.

The bridegroom answered, "Next Sunday you must come and
see me without fail. I have invited some other guests, and, so that
you may be able to find the way, I will strew some ashes to guide
you."

When Sunday came, and the maiden was about to start, she was
frightened, though she did not know why. So that she should be
sure of finding her way back she filled her pockets with peas and
lentils. At the entrance to the forest she found the track of ashes,
and followed it, but every step or two she scattered a few peas right
and left.

She walked nearly the whole day, right into the midst of the forest, where it was almost dark. Here she saw a solitary house, which she did not like. It was so dark and dismal. She went in, but found nobody, and there was dead silence. Suddenly a voice cried—

> "Turn back, turn back, thou bonnie bride,
> Nor in this house of death abide."

The maiden looked up, and saw that the voice came from a bird in a cage hanging on the wall. Once more it made the same cry—

> "Turn back, turn back, thou bonnie bride,
> Nor in this house of death abide."

The beautiful bride went from room to room, all over the house, but they were all empty; not a soul was to be seen. At last she reached the cellar, and there she found an old, old woman with a shaking head.

"Can you tell me if my bridegroom lives here?"

"Alas! poor child," answered the old woman, "little do you know where you are; you are in a murderer's den. You thought you were about to be married, but death will be your marriage. See here, I have had to fill this kettle with water, and when they have you in their power they will kill you without mercy, cook, and eat you, for they are eaters of human flesh. Unless I take pity on you and save you, you are lost." Then the old woman led her behind a great cask, where she could not be seen. "Be as quiet as a mouse," she said. "Don't stir, or all will be lost. Tonight, when the murderers are asleep, we will fly. I have long waited for an opportunity."

Hardly had she said this when the riotous crew came home. They dragged another maiden with them, but as they were quite drunk they paid no attention to her shrieks and lamentations. They gave her wine to drink, three glasses full—red, white, and yellow. After she had drunk them she fell down dead. The poor bride hidden behind the cask was terrified; she trembled and shivered, for she saw plainly to what fate she was destined.

One of the men noticed a gold ring on the little finger of the murdered girl, and as he could not pull it off he took an axe and chopped the finger off, but it sprang up into the air, and fell right into the lap of the bride behind the cask. The man took a light to look for it, but he could not find it. One of the others said, "Have you looked behind the big cask?"

But the old woman called out, "Come and eat, and leave the search till tomorrow; the finger won't run away."

The murderer said, "The old woman is right," and they gave up the search and sat down to supper. But the old woman dropped a sleeping draught into their wine, so they soon lay down, went to sleep, and snored lustily.

When the bride heard them snoring she came out from behind the cask, but she was obliged to step over the sleepers, as they lay in rows upon the floor. She was dreadfully afraid of touching them, but God helped her, and she got through without mishap. The old woman went with her and opened the door, and they hurried away as quickly as they could from this vile den.

All the ashes had been blown away by the wind, but the peas and lentils had taken root and shot up, and showed them the way in the moonlight.

They walked the whole night, and reached the mill in the morning. The maiden told her father all that she had been through.

When the day which had been fixed for the wedding came, the bridegroom appeared, and the miller invited all his friends and relations. As they sat at table, each one was asked to tell some story. The bride was very silent, but when it came to her turn, and the bridegroom said, "Come, my love, have you nothing to say? Pray tell us something," she answered:

"I will tell you a dream I have had. I was walking alone in a wood, and I came to a solitary house where not a soul was to be seen. A cage was hanging on the wall of one of the rooms, and in it there was a bird that cried—

"Turn back, turn back, thou bonnie bride,
Nor in this house of death abide.

It repeated the same words twice. This was only a dream, my love! I walked through all the rooms, but they were all empty and dismal. At last I went down to the cellar, and there sat a very old woman, with a shaking head. I asked her, 'Does my bridegroom live here?' She answered, 'Alas, you poor child, you are in a murderer's den! Your bridegroom indeed lives here, but he will cut you to pieces, cook you, and eat you.' This was only a dream, my love! Then the old woman hid me behind a cask, and hardly had she done so when the murderers came home, dragging a maiden with them. They gave her three kinds of wine to drink—red, white, and yellow, and after drinking them she fell down dead. My love, I was only dreaming this! Then they took her things off and cut her to pieces. My love, I was only dreaming! One of the murderers saw a gold ring on the girl's little finger, and, as he could not pull it off, he chopped off the finger, but the finger bounded into the air, and fell behind the cask on to my lap. Here is the finger with the ring."

At these words she produced the finger and showed it to the company.

When the bridegroom heard these words, he turned as pale as ashes, and tried to escape, but the guests seized him and handed him over to justice. And he and all his band were executed for their crimes.

TOM THUMB

A POOR PEASANT SAT ONE evening by his hearth and poked the fire, while his wife sat opposite spinning. He said, "What a sad thing it is that we have no children. Our home is so quiet, while other folk's houses are noisy and cheerful."

"Yes," answered his wife, and she sighed. "Even if it were an only one, and if it were no bigger than my thumb, I should be quite content. We would love it with all our hearts."

Now, some time after this, she had a little boy who was strong and healthy, but was no bigger than a thumb. Then they said, "Well, our wish is fulfilled, and, small as he is, we will love him dearly"; and because of his tiny stature they called him Tom Thumb. They let him want for nothing, yet still the child grew no bigger, but remained the same size as when he was born. Still, he looked out on the world with intelligent eyes, and soon showed himself a clever and agile creature, who was lucky in all he attempted.

One day, when the peasant was preparing to go into the forest to cut wood, he said to himself, "I wish I had some one to bring the cart after me."

"O Father!" said Tom Thumb, "I will soon bring it. You leave it to me; it shall be there at the appointed time."

Then the peasant laughed, and said, "How can that be? You are much too small even to hold the reins."

"That doesn't matter, if only Mother will harness the horse," answered Tom. "I will sit in his ear and tell him where to go."

"Very well," said the father. "We will try it for once."

When the time came, the mother harnessed the horse, set Tom in his ear, and then the little creature called out, "Gee-up" and "Whoa" in turn, and directed it where to go. It went quite well, just as though it were being driven by its master; and they went the right way to the wood. Now it happened that while the cart was turning a corner, and Tom was calling to the horse, two strange men appeared on the scene.

"My goodness," said one, "what is this? There goes a cart, and a driver is calling to the horse, but there is nothing to be seen."

"There is something queer about this," said the other. "We will follow the cart and see where it stops."

The cart went on deep into the forest, and arrived quite safely at the place where the wood was cut.

When Tom spied his father, he said, "You see, Father, here I am with the cart; now lift me down." The father held the horse with his left hand, and took his little son out of its ear with the right. Then Tom sat down quite happily on a straw.

When the two strangers noticed him, they did not know what to say for astonishment.

Then one drew the other aside, and said, "Listen, that little creature might make our fortune if we were to show him in the town for money. We will buy him."

So they went up to the peasant, and said, "Sell us the little man. He shall be well looked after with us."

"No," said the peasant. "He is the delight of my eyes, and I will not sell him for all the gold in the world."

But Tom Thumb, when he heard the bargain, crept up by the folds of his father's coat, placed himself on his shoulder, and whispered in his ear, "Father, let me go. I will soon come back again."

Then his father gave him to the two men for a fine piece of gold.

"Where will you sit?" they asked him.

"Oh, put me on the brim of your hat, then I can walk up and down and observe the neighborhood without falling down."

They did as he wished, and when Tom had said good-bye to his father, they went away with him.

They walked on till it was twilight, when the little man said, "You must lift me down."

"Stay where you are," answered the man on whose head he sat.

"No," said Tom. "I will come down. Lift me down immediately."

The man took off his hat and set the little creature in a field by the wayside. He jumped and crept about for a time, here and there among the sods, then slipped suddenly into a mouse-hole which he had discovered.

"Good evening, gentlemen, just you go home without me," he called out to them in mockery.

They ran about and poked with sticks into the mouse-hole, but all in vain. Tom crept further and further back, and, as it soon got quite dark, they were forced to go home, full of anger, and with empty purses.

When Tom noticed that they were gone, he crept out of his underground hiding-place again. "It is dangerous walking in this field in the dark," he said. "One might easily break one's leg or one's neck." Luckily, he came to an empty snail shell. "Thank goodness," he said. "I can pass the night in safety here," and he sat down.

Not long after, just when he was about to go to sleep, he heard two men pass by. One said, "How shall we set about stealing the rich parson's gold and silver?"

"I can tell you," interrupted Tom.

"What was that?" said one robber in a fright. "I heard some one speak."

They remained standing and listened.

Then Tom spoke again, "Take me with you and I will help you."

"Where are you?" they asked.

"Just look on the ground and see where the voice comes from," he answered.

At last the thieves found him, and lifted him up. "You little urchin, are *you* going to help us?"

"Yes," he said. "I will creep between the iron bars in the pastor's room, and will hand out to you what you want."

"All right," they said, "we will see what you can do."

When they came to the parsonage, Tom crept into the room, but called out immediately with all his strength to the others, "Do you want anything that is here?"

The thieves were frightened, and said, "Do speak softly, and don't wake any one."

But Tom pretended not to understand, and called out again, "What do you want? Everything?"

The cook, who slept above, heard him and sat up in bed and listened. But the thieves were so frightened that they retreated a little way. At last they summoned up courage again, and thought to themselves, "The little rogue wants to tease us." So they came back and whispered to him, "Now, do be serious, and hand us out something."

Then Tom called out again, as loud as he could, "I will give you everything if only you will hold out your hands."

The maid, who was listening intently, heard him quite distinctly, jumped out of bed, and stumbled to the door. The thieves turned and fled, running as though wild huntsmen were after them. But the maid, seeing nothing, went to get a light. When she came back with it, Tom, without being seen, slipped out into the barn, and the maid, after she had searched every corner and found nothing, went to bed again, thinking she had been dreaming with her eyes and ears open.

Tom Thumb climbed about in the hay, and found a splendid place to sleep. There he determined to rest till day came, and then to go home to his parents. But he had other experiences to go through first. This world is full of trouble and sorrow!

The maid got up in the grey dawn to feed the cows. First she went into the barn, where she piled up an armful of hay, the very

bundle in which poor Tom was asleep. But he slept so soundly that he knew nothing till he was almost in the mouth of the cow, who was eating him up with the hay.

"Heavens!" he said, "however did I get into this mill?" but he soon saw where he was, and the great thing was to avoid being crushed between the cow's teeth. At last, whether he liked it or not, he had to go down the cow's throat.

"The windows have been forgotten in this house," he said. "The sun does not shine into it, and no light has been provided."

Altogether he was very ill-pleased with his quarters, and, worst of all, more and more hay came in at the door, and the space grew narrower and narrower. At last he called out, in his fear, as loud as he could, "Don't give me any more food. Don't give me any more food."

The maid was just milking the cow, and when she heard the same voice as in the night, without seeing any one, she was frightened, and slipped from her stool and spilt the milk. Then, in the greatest haste, she ran to her master, and said, "Oh, your reverence, the cow has spoken!"

"You are mad," he answered, but he went into the stable himself to see what was happening.

Scarcely had he set foot in the cow-shed before Tom began again, "Don't bring me any more food."

Then the pastor was terrified too, and thought that the cow must be bewitched, so he ordered it to be killed. It was accordingly slaughtered, but the stomach, in which Tom was hidden, was thrown into the manure heap. Tom had the greatest trouble in working his way out. Just as he stuck out his head, a hungry wolf ran by and snapped up the whole stomach with one bite. But still Tom did not lose courage. "Perhaps the wolf will listen to reason," he said. So he called out, "Dear wolf, I know where you would find a magnificent meal."

"Where is it to be had?" asked the wolf.

"Why, in such and such a house," answered Tom. "You must squeeze through the grating of the storeroom window, and there you will find cakes, bacon, and sausages, as many as you can possibly eat," and he went on to describe his father's house.

The wolf did not wait to hear this twice, and at night forced himself in through the grating, and ate to his heart's content. When he was satisfied, he wanted to go away again, but he had grown so fat that he could not get out the same way. Tom had reckoned on this, and began to make a great commotion inside the wolf's body, struggling and screaming with all his might.

"Be quiet," said the wolf. "You will wake up the people of the house."

"All very fine," answered Tom. "You have eaten your fill, and now I am going to make merry," and he began to scream again with all his might.

At last his father and mother woke up, ran to the room, and looked through the crack of the door. When they saw a wolf, they went away, and the husband fetched his axe, and the wife a scythe.

"You stay behind," said the man, as they came into the room. "If my blow does not kill him, you must attack him and rip up his body."

When Tom Thumb heard his father's voice, he called out, "Dear Father, I am here, inside the wolf's body."

Full of joy, his father cried, "Heaven be praised! Our dear child is found again," and he bade his wife throw aside the scythe that it might not injure Tom.

Then he gathered himself together, and struck the wolf a blow on the head, so that it fell down lifeless. Then with knives and shears they ripped up the body, and took their little boy out.

"Ah," said his father, "what trouble we have been in about you."

"Yes, Father, I have traveled about the world, and I am thankful to breathe fresh air again."

"Wherever have you been?" they asked.

"Down a mouse-hole, in a cow's stomach, and in a wolf's maw," he answered. "And now I shall stay with you."

"And we will never sell you again, for all the riches in the world," they said, kissing and fondling their dear child.

Then they gave him good and drink, and had new clothes made for him, as his own had been spoilt in his travels.

RUMPELSTILTSKIN

THERE WAS ONCE A MILLER who was very poor, but he had a beautiful daughter. Now, it fell out that he had occasion to speak with the King, and, in order to give himself an air of importance, he said, "I have a daughter who can spin gold out of straw."

The King said to the miller, "That is an art in which I am much interested. If your daughter is as skillful as you say she is, bring her to my castle tomorrow, and I will put her to the test."

Accordingly, when the girl was brought to the castle, the King conducted her to a chamber which was quite full of straw, gave her a spinning-wheel and winder, and said, "Now, set to work, and if between tonight and tomorrow at dawn you have not spun this straw into gold you must die." Thereupon he carefully locked the door of the chamber, and she remained alone.

There sat the unfortunate miller's daughter, and for the life of her did not know what to do. She had not the least idea how to spin straw into gold, and she became more and more distressed, until at last she began to weep. Then all at once the door sprang open, and in stepped a little mannikin, who said, "Good evening, Mistress Miller, what are you weeping so for?"

"Alas!" answered the maiden, "I've got to spin gold out of straw, and don't know how to do it."

Then the mannikin said, "What will you give me if I spin it for you?"

"My necklace," said the maid.

The little man took the necklace, sat down before the spinning-wheel, and whir—whir—whir, in a trice the reel was full.

Then he fixed another reel, and whir—whir—whir, thrice round, and that too was full; and so it went on until morning, when all the straw was spun and all the reels were full of gold.

Immediately at sunrise the King came, and when he saw the gold he was astonished and much pleased, but his mind became only the more avaricious. So he had the miller's daughter taken to another chamber, larger than the former one, and full of straw, and he ordered her to spin it also in one night, as she valued her life.

The maiden was at her wit's end, and began to weep. Then again the door sprang open, and the little mannikin appeared, and said, "What will you give me if I spin the straw into gold for you?"

"The ring off my finger," answered the maiden.

The little man took the ring, began to whir again at the wheel, and had by morning spun all the straw into gold.

The King was delighted at the sight of the masses of gold, but was not even yet satisfied. So he had the miller's daughter taken to a still larger chamber, full of straw, and said, "This you must tonight spin into gold, but if you succeed you shall become my Queen." "Even if she is only a miller's daughter," thought he, "I shan't find a richer woman in the whole world."

When the girl was alone the little man came again, and said for the third time, "What will you give me if I spin the straw for you this time?"

"I have nothing more that I can give," answered the girl.

"Well, promise me your first child if you become Queen."

"Who knows what may happen," thought the miller's daughter, but she did not see any other way of getting out of the difficulty, so she promised the little man what he demanded, and in return he spun the straw into gold once more.

When the King came in the morning, and found everything as he had wished, he celebrated his marriage with her, and the miller's daughter became Queen.

About a year afterwards a beautiful child was born, but the Queen had forgotten all about the little man. However, he suddenly entered her chamber, and said, "Now, give me what you promised."

The Queen was terrified, and offered the little man all the wealth of the kingdom if he would let her keep the child. But the mannikin said, "No, I would rather have some living thing than all the treasures of the world." Then the Queen began to moan and weep to such an extent that the little man felt sorry for her. "I will give you three days," said he, "and if within that time you discover my name you shall keep the child."

Then during the night the Queen called to mind all the names that she had ever heard, and sent a messenger all over the country to inquire far and wide what other names there were. When the little man came on the next day, she began with Caspar, Melchoir, Balzer, and mentioned all the names that she knew, one after the other. But at every one the little man said, "No, that's not my name."

The second day she had inquiries made all round the neighborhood for the names of people living there, and suggested to the little man all the most unusual and strange names.

"Perhaps your name is Cowribs, Spindleshanks, or Spiderlegs?"

But he answered every time, "No, that's not my name."

On the third day the messenger came back and said, "I haven't been able to find any new names, but as I came round the corner of a wood on a lofty mountain, where the fox says good-night to the hare, I saw a little house, and in front of the house a fire was burning, and around the fire an indescribably ridiculous little man was leaping, hopping on one leg, and singing:

"'Today I bake, tomorrow I brew my beer;
The next day I will bring the Queen's child here.

> Ah! lucky 'tis that not a soul doth know
> That Rumpelstiltskin is my name, ho! ho!'"

Then you can imagine how delighted the Queen was when she heard the name, and when presently afterwards the little man came in and asked, "Now, your majesty, what is my name?" at first she asked:

"Is your name Tom?"

"No."

"Is it Dick?"

"No."

"Is it, by chance, Rumpelstiltskin?"

"The devil told you that! The devil told you that!" shrieked the little man, and in his rage stamped his right foot into the ground so deep that he sank up to his waist.

Then, in his passion, he seized his left leg with both hands, and tore himself asunder in the middle.

THE TWELVE HUNTSMEN

THERE WAS ONCE A PRINCE, who was betrothed to a maiden, the daughter of a King, whom he loved very much. One day when they were together, and very happy, a messenger came from the Prince's father, who was lying ill, to summon him home as he wished to see him before he died. He said to his beloved, "I must go away, and leave you now, but I give you this ring as a keepsake. When I am King, I will come and fetch you away."

Then he rode off, and when he got home he found his father on his deathbed. His father said, "My dear son, I wanted to see you once more before I die. Promise to marry the bride I have chosen for you," and he named a certain Princess.

His son was very sad, and without reflecting promised to do what his father wished, and thereupon the King closed his eyes and died.

Now, when the Prince had been proclaimed King, and the period of mourning was past, the time came when he had to keep his promise to his father. He made his offer to the Princess, and it was accepted. His betrothed heard of this, and grieved so much over his faithlessness that she very nearly died. The King her father asked, "Dear child, why are you so sad? You shall have whatever you desire."

She thought for a moment, then said, "Dear Father, I want eleven maidens all exactly like me in face, figure, and height."

The King said, "If it is possible, your wish shall be fulfilled."

Then he caused a search to be made all over his kingdom, till the eleven maidens were found, all exactly like his daughter. The

Princess ordered twelve huntsmen's dresses to be made, which she commanded the maidens to wear, putting on the twelfth herself. Then she took leave of her father, and rode away with the maidens to the court of her former bridegroom whom she loved so dearly. She asked him if he wanted any huntsmen, and whether he would take them all into his service. The King did not recognize her, but, as they were all so handsome, he said yes, he would engage them. So they all entered the King's service.

Now, the King had a lion which was a wonderful creature, for he knew all secret and hidden things. He said to the King one evening, "You fancy you have twelve huntsmen there, don't you?"

"Yes," said the King.

"You are mistaken," said the lion. "They are twelve maidens."

The King answered, "That can't be true! How can you prove it?"

"Oh, have some peas strewn in your anteroom tomorrow, and you will soon see. Men have a firm tread, and when they walk on peas they don't move, but maidens trip and trot and slide, and make the peas roll about."

The King was pleased with the lion's advice, and ordered the peas to be strewn on the floor.

There was, however, a servant of the King who favored the huntsmen, and when he heard that they were to be put to this test, he went and told them all about it, and said, "The lion is going to prove to the King that you are maidens."

The Princess thanked him, and said afterwards to her maidens, "Do your utmost to tread firmly on the peas."

Next morning, when the King ordered them to be called, they walked into the antechamber with so firm a tread that not a pea moved. When they had gone away, the King said to the lion, "You lied. They walked just like men."

But the lion answered, "They had been warned of the test, and were prepared for it. Just let twelve spinning-wheels be brought into the antechamber, and they will be delighted at the sight, as no man would be."

This plan also pleased the King, and he ordered the spinning-wheels. But again the kind servant warned the huntsmen of the plan. When they were alone, the Princess said to her maidens, "Control yourselves, and don't so much as look at the spinning-wheels."

When the King next morning sent for the huntsmen, they walked through the antechamber without even glancing at the spinning-wheels.

The the King said to the lion, "You lied to me. They *are* men; they never looked at the spinning-wheels."

The lion answered, "They knew that they were on their trial, and restrained themselves."

But the King would not believe him any more.

The twelve huntsmen always went with the King on his hunting expeditions, and the longer he had them, the better he liked them. Now, it happened one day when they were out hunting, that the news came of the royal bride's approach.

When the true bride heard it, the shock was so great that her heart nearly stopped, and she fell down in a dead faint. The King, thinking something had happened to his favorite huntsman, ran to help him, and pulled off his glove. Then he saw the ring that he had given to his first betrothed, and when he looked her in the face he recognized her. He was so moved that he kissed her, and when she opened her eyes he said, "You are mine, and I am yours, and nobody in the world shall separate us."

Then he sent a messenger to the other bride, and begged her to go home, as he already had a wife, and he who has an old dish does not need a new one. Their marriage was then celebrated, and the lion was taken into favor again, as, after all, he had spoken the truth.

THE LITTLE PEASANT

THERE WAS ONCE A VILLAGE in which there was only one poor peasant; all the others were very well-to-do, so they called him the Little Peasant. He had not even got a single cow, far less money with which to buy one, though he and his wife would have been so glad to possess one.

One day he said to his wife, "Look here, I have a good idea. There is my godfather, the joiner, he shall make us a wooden calf and paint it brown, so that it looks like a real one, and perhaps some day it will grow into a cow."

This plan pleased his wife, so his godfather, the joiner, cut out and carved the calf and painted it properly, and made its head bent down to look as if it were eating.

Next morning, when the cows were driven out, the Little Peasant called the cowherd in, and said, "Look here, I have a little calf, but it is very small and has to be carried."

The cowherd said, "All right," took it in his arms, carried it to the meadow, and put it down in the grass.

The calf stood there all day and appeared to be eating, and the cowherd said, "It will soon be able to walk by itself; see how it eats."

In the evening, when he was going home, he said to the calf, "If you can stand there all day and eat your fill, you may just walk home on your own legs, I don't mean to carry you!"

But the Little Peasant was standing by his door waiting for the calf, and when the cowherd came through the village without it, he at once asked where it was.

The cowherd said, "It is still standing there; it would not stop eating to come with us."

The Little Peasant said, "But I must have my little calf back."

So they went back together to the field, but some one had stolen the calf in the meantime, and it was gone.

The cowherd said, "It must have run away."

But the Little Peasant said, "Nothing of the kind," and he took the cowherd up before the bailiff, who condemned him, for his carelessness, to give the Little Peasant a cow, in place of the lost calf.

So at last the Little Peasant and his wife had the long-wished-for cow; they were delighted, but they had no fodder and could not give it anything to eat, so very soon they had to kill it.

They salted the meat, and the man went to the town to sell the hide, intending to buy another calf with the money he got for it. On the way he came to a mill, on which a raven sat with a broken wing. He took it up out of pity and wrapped it in the hide. Such a storm of wind and rain came on that he could go no further, so he went into the mill to ask for shelter.

Only the miller's wife was at home, and she said to the Little Peasant, "You may lie down in the straw there." And she gave him some bread and cheese to eat.

The Little Peasant ate it, and then lay down with the hide by his side.

The miller's wife thought, "He is tired, and won't wake up."

Soon after a priest came in, and he was made very welcome by the woman, who said, "My husband is out, so we can have a feast."

The Little Peasant was listening, and when he heard about the feast he was much annoyed, because bread and cheese had been considered good enough for him.

The woman then laid the table, and brought out a roast joint, salad, cake, and wine. They sat down, but just as they were beginning to eat, somebody knocked at the door.

The woman said, "Good heavens, that is my husband!"

She quickly hid the joint in the oven, the wine under the pillow, the salad on the bed, and the cake under the bed, and, last of all, she hid the priest in the linen chest. Then she opened the door for her husband, and said, "Thank heaven you are back. The world might be coming to an end with such a storm as there is!"

The miller saw the Little Peasant lying on the straw, and said, "What is that fellow doing there?"

"Oh!" said his wife, "the poor fellow came in the middle of the storm and asked for shelter, so I gave him some bread and cheese, and told him he might lie on the straw!"

"He's welcome as far as I'm concerned," said the man, "but get me something to eat, wife. I'm very hungry."

His wife said, "I have nothing but bread and cheese."

"Anything will please me," said the man. "Bread and cheese is good enough." And his eyes falling on the Little Peasant, he said, "Come along and have some too."

The Little Peasant did not wait for a second bidding, but got up at once, and they fell to.

The miller noticed the hide on the floor in which the raven was wrapped, and said, "What have you got there?"

"I have a soothsayer there," answered the Little Peasant.

"Can he prophesy something to me?" asked the miller.

"Why not?" answered the Little Peasant. "But he will only say four things, the fifth he keeps to himself."

The miller was inquisitive, and said, "Let me hear one of his prophecies."

The Little Peasant squeezed the raven's head and made him croak.

The miller asked, "Why did he say?"

The Little Peasant answered, "First he said that there was a bottle of wine under the pillow."

"That's a bit of luck!" said the miller, going to the pillow and finding the wine. "What's next?"

The Little Peasant made the raven croak again, and said,

"Secondly, he says there is a joint in the oven."

"That's a bit of luck!" said the miller, going to the oven and finding the joint.

The Little Peasant again squeezed the raven to make him prophesy, and said, "Thirdly, he says there is some salad in the bed."

"That's a bit of luck!" said the miller, finding the salad.

Again the Little Peasant squeezed the raven to make him croak, and said, "Fourthly, he says there is a cake under the bed."

"That's a bit of luck!" cried the miller, as he found the cake.

Now the two sat down at the table together, but the miller's wife was in terror. She went to bed, and took all the keys with her.

The miller would have liked to know what the fifth prophecy could be, but the Little Peasant said, "We will quietly eat these four things first, the fifth is something dreadful."

So they went on eating, and then they bargained as to how much the miller should pay for the fifth prophecy, and at last they agreed upon three hundred thalers.

Then again the Little Peasant squeezed the raven's head and made him crow very loud.

The miller said, "What does he say?"

The Little Peasant answered, "He says the devil is hidden in the linen chest."

The miller said, "The devil will have to go out." And he opened the house door and made his wife give up the keys. The Little Peasant unlocked the linen chest, and the priest took to his heels as fast as ever he could.

The miller said, "I saw the black fellow with my own eyes; there was no mistake about it."

The Little Peasant made off at dawn with his three hundred thalers.

After this the Little Peasant began to get on in the world; he built himself a pretty new house and the other peasants said, "He must have been where the golden snow falls and where one brings home gold in bushels."

Then he was summoned before the bailiff to say where he got all his riches.

He answered, "I sold my cowhide in the town for three hundred thalers."

When the other peasants heard this they all wanted to enjoy the same good luck, so they ran home, killed their cows, and took the hides off to get the same price for them.

The bailiff said, "My maid must have the first chance." When she reached the town the buyer only gave her three thalers for the hide, and he did not even give the others so much, for he said, "What on earth am I to do with all these hides?"

Now the peasants were enraged at the Little Peasant for having stolen a march upon them, and to revenge themselves they had him up before the bailiff and accused him of cheating.

The innocent Little Peasant was unanimously condemned to death; he was to be put into a cask full of holes and rolled into the water. He was led out, and a priest was brought to read a mass, and all the people had to stand at a distance.

As soon as the Little Peasant looked at the priest, he knew he was the man who had been at the miller's. He said to him, "I saved you out of the chest, now you must save me out of the cask."

Just then a shepherd came by driving a flock of sheep, and the Little Peasant knew that he had long wanted to be bailiff himself. So he called out as loud as he could, "No, I will not, and if all the world wished it I would not."

The shepherd, who heard what he said, came and asked, "What's the matter, what will you not do?"

The Little Peasant said, "They want to make me bailiff if I will sit in this cask, but I won't."

"If that is all," said the shepherd, "I will get into the cask myself."

The Little Peasant said, "If you will get into the cask you shall be made bailiff."

The shepherd was delighted, and got in, and the Little Peasant fastened down the cover upon him. The flock of sheep he took for himself, and drove them off.

Then the priest went back to the peasants and told them the mass was said; so they went and rolled the cask into the water.

When it began to roll the shepherd cried out, "I am quite ready to be bailiff!"

The peasants thought that it was only the Little Peasant crying out, and they said, "Very likely. But you must go and look about you down below first." And they rolled the cask straight into the water.

Thereupon they went home, and when they entered the village what was their surprise to meet the Little Peasant calmly driving a flock of sheep before him, as happy as could be. They cried, "Why, you Little Peasant, how do you come here again? How did you get out of the water?"

"Well," said the Little Peasant, "I sank deep, deep down till I touched the bottom. Then I knocked the head of the cask off, crept out, and found myself in a beautiful meadow in which numbers of lambs were feeding, and I brought this flock back with me."

The other peasants said, "Are there any more?"

"Oh yes, plenty," answered the Little Peasant, "more than we should know what to do with."

Then the other peasants planned to fetch some of these sheep for themselves; they would each have a flock.

But the bailiff said, "I go first."

They all ran together to the water; the sky just then was flecked with little fleecy clouds and they were reflected in the water. When the peasants saw them, they cried, "Why, there they are! We can see the sheep below the water!"

The bailiff pressed forward, and said, "I will be the first to go down to look about me. I will call you if it is worthwhile." So he sprang into the water with a great splash.

The others thought he cried, "Come along!" and the whole party plunged in after him.

So all the peasants perished, and, as the Little Peasant was the sole heir, he became a rich man.